To Hugh,

with best wishes &

lots more good rugby

together

Ros

15 Sept '91

RUNNING
WITH THE BALL

The Sixth Match (George Barnard, 1852)

RUNNING WITH THE BALL

The Birth of Rugby Football

JENNY MACRORY

foreword by M R Steele-Bodger

CollinsWillow
An Imprint of HarperCollins*Publishers*

All rights reserved

First published in 1991 by
Collins Willow
an imprint of HarperCollins Publishers
London

© Jenny Macrory 1991

A CIP catalogue record for this book is available from the British Library

ISBN 0 00 218402 8

Set in Bembo by Phoenix Photosetting, Chatham, Kent
Designed by Judith Gordon
Printed and bound in Great Britain by Butler and Tanner Ltd,
Frome, Somerset

CONTENTS

ACKNOWLEDGEMENTS

My thanks are due to Rugby School, and in particular to all those early football enthusiasts whose writings and illustrations have inspired this book; to the Governing Body for permission to reproduce the pictures, all but two of which are to be found in the School's collection (the opening pictures in Chapters 2 and 3 are from the Mary Evans Picture Library); and to Headmasters Richard Bull and Michael Mavor for their encouragement. Bill Reesby has undertaken the photographic work with patience and promptitude, and Kay Jennings has given invaluable help throughout. I am grateful to John Griffiths for his constructive criticism of the text, Micky Steele-Bodger for kindly agreeing to write the foreword, and to my family, especially Jessica, another Rugbeian, for all their practical help and support.

Jenny Macrory
February, 1991

FOREWORD

This book makes fascinating reading for anyone interested in rugby football. Jenny Macrory, through careful and detailed research, has vividly described the growth and development of the game and in so doing has re-emphasized the important role that Rugby School played in the spread of rugby throughout the country.

The documented evidence explains the essential difference between running with the ball and running in, the latter at first merely allowing the team to have a 'try at goal', whereas after 1883 it became a try in its own right. The white jersey which England adopted came from the School as did the idea of caps, first worn to please Queen Adelaide – royalty attended matches even in those days. It is extraordinary to appreciate how there was almost only one football code, a combination of dribbling and handling until the questioned legality of hacking led to the formation of the Football Association. As a previous member of the International Rugby Football Board, the supreme lawmaking authority in the rugby world, and remembering only too well the work involved in formulating the laws, I particularly enjoyed the thought of a panel of Rugby schoolboys being asked to settle all differences of opinion and disputes relating to the laws and doing so for some thirty years.

Indeed it is somewhat ironic that rugby footballers from all over the world now compete for a World Cup – the Webb Ellis Trophy, so named after a boy who was by common consent of his contemporaries not the friendly gregarious type usually associated with this most social of games.

This book has greatly widened my own knowledge of the history of rugby football, and made me even more proud to have been a pupil at the school which gave the sporting world such a great game.

Micky Steele–Bodger

INTRODUCTION

'A grand game, as I used to consider it.' This was the affectionate memory of a ninety-three year old man looking back on his schooldays at Rugby. His sentiments have been echoed by generations of players for whom Rugby football has brought a lifetime of pleasure, whether on the field or the touchline, or recollected in the tranquillity of a comfortable armchair. Thomas Harris was seven years old when he first entered Rugby School in 1819. The game he knew resembled modern Rugby football more in spirit than in science and he, like every generation before him and since, believed the game played in his day to have been the best one of all.

The lifetime of Thomas Harris coincided exactly with the period during which Rugby football grew from its first recorded play into the modern, fifteen aside game which, by the end of his century, had reached maturity and international renown. Harris had been there at the beginning. He played the same game that William Webb Ellis played, in which the ball could be caught but not carried. The objective was then, as it is today, to score by kicking goals over a high cross-bar, and in the course of play there was 'plenty of hacking, but little struggling'. A fair catch entitled the player to make his mark and take an unimpeded kick, and since the number of players was limited only by the extent of the school roll call, it was this advantage which allowed most goals to be scored.

Running with the Ball follows the development of football at Rugby School during the fifty years between the introduction of carrying in the 1820s and the formation of the Rugby Football Union in 1871 when the game may be said to have reached maturity. During most of this time the schoolboys at Rugby were unconcerned about football in other schools or in the wider world. Cricket they played competitively against outsiders, but football was an entirely domestic affair. Games were arranged by the boys themselves with virtually no interference from masters, though some, particularly those who were themselves Old Rugbeians, would join in and play alongside the pupils for their own pleasure.

This book attempts to answer why the game developed its peculiar characteristics, and why the Rugby game alone, among the many versions of football played at equally distinguished English schools, should have survived as a national and international sport. Running with the ball has been described as the most distinctive feature of the game, but it is by no means the only important difference between Rugby and other football games. The high goal, oval ball and degree of contact during play are equally unusual, and in the early days the large numbers involved and the unequal distribution of sides contributed substantially to the nature of the game played at Rugby.

A close look at the way in which the school itself changed in its organization and ethics, particularly under the Headmastership of Dr Thomas Arnold, is essential to any study of the game's development. The chapters in this book which discuss the evolution of Rugby football at the school have been based entirely upon sources from the archives in the school library. As far as possible evidence has been derived from contemporary documents and accounts written by Rugbeians of the game as they knew it in their schooldays.

Many of these sources were printed in private publications and are now rare. The principal documents have therefore been reproduced, and are interspersed with the commentary so that readers may gain a better understanding of early Rugby football through the eyes of contemporary players. The illustrations are also taken chiefly from the collection at the school, and the series of schoolboy drawings by CH Chambers, which are thought to be the first detailed drawings of the game, are as important a source of information as the letters and articles.

The question of the spread of the Rugby game into the wider world is discussed in the second part of the book. It would, of course, take a volume of encyclopaedic proportions to look at this in detail. The short answer is that energetic and enthusiastic players carried the game out of the schools and into the universities. In adult life they arranged matches and formed clubs so that they could continue to play wherever they happened to find themselves. It is through an investigation of the people involved in the formation of early clubs at home and abroad that the story can be unfurled. For the sake of clarity and continuity the particular influence of Old Rugbeians is indicated in the brief accounts given of the many channels through which the game flowed into the wider world during the second half of the nineteenth century. By then players, many of whom matched in enthusiasm the Old Rugbeians, were emerging from many other schools, as well as from the universities, the armed services and the clubs, and they too were energetic in their promotion of the game. This book can only attempt to examine the means by which Rugby football was disseminated, and space does not allow credit to be given to all those individuals who played a part. JRA Daglish's short history of the Liverpool club, *Red, Black and Blue* is an excellent example of the way in which the careful study of the people involved in the early organization of a club can reveal the reasons for its foundation.

One of the questions which any club historian must ask is why the Rugby game rather than Association football should have been played. There is frequent confusion over the split between the two games, and it is often assumed that a form of modern soccer was being played at Rugby School in 1823 when Webb Ellis violated the rules and ran forward with the ball. This was far from the truth. Most of the leading schools played football of one sort or another according to their own rules. When their old boys at the universities tried to play one another there was considerable confusion, and the difficulty was exaggerated when open clubs were formed and wished to play matches. There followed discussions aimed at finding a common code, and the intransigence of the schools in insisting upon their own games led the London clubs to try and draw up a new set of rules for their own use. It proved impossible to adapt the rather complex rules which the various schools had developed, so eventually the Football Association, following the pattern set at Cambridge, drew up a new game from scratch to accommodate the requirements of the clubs. This code satisfied players who favoured the dribbling game, but was too far removed from the Rugby game to be acceptable to Blackheath and other followers of the Rugby code. It was therefore in 1863, not 1823, that the game of football finally diverged into two distinct sports. For this reason the events leading up to the formation of the

Football Association were crucial to the survival of the Rugby game, and have therefore been included in this account.

The primitive games which had been played for hundreds of years were the origin of football play in general. These games were usually annual matches having in common the objective of kicking or carrying a ball to a goal. Such games, where they existed, were entirely local, and in many of them it is possible to trace aspects of modern play. A representative few of these town and village games are described to give a general background to the much more organized and structured nineteenth century games from which modern football has grown.

CHAPTER 1 *THE LOCAL DERBY*

Football in Sixteenth Century Italy

Football is a game of ancient lineage. It is known to have been played by the Greeks and Romans, and may well have first been introduced to the British Isles during the Roman occupation. If this was so, then the Roman legionaries behaved very much as their nineteenth century British military counterparts were later to do in seeking to relieve the boredom of prolonged overseas postings by amusing themselves playing games of football. The Greek origins of the Roman game are indicated in its name, *harpastum*, which is derived from a Greek word meaning 'to snatch'. It was an organized field game in which play was started by throwing the ball into the air between two sets of players, whose objective was to carry the ball over the goal lines marked at either end of the pitch.

A very similar game survived until the nineteenth century in the Eastern counties of England, where there had been a strong Roman presence centred upon Lincoln, Colchester and St Albans. This game was known as *camp ball*, and was played on a defined pitch between eighty and a hundred yards long with narrow goals, just two or three feet wide, at either end. Players had to attempt to carry or throw the ball between the goals without being caught in possession, a *snotch* being lost whenever a player was held. The game was completed after seven or nine *snotches* had been scored. When a small ball was used the game was principally a carrying one, but if there was a large ball it became *kicking camp*. Shoes were worn in yet another variation, the nature of which may perhaps be deduced from its name – *savage camp*. Many historians of football prefer to ignore this last version of camp ball, but the tripping or hacking which its name implies were an integral part of several of the early public school games in which the modern codes have their origins.

Carew's *Survey of Cornwall* published in 1602 describes the local sport of *hurling* which, in one of its forms known as *hurling to goales*, closely resembles camp ball. 'Fifteen, twenty or thirty players chosen on each side . . . strip themselves to their lightest apparel, and then join hands in ranks against one another'. Each man was then paired with an opponent, sticks placed eight or ten feet apart at either end of a pitch some 200 or 240 yards long and play began when a neutral party threw the ball into the air between the teams. The object of the game was to carry the ball through the opposite goal.

Camp ball and hurling to goals were unusual in their restriction to a defined field of play. They appear to have been played simply for enjoyment, the sides being chosen from players who had elected to join in, and the numbers involved seem to have been limited and evenly matched. The alternative Cornish game, known as *hurling over country* was more closely aligned to the village games played elsewhere in Britain. These were usually annual contests between neighbouring parishes in which a ball was propelled across country by an unlimited number of participants between 'goals' which were often several miles apart.

The Welsh game of Cnapan, traditionally played on holidays and feast days, was in its earliest recorded form more closely akin to a battle than to a game. Brian John, in his booklet *The Ancient Game of Cnapan*, examines its development beginning with the extraordinary account written in 1603 by George Owen of Pembrokeshire. In his day the game was already thought to be 'of great antiquity'. The ball, which was small, round and made of wood, was designed to be carried in the hand and thrown, not kicked. Indeed with around two thousand participants sometimes taking part, a kicking game would scarcely have been practicable, particularly as the players were bare footed. There were also horsemen carrying 'monstrous cudgels of three foot and a half long' who would gallop away with the ball towards their own country if they could get hold of it, but they were not allowed to cause the footmen 'annoyance' by coming among them. Any horseman breaking the rules was liable to incur immediate rough justice and to have stones hurled at him to chase him away. The game seems to have been kept moving by obliging the holder of the ball to throw it when demanded to do so. Failure to respond on the third time of asking rendered him liable to the 'bastinado' of fists and cudgels which must have proved a powerful incentive to let go.

These free-for-all cross country games gradually declined as society in general became gentler, and as the ancient open landscapes were gradually enclosed. Play in many cases was removed to the beaches and to the streets of the towns, and the wooden ball gave way to an inflated bladder. Street football in Neath survived until 1884, and the last cross-country Cnapan game took place between Llandysul and Llanwenog in 1922.

While it can hardly be claimed that modern Rugby football is descended any more directly from Cnapan than from the many other rural games, there can be no doubt that when Rugby football was introduced to South Wales in the 1870s it was readily accepted as a natural successor to Cnapan, and quickly found favour in a society which had long enjoyed a tradition in ball games.

Cnapan may have been a 'carrying' game, but this was probably significant only insofar as there was no natural resistance to the concepts of physical contact or handling when the first Rugby football clubs were formed. A far closer analogy between the ancient and the modern games lies in George Owen's description of the spirit in which the games were played.

They contend not for any wager or valuable thing, but for glory and renown – first for the fame of their country in general, next every particular to win praise for his activity and prowess, which two considerations ardently inflameth the minds of the youthful people to strive to the death for glory and fame, which they esteem dearer to them than worldly wealth. Their matches are commonly made without stint or number, but as they happen to come, wherein also appeareth a policy . . . for the weaker number to save the glory of their country against the greater multitude.

The desire of the Welsh players to achieve renown strongly echoes the sentiments expressed in accounts of the matches played at Rugby School in the mid-nineteenth century in which numerically smaller sides motivated by a strong sense of loyalty were frequently successful against all the odds.

Many of the Welsh games were traditionally played on high days and holidays, and the association of football games with traditionally rowdy festivities was commonplace. Shrove Tuesday was the most popular date for many such local matches, all of which were played to different rules but served the same purpose in providing an excuse for the contenders to try their strength and stamina in competition with their neighbours. The Derby game, which gave rise to the expression 'a local Derby', is one of the best known village contests. It was played between the neighbouring parishes of St Peter's and All Saints, Derby, and was fabled to have had its roots in a victory celebration following the defeat of a cohort of Roman soldiers in 217 AD by the people of Little Chester.

SOURCE 1   *The Derby Game*

FROM GLOVER'S *HISTORY OF DERBYSHIRE*, 1829

The players are young men from eighteen to thirty or upwards, married as well as single, and many veterans who retain a relish for the sport are occasionally seen in the very heat of the conflict. The game commences in the market place, where the partisans of each parish are drawn up on each side, and about noon a large ball is tossed up in the midst of them. This is seized upon by some of the strongest and most active men of each party. The rest of the players immediately close in upon them, and a solid mass is formed. It then becomes the object of each party to impel the course of the crowd towards their particular goal. The struggle to obtain the ball, which is carried in the arms of those who have possessed themselves of it, is then violent, and the motion of the human side heaving to and fro without the least regard to consequences is tremendous. Broken shins, broken heads, torn coats and lost hats are amongst the minor accidents of this dreadful contest, and it frequently happens that persons fall, owing to the intensity of pressure, fainting and bleeding beneath the feet of the surrounding mob. . . . Still the crowd is encouraged by respectable persons attached to each party, who take a surprising interest in the result of the day's sport, urging on the players with shouts, and even handing those who are exhausted oranges and other refreshments. The object of the St Peter's party is to get the ball into the water down the Morledge brook and into the Derwent as soon as they can; while the All Saints' party endeavour to prevent this and urge the ball westward. The St Peter's players are considered to be equal to the best water spaniels, and it is certainly curious to see two or three hundred men up to their chins in the Derwent continually ducking each other. The numbers engaged on both sides exceed a thousand, and the streets are crowded with lookers on. The shops are closed, and the town presents the aspect of a place suddenly taken by storm.

CHAPTER 2 *NO FOOTBALL PLAYING IN YE STREET*

Shrove Tuesday at Dorking

It is hardly surprising that a year was considered a suitable interval between games, and the contestants must have woken up to Ash Wednesday feeling very much the same as the citizens of Rio or Trinidad do the morning after their Carnival celebrations. The opportunity which such football games offered to the people to settle local differences, and generally to release any head of steam which may have been building up over the winter, closely parallels the traditional function of Mardi Gras festivities in other parts of the world. The involvement of spectators as well as players, and the encouragement of 'respectable persons' contributed to the cathartic value of such events within close-knit communities. Feelings may have run high, but custom placed some restraint on unbridled violence.

For the young men these annual contests provided an opportunity to demonstrate their strength and courage in the public arena. They were joined by those 'veterans who retain a relish for the sport' whose counterparts are still in evidence in club play worldwide. It is interesting that Glover specifically remarks upon the fact that 'married men as well as single' took part. Reference is made in several of the local games to the association of football with the bachelor state. The implication is that a good performance at football might attract the attention of a suitable bride, or might possibly help in winning the approval of her father.

In Scotland on Shrove Tuesday a game was played in the parish of Scone in which the bachelors challenged the married men to carry the ball, not to kick it, between the Cross of Scone and a hole on the moor on the one hand and the river on the other. The game seems to have been a 'no holds barred' affair lasting from 2 o'clock in the afternoon until sunset. While the custom lasted, every man in the parish 'the gentry not excepted' was obliged to turn out and support the side to which he belonged on pain of a fine if he failed to do so. The married women of Inverness found themselves similarly aligned against the spinsters in a game invariably won by the matrons.

The association between football and the marital status of the participants also occurs in the annual Shrove Tuesday game played by the Marblers of Purbeck at Corfe Castle in Dorset. There the most recently married man had to 'bring a footballe according to the custom of our companie' , and from Brand's *Popular Antiquities* we learn that in the North of England among colliers 'it is customary to watch for the bridegroom's coming out of church after the ceremony in order to demand money for a football.'

The ball itself was clearly a prized possession, and indeed at Alnwick Castle in Northumberland the object of the Shrove Tuesday game was not to convey the ball to a specified goal, but to obtain and carry it off as a personal prize. In another northern game the pupils of Bromfield Free School in Cumberland were allowed to celebrate with a football match if they succeeded in barring out the schoolmaster for three days. The peace terms traditionally agreed between master and boys included the privilege of holding first a cock fight and then a football game in which the goals were the houses of the team captains, usually some miles apart from one another.

Coal miners seem to have had a marked enthusiasm for football, a predilection demonstrated when modern, organized football enjoyed rapid growth in the late nineteenth century in the mining areas of Lancashire, Yorkshire and South Wales. In the Warwickshire coalfields, where inter-parish games were played, a special day known as 'Football Day' was set aside, often on the first day of the local 'wakes' or holidays. These games seem to have been predominantly kicking games in which carrying was prohibited, though hand-ling the ball was allowed. Success depended on *piggling* [presumably dribbling], and speed in running. There was an element of tactical organization in the allocation of a defensive role to 'reserve men' and 'goal men', and custom clearly allowed some moves and banned others. In an article in *The Sporting Gazette* written in 1863, John Cartwright described one such Warwickshire game in which a player defied customary practice in a way which echoed the famous exploit of William Webb Ellis.

On one occasion a swift runner playing for a village near Atherstone, caught up the ball in his hands, and at a turn in the roadway which obscured him from his followers, leapt the fence into the fields, and by a short cut gained the village, where he deposited the ball. The opponents and the other players followed along the road. Their reserved men had, of course, heard and seen nothing of the ball, and the man had not passed the goal men. En masse the two sides proceeded to the village, where they found the delin-quent smoking his pipe outside the ale-house, the ball lying at his feet.

Not surprisingly disorder and broken heads followed, and Football Day was banned thereafter by the magistrate. In this instance it was probably not so much the carrying of the ball which aroused the fury of the opposition as the blatant cheating in taking the ball by a route other than that established by custom and so ruining the day's play for the other contestants. Webb Ellis' disregard for the rules invoked similar disapproval from his fellows, so much so that seventy years later a contemporary at Rugby, Thomas Harris, could still remember perfectly in his old age that Ellis had been generally regarded as 'inclined to take unfair advantages at football'.

Football was not confined to parish rivalries. In towns and cities there were traditional games played in the streets. One such annual game was played at Chester, where the shoemakers were required to deliver a 'ball of leather, called a football, of the value of three shillings and fourpence or above' to the drapers 'to play at from thence to the common hall of the same city'. Tradition had it that the precursor of the leather ball was the head of a captured Dane. London, too, played host to football games. In the reign of Henry II, FitzStephen refers to schoolboys playing ball in the fields immediately after dinner on Shrove Tuesday, and Samuel Pepys recorded in his diary for 2 January 1665, 'to my Lord Brounker's, by appointment, in the Piazza, Covent Garden. The street full of footballs, it being a great frost.' Westminster School and Charterhouse [then still a London school], each had their own football games and in the nineteenth century were influential in the discussions leading to more formal regulation of the sport.

Just outside London in the boroughs of Twickenham, Bushey, Hampton and Kingston, street football was played on Shrove Tuesday, though there is no evidence in William Hone's account of play in 1815 that the game involved any element of contest, except perhaps for a traditional battle with the glass windows lining the route. These Shrove Tuesday games increasingly met with disapproval in the better ordered society of the mid-nineteenth century, and the damage and disorder they caused provoked attempts to prevent them. The formation of the police force by Sir Robert Peel enabled the prohibitions of magistrates to be enforced effectively, and Shrove Tuesday football gradually died out, first in the urban areas and then in the countryside, leaving only a handful of traditional games to survive to the present day.

In Northamptonshire a football game was called for an unusual purpose in 1765. An advertisement had appeared in the Northampton Mercury on 29 July announcing that there would be a Foot Ball Play for a prize of considerable value on the following Thursday and Friday. Gentlemen players were invited to present themselves between ten and twelve o'clock at any of the public houses in the village of West Haddon where they would be welcomed and entertained. The advertisement aroused no suspicion, and it may therefore be assumed that football was not an unusual occurrence. However the real reason for the assembly was to stage a mass protest against the Bill for the Inclosure of the Common Fields and Heath of West Haddon which had been passed by Parliament in April of the previous year. The Inclosure Acts were designed to replace the ancient rights of farmers and cottagers to graze animals and raise crops on common land by the allocation of plots of land to individuals. The average Cottager in West Haddon had received just over an acre, and this was considered to be of less value to him than his old Rights to Common Land. Not only could he produce less from it, but he was required by law to pay for the fencing of his property, a cost which he could ill afford. The cottagers and small farmers were therefore discontented with their settlements, and the football game, whether it had been designed as a protest or not, quickly degenerated into a riot. Damage in football games was, as we have seen, not unusual, and at West Haddon anger at the inclosures was vented by the destruction of the fences put up round the new fields and the burning of stacks of posts and rails awaiting erection. In his article in *Northamptonshire Past and Present* (1968) JW Anscombe goes on to describe how General Mordaunt's Dragoons were sent to quell the disturbance. Arrests were made and urgent attempts were made to trace the organizers who had committed 'The Black Act of Felony', an offence which could attract the sentence of death without benefit of Clergy. The men who placed the advertisement absconded, but a number of others were gaoled. This specific use of football as a vehicle for united political protest is unusual, but there is no doubt that local disagreements were often avenged during the course of traditional games.

Historians of football frequently go to considerable lengths to claim an exclusive line of descent for one modern game or another from what they describe rather broadly as 'the primitive game'. This is a fruitless exercise as there was no uniformity in football play before the second half of the nineteenth century. The many different local games played from Scotland to Cornwall, and from Wales to East Anglia, included kicking, handling and carrying in various combinations. These games formed the common ancestry for all the modern codes of football which were later to develop in response to the changing social and economic circumstances of an increasingly organized and industrialized society.

The Rugby game in particular has been regularly portrayed as a survival of 'primitive' football, generally on the grounds that carrying the ball is permitted. Certainly football was played in the town of Rugby in the middle of the eighteenth century. The Constable's books indicate that New Year's Eve rather than Shrove Tuesday brought football trouble to Rugby, and the entry for 31 December, 1743/4 reads 'Pd Baxter for Crying no football play in ye street, 2d'. Whatever form this local game may have taken it certainly did not result in the direct translation of the carrying game to the playing fields of the school, where the game played at the turn of the century distinctly forbade running with the ball.

SOURCE 2　　*Football Day at Kingston-upon-Thames*　　*[1815]*

An early mention of Twickenham

FROM *THE EVERY DAY BOOK*, 1845 EDITED BY WILLIAM HONE

Having some business which called me to Kingston-upon-Thames on the day called Shrove Tuesday, I got upon the Hampton Court coach to go there. We had not gone four miles when the coachman exclaimed to one of the passengers, 'It's football day!' Not understanding the term I questioned him what he meant by it; his answer was that I should see what he meant where I was going. Upon entering Teddington, I was not a little amused to see all the inhabitants securing the glass of all their front windows *from the ground to the roof*, some by placing hurdles before them, and some by nailing laths across the frames. At Twickenham, Bush[e]y and Hampton Wick they were all engaged in the same way. Having to stop a few hours at Hampton Wick and Kingston, I had an opportunity of seeing the whole custom, which is to carry a football from door to door and beg money; at about twelve o'clock the ball is turned loose, and those who can kick it. In the town of Kingston all the shops are purposely kept shut on that day; there are several balls in the town, and of course several parties. I observed some persons of respectability following the ball. The game lasts about four hours, when the parties retire to the public houses and spend the money they before collected in refreshments. I understand the corporation of Kingston attempted to put a stop to this game, but the judges confirmed the right to the game, and it now legally continues, to the no small annoyance of some of the inhabitants, besides the expense and trouble they are put to in securing all their windows.

CHAPTER 3 *THE EXERCISE OF YOUNG GENTLEMEN*

No account of the football game played in the streets of Rugby town has survived, and it is probably safe to assume that it was little more than a rowdy free for all to see the old year out. The boys of Rugby School were no doubt involved, and may well have entered the fray against the lads of the town. An ancient rivalry between town and gown survived late into the nineteenth century in the form of keenly anticipated and hard fought snowball fights after the first suitable snowfall of the winter. These battles in many ways resembled the traditional village football games with the school gates as the goal. The town boys would attempt to storm the gates under a barrage of snowballs, and considered themselves victorious if they gained access to the quadrangle behind. In a return encounter on Guy Fawkes day the schoolboys would endeavour to get to the bonfire built in the market place by the town boys and to set it alight ahead of schedule.

The old schoolhouse which Rugby School had occupied since its foundation in 1567 was in the centre of the little town directly opposite the parish church. It had no playground and the pupils were obliged to take their exercise where they could – usually in the churchyard (which was not encouraged), or on a small area of ground beyond. By the middle of the eighteenth century the old building had

16

become 'so ruinous as not to be worth effectual repair' and the Trustees applied to Parliament in 1748 for permission to seek new premises. In their submission the Trustees argued that not only were the old buildings inadequate for the expanding school, but that its situation was 'in a place too much confined, and without any ground or inclosure adjoining, for the recreation of the youth therein educated, and consequently attended with, and liable to, many inconveniences both to the master and scholars.'

Not least among those inconveniences were the complaints made by neighbours about the activities of the pupils in their free time. It was therefore viewed as a great benefit when the Trustees bought the

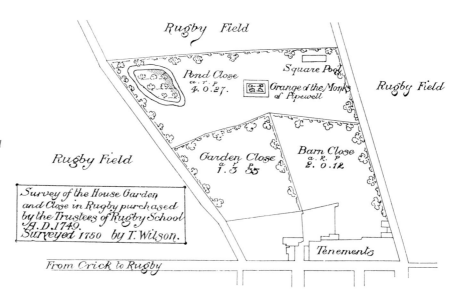

Survey of the Rugby School site (T Wilson, 1750)

old Manor House on the edge of the town which had with it about eight acres of land divided into three fields. One of these, the Barn Close, was given over as a playground 'affording every accommodation that could be required for the exercise of the young gentlemen.' From 1750 this two acre paddock was used for cricket and football games and thereafter all mention of street football in the Constable's records ceased.

There are a few passing references to football before 1800, but on the whole the boys preferred to spend their free time in other ways. Marbles were popular with the younger boys, and 'carting' was in vogue for a while. This involved the building of a kind of go-kart which would be harnessed to four small boys and driven by an older pupil in races round the Close. The senior boys took it for granted that they could commandeer the juniors to assist them with the more boring aspects of their sports, and not only used them as racehorses, but would send them off at all hours of the day and night to attend to fishing lines set on the River Avon, carry nets and rods, tear up paper for paper chases, field for them in the cricket nets [which had no side netting in those days] and generally to be in attendance when they were needed. By and large half holidays would be spent in the kind of pursuits enjoyed by young countrymen anywhere in England at that time. The seasons dictated many activities, with swimming and skating at the appropriate times, and field sports whenever possible. The headmaster's rule book in the 1790s specifically forbade badger baiting, cock fighting and 'suchlike activities unbecoming to a gentleman', and a rather indifferent pack of hounds kept by the boys for hunting was finally (and mercifully) abandoned on Dr Arnold's orders when he first arrived at the school in 1828.

In their leisure time the boys organized their own activities with little interference from the masters except for regulations designed to ensure that they did not stray too far afield or do any serious damage. There were inevitable clashes with local landowners when the boys were caught poaching fish or game, or even hooking the occasional chicken or goose on a baited line cast over a farmyard wall. The food provided by the school seems not to have been particularly ample or edible, so any sport which resulted in the wherewithal for a feast at one of the 'guttle shops' in the town was bound to be popular. The headmaster threatened in vain to put out of bounds any establishment where meat was roasted for the pupils, and hunting flourished. For the headmaster the half holidays on which his pupils decided to play football must have been relatively peaceful, since on those days at least he could be sure that they would spend the afternoon within the confines of the school grounds.

The game played in the first quarter of the nineteenth century was spontaneous and uncomplicated. The rules were not written down because there was no need for it. The players were all members of the same institution, played on the same single pitch, and were taught the code by word of mouth and by example. The practice of requiring the junior boys or 'fags' to take part in the sports of their elders applied equally to football where they were duly dispatched en masse to be goalkeepers. Thus they were obliged to watch the game and occasionally to take part from their earliest days at school – which could at that time have been as young as six or seven years old. By the time they were considered old enough to take a full part in the play most Rugby boys would have served a considerable apprenticeship out of harm's way between the goalposts, and would have been thoroughly familiar with the accepted regulations. This method of teaching the coming generations by giving them all a small part to play alongside the more experienced players was in marked contrast to the games in many other schools where limited numbers on each side were customary. At Rugby frequent changes in methods and rules of play could easily be introduced to suit the prevailing conditions with no more complication than the agreement of the leading players meeting at the end of the day's play. Their decisions were then implemented with a minimum of formality in the following game. The system of 'Fagging in goal' not only gave the younger boys the opportunity to learn by watching, but also provided them with a chance to practise among themselves. There were long intervals when the ball would be at the other end of the field and the goalkeepers, bored and cold, would take their chance to play a mini game of their own using a spare puntabout or practice ball if they could grab one, or even, in the absence of a ball, an old glove stuffed with leaves.

The classic account of a football game at Rugby as it was played by William Webb Ellis and his contemporaries appeared in the school magazine, the *Meteor*, in 1880. The author was Matthew Bloxam, a solicitor and well-known antiquarian who had lived in the town close to the school all his life. His father was a master and he and his five brothers were all Rugbeians. He had entered in 1813 at the age of eight and left in 1821, but remained in daily contact after he left through his younger brother who was still at the school and through the pupils living in his father's boarding house. Right up until his death in 1888 he was in touch with both boys and masters, giving talks and writing articles about the history of Rugby and his recollections of his boyhood. As an antiquarian and historian he was painstakingly accurate, and there is no reason to disbelieve his description, which is the only surviving eye witness account of the football game current at Rugby when William Webb Ellis entered the school in 1816.

SOURCE 3   *Football in the 1820s*

FROM AN ARTICLE BY MH BLOXAM PUBLISHED IN
THE *METEOR*, 12 DECEMBER 1880

A leading article in *The Times* newspaper, the leading journal of Europe, a few weeks past, on the Rugby School Football Rules and Play, as contrasted with the Association Rules, has prompted me to write a few words on the game of football, as played at Rugby in my time, 1813–20. The last time I played at Bigside in the Close was just 60 years ago, and my recollections of the game extend to 67 years.

When I was entered at the School, after the summer holidays of 1813, a considerable portion of the Close south of the wall of the Headmaster's garden, was parted off by a paling and the space thus enclosed filled with the *débris* of building materials, for the School House and School buildings, as originally designed, were just finished. A range of barns, partly tiled, partly thatched, adjoining the Dunchurch Road, fitted up temporarily as Schoolrooms, were in existence and used as such, and near to these stood the famous 'Treen's Tree.' The published views of the Schools, sheds and buildings, as they appeared in 1809, we owe to Mr. Edward Pretty, then the Drawing Master of the School. He was one who did much for the School in preserving its features as it existed in 1809, and subsequently as the new Schools were gradually engrafted on the site of the old Schools. I think, therefore, that his memory ought to be preserved and not consigned to oblivion. He failed from want of patronage to complete a work he had commenced on the History of the School, the credit of which has been given to another.

In 1813 the available space for the playground was not more than four acres at the most. There was an island, the mound is still existing but the moat is gone, and the appearance altogether sadly altered from the past, and not for the better. The island was in a separate field from the Close, and the southern part of the present Close was divided into fields, and formed a small dairy farm. Cricket and Football at Bigside were played at the north-west corner of the Close, adjoining the Dunchurch Road. One of the goals was erected on the site of the Chapel, not then in existence.

When preparations for the erection of the Chapel were made, and the ground enclosed for that purpose, *circa* A.D. 1817–18, Bigside both at Cricket and Football was removed to that part of the Close lying immediately south of the Headmaster's garden wall. The procedure at Bigside of Football was then as follows: all fags were stopped on going out after three o'clock calling-over (I should add that the Fifth Form only, which was then next to the Sixth Form, was exempt from fagging) and compelled to go into the Close, except those specially exempt, by having to attend the French

Master, Drawing Master, or Drill Sergeant, the times for which, being extras, were taken out of the half-holidays, and consequently little was learned. When, then, all had assembled in the Close, two of the best players in the School commenced choosing in, one for each side. One of these players in my time was an athlete in the Lower Fourth Form, then the lowest form in the Upper School. After choosing in about a score on each side, a somewhat rude division was made of remaining fags, half of whom were sent to keep goal on the one side, the other half to the opposite goal for the same purpose. Any fag, though not specially chosen in, might follow up on that side to the goal of which he was attached. Some of these were ready enough to mingle in the fray, others judiciously kept half-back, watching their opportunity for a casual kick, which was not unfrequently awarded them. Few and simple were the rules of the game: touch on the sides of the ground was marked out, and no one was allowed to run with the ball in his grasp towards the opposite goal. It was Football, and not handball, plenty of hacking but little struggling. As to costume, there were neither flannels nor caps, the players simply doffed their hats, and coats, or jackets, which were heaped together on either side near the goals till the game was over. All were scratch matches, one boarding-house was never pitted against another, and there was no Cock House. There were no Old Rugbeian matches; Railways had not commenced to pervade the land, and Rugby was a good twelve hours journey from London. With Oxford there was no direct communication. Once a year, at the Easter speeches, the School used to be re-visited by Old Rugbeians from Oxford, but these never amounted to more than a score in number, if so many. After the games of the day were concluded, however vigorously they may have been contended, all further remembrance of the game was consigned to the limbo of oblivion, our tasks to be learned that night were sufficiently onerous to allow little leisure for discussion, and there was no *Meteor* in which the incidents of each game could be recorded.

In the latter half-year of 1823, some fifty-seven years ago, originated though without premeditation, that change in one of the rules, which more than any other has since distinguished the Rugby School game from the Association Rules.

A boy of the name Ellis – William Webb Ellis – a town boy and a foundationer, who at the age of nine entered the School after the midsummer holidays in 1816, who in the second half-year of 1823, was, I believe, a praeposter, whilst playing Bigside at football in that half-year, caught the ball in his arms. This being so, according to the then rules, he ought to have retired back as far as he pleased, without parting with the ball, for the combatants on the opposite side could only advance to the spot where he had caught the ball, and were unable to rush forward till he had either punted it or had placed it for some one else to kick, for it was by means of these placed kicks that most of the goals were in those days kicked, but the moment the ball touched the ground, the opposite side might rush on. Ellis, for the first time, disregarded this rule, and on catching the ball, instead of retiring backwards, rushed forwards with the ball in his hands towards the opposite goal, with what result as to the game I know not, neither do I know how this infringement of a well-known rule was followed up, or when it became, as it is now, a standing rule. Mr. Ellis was high up in the School, and as to scholarship of fair average abilities. He left School in the summer of 1825, being the second Rugby Exhibitioner of that year, and was entered at Brasenose College, Oxford. He subsequently took Holy Orders, and at a later period became incumbent of the church of St. Clement Danes, Strand, London. He died on the continent some years ago. When at School, though in a high Form, Mr. Ellis was not what we should call a 'swell,' at least none of his compeers considered him as such; he had, however, no lack of assurance, and was ambitious of being thought something of. In fact he did an act which if a fag had ventured to have done, he would probably have received more kicks than commendations. How oft it is that such small matters lead to great results!

CHAPTER 4 *THE DISREGARDED RULE*

In 1887 Mr Montague Shearman contributed the *Athletics and Football* volume to the popular *Badminton Library of Sports and Pastimes*. In an otherwise carefully researched account of the football games played in major schools he made one seemingly insignificant error. In an earlier work, *Football: its History for Five Centuries*, he had reached the conclusion that 'in each particular school the rules of the game were settled by the capacity of the playground: and that as these were infinitely various in character, so were the games various.' He had a point. There is no doubt that the size, shape and surface of the playgrounds strongly influenced the way in which school games evolved, and this was undoubtedly as true of Rugby as it was of Eton, Harrow, Winchester and the rest. However in contrasting Rugby with other schools where football was played in confined or walled areas, often with hard, flagged surfaces, Shearman stated:

One school alone seems to have owned, almost from its foundation, a wide open grass play-ground of ample dimensions, and that School was Rugby; hence it happens, as we should have expected, that at Rugby School alone do we find that the original game survived almost in its primitive shape.

Here he was wrong. As we have seen it was not until 1750 that Rugby had any kind of playground at all. Indeed one of the major complaints about the old school house was that it was in 'a place too much confined' for the pupils to take exercise, and it was not until after the migration to the edge of the town that a field was available for recreation. Shearman went on to say that,

As far as we can discover . . . no School but Rugby played the old game where every player was allowed to pick up the ball and run with it, and every adversary could stop him by collaring, hacking over, and charging, or by any other means he pleased. It is tolerably plain that the Rugby game was originally played at Rugby alone, while other schools adopted a more or less modified kicking game.

In fact it is perhaps surprising that the old street game was not simply transferred on to the newly available Barn Close in the middle of the eighteenth century, but Matthew Bloxam is perfectly clear that until at least 1821 when he left the school the game played was 'football, not handball', and closely resembled the kicking games current in other schools at that time. He twice wrote articles describing the game as he knew it, and both were published well before either of Shearman's books. He first mentioned William Webb Ellis in a letter to the *Meteor* in October, 1876 in response to a letter in the *Standard* newspaper which had expressed the belief that the Rugby game was of great and unknown antiquity. Bloxam had originally responded that running with the ball had been introduced sometime after Dr Arnold became Headmaster in 1828. However he had made further enquiries and then he,

ascertained that this change originated with a Town boy or Foundationer of the name of Ellis, William Webb Ellis. . . . It must, I think, have been in the second half-year of 1823 that this change from the former system, in which the football was not allowed to be taken up and run with, commenced.

Poor Bloxam! His integrity has since been called into account in numerous books, articles and broadcasts, yet he can have had no possible reason to invent the story. He was only correcting, in a thoroughly gentlemanly way, his own previous mis-statement in his reply to the *Standard*'s correspondent. It is a great pity that Bloxam did not see fit to name the source of his newly acquired information, but it would have been entirely natural if his brother John, who was an exact contemporary of Ellis at Rugby and at Oxford, had seen the letters and come forward with his own recollections. Matthew sought only to set the record straight in a note to the school magazine, and was certainly not attempting to set Ellis up as some kind of hero.

Matthew Bloxam

On the contrary, his later article for the *Meteor* in 1880 implies a certain dislike both of the boy and of his innovation.

In this second article, prompted by a recent *Times* leader about the differences between the rules of the Rugby and Association games, Bloxam expands his account of Ellis' action and explains precisely both what the rules required he should have done and how he transgressed.

A boy of the name of Ellis, William Webb Ellis, . . . who in the second half-year of 1823, was, I believe, a praeposter, whilst playing Bigside at football in that half-year, caught the ball in his arms. This being so, according to the then rules, he ought to have retired back as far as he pleased, without parting from the ball, for the combatants on the opposite side could only advance to the spot where he had caught the ball, and were unable to rush forward until he had either punted it or had placed it for some one else to kick, for it was by means of these placed kicks that most of the goals were in those days kicked, but the moment the ball touched the ground the opposite side might rush on. Ellis for the first time disregarded this rule, and on catching the ball, instead of retiring backwards, rushed forwards with the ball in his hands towards the opposite goal, with what result as to the game I know not, nor do I know how this infringement of a well known rule was followed up, or when it became as it is now, a standing rule.

Bloxam's account of the play seems to leave no doubt that Shearman was mistaken in assuming that the carrying game at Rugby represented a survival of old-style play. The Old Rugbeian Society politely suggested Mr Shearman's statements were 'misleading, if not altogether erroneous', and in 1895 formed a committee to investigate the matter. The committee's report, published in 1897, took the form of a booklet entitled *The Origin of Rugby Football* reproducing the correspondence which their enquiries had generated, and pointing out that running with the ball was introduced to the game during the 1820s and 1830s and was unknown at Rugby School before then. They took particular care to follow up the Webb Ellis story, and were understandably in some difficulty extracting clear recollections from the very few surviving contemporaries, all of whom were by then well over eighty years old.

What is, however, made abundantly clear in all the published letters is the fact that running in with the ball was still regarded as an exceptional occurrence gradually gaining customary status during the 1830s, and was not regularly practised until after 1841 when it was officially legalized. There can be no doubt that it was not an integral part of the original Rugby game and that the innovation took fifteen or twenty years to become fully established.

The oldest Rugbeian traced by the committee was Mr Thomas Harris who had entered the school in 1819 at the age of seven, and left in 1828. His memory of the rules under which he played corresponds closely with Bloxam. In a letter written in May 1895 he says:

1. Picking up and running with the ball in hand was distinctly forbidden. If a player caught the ball on a rebound from the ground, or from a stroke of the hand, he was allowed to take a few steps so as to give effect to a drop kick, but no more: subject of course to interruption from the adverse players. I remember Mr William Webb Ellis perfectly. He was an admirable cricketer, but was generally regarded as inclined to take unfair advantages at football. I should not quote him in any way as an authority.
2. If the ball was caught in the hands from a kick, the catcher was entitled to a 'place try' at goal, retiring a sufficient distance from the place where the catch was made.
3. All laying hands upon and holding a player was strictly forbidden under any circumstances.

In a postscript Harris remarks fondly 'a grand game, I used to consider it', and in a further letter a few days later he confirms his statement that Webb Ellis was regarded as unfair by the leading players of the day, and goes on to make the interesting comment that 'in the matches played in the lower part of the school when I was myself a junior, the cry of 'Hack him over' was always raised against any player who was seen to be running with the ball in his hands.' So, legitimately or not, boys *did* from time to time try to carry the ball in the early 1820s, and the remedy for their audacity was an immediate and orchestrated attempt to stop them in their tracks. Harris corroborates Bloxam's evidence about the rules of play, and in recalling that Ellis was 'an admirable cricketer' he proved that there was nothing wrong with his memory, since Webb Ellis had later played in the Oxford University XI.

So how true is the Webb Ellis story?

SOURCE 4 *Ackermann's History of Rugby School [1816]*

The house purchased was the property of a Mrs. Pennington, and had before belonged to, and been occupied by Mr. Burnaby, the then Lord of the Manor of Rugby. It does not, however, necessarily follow that this was the Manor House, but a very ancient inhabitant of Rugby states that it certainly was so. *But what made the purchase in the highest degree desirable, was some old enclosures annexed to it, which were capable of affording every accommodation that could be required for the exercise of the young gentlemen.* In the infant state of the school one of these closes was amply sufficient for the purpose, but the present vast increase in the number of the boys has pointed out the necessity of *extending the limits of the play-ground*; and the trustees in the course of the present year (1816), have ordered all the fences between these closes to be removed, the ditches filled up, and the ground levelled: *thus a plot of eight acres is now given up to the entire use of the young men in their various amusements.* This is an improvement that cannot but be approved and admired: it is now indeed a play-ground altogether worthy of the noble buildings which stand by the side of it; and it must naturally be viewed with more interest, when it is considered that it is a kind of natural plan of the Middlesex property, from which itself and all its appendages are derived. The present play-ground at Rugby is the exact size of the 'Conduit Close' which came to the school by the bequest of the Founder: it is eight acres within a few perches, as appears from the account of the allotment drawn up and left by the surveyors at the conclusion of the business of the enclosure.

CHAPTER 5 *A BOY OF THE NAME*
OF ELLIS

William Webb Ellis

Extraordinary motives have, in recent years, been attributed to Matthew Bloxam and to the committee of Old Rugbeians who sought to confirm his findings about the origin of the carrying game at Rugby School. Yet Bloxam, as we have already seen, was a thoroughly honest antiquarian with an impeccable reputation for careful, scholarly investigation. He was a lawyer by profession and the author of a meticulous standard work on Gothic Architecture which ran to eleven editions. Matthew's school career had overlapped with that of William Webb Ellis for five years, while his younger brother John spent nine years level-pegging with Ellis as they made their way up the school never more than a few places apart. The family knew Ellis well, and they did not like him at all.

According to Bloxam's picture of him William Webb Ellis was far from the stuff of which even schoolboy heroes are made. 'Mr Ellis', he wrote, 'was high up in the school, and as to scholarship of fair average abilities. He left school in the summer of 1825, being the second Rugby Exhibitioner of that year, and was entered at Brasenose College, Oxford.'

Now to win the second leaving Exhibition, which was a valuable award providing a substantial sum of money annually for the duration of his undergraduate career, was no mean achievement. The Exhibitions were fiercely competed for, and in coming second in the examination Ellis displayed an academic aptitude deserving of more enthusiastic commendation than Bloxam's grudging 'fair average'.

When at school, though in a high form, Mr Ellis was not what we should call a *swell*, at least none of his compeers considered him as such; he had, however, no lack of assurance, and was ambitious of being thought something of. In fact he did an act which if a fag had ventured to have done, he would probably have received more kicks than commendations. How oft it is that such small matters lead to great results!

One other recollection of a contemporary confirms Bloxam's view that Ellis, in spite of his academic success and his cricketing ability, was not particularly popular with his schoolboy contemporaries. Thomas Harris wrote to the investigating committee,

As to Mr W. Webb Ellis and his practices, you must observe that I was several years his junior, and had not either reasons or opportunities for closely observing his manner of play. *I am sure, however, that it was very generally regarded as unfair by the leading players of his day.* It may be that his practice of running with the ball, which Mr Bloxam speaks of as having been invented by him was the point objected to; but of this I cannot speak of my own observation.

There is only one mention of Ellis in a directly contemporary document that has so far come to light, and while it does not concern football, it nevertheless endorses the disapproving tone of the other comments. On 3 April, 1822, Thomas Lawrence Bloxam wrote to his brother Andrew at Oxford immediately the results were declared to tell him the winners of the English and Latin Prizes at Rugby. The stakes were high with £10 10s, a huge sum amounting to the equivalent of about two months' salary for an assistant master, for the best entries. Competition was intense, and excitement widespread among the pupils, most of whom had placed bets on the outcome. Thomas begins his letter by quoting the starting prices of the favourites in the English prize, which had a neck and neck finish, and then goes on to say,

Cheshire won the other race in a canter – Ellis got the wooden spoon, in plain terms was the last horse that was placed. He had taken for his Latin Motto for the Latin Prize *Dux Femina Facti* [which may be loosely translated as *cherchez la femme*], which the masters thought was a broad hint that his Mother had been helping him in the composition.

In view of the very substantial prize money involved the implication of cheating amounted to a serious matter and was obviously no secret. The mention of Mrs Ellis is interesting. She was an enterprising woman who wanted the best for her sons after the death of her husband James Ellis, of the 3rd Dragoon Guards, at the Battle of Albuera on 16 May, 1812. She had been left 'totally unprovided for' except for a small army pension of £10 for each child, but knew, possibly because her own family were natives of the area, that if she moved to Rugby her two boys would be eligible to become foundationers at the Great School where they would receive a good education at no cost. It was not at all unusual for widows or the wives of serving officers to take up residence in the town in order to obtain for their children an education which they otherwise might not be able to afford. Once they were entered at the school Mrs Ellis maintained a close interest in her sons' progress, and her reputation with the masters must have been such that they thought her not only willing but *able* to help William with Latin to the very high standard achieved by senior pupils. She stayed in Rugby at least for a while after her sons left the school and is remembered by George Benn in his communication with the *Origins* committee, though he was too young to have known her son. Later she moved to live with William, and when she died he erected an affectionately worded memorial to her in St Clement Dane's in the Strand, London, where he was Rector.

A mother, whose piety is recorded in Heaven and requires no praise upon earth . . . Her spirit rejoices in God her Saviour. Let my last end be like hers.

Unfortunately the church was badly bombed during the Second World War and the memorial to Mrs Ellis was destroyed, though a tablet to the memory of her son was erected by the Rugby Football Union of the Royal Air Force after the church was restored .

No doubt Ellis owed something of the 'ambition to be thought something of' to his mother's influence. He was not without ability as both a scholar and an athlete – his Exhibition and his place in the Oxford University Cricket XI are proof of that – but he had damaged his reputation on the football field and in the Latin Prize too much for his successes to be wholeheartedly welcomed. What *does* emerge

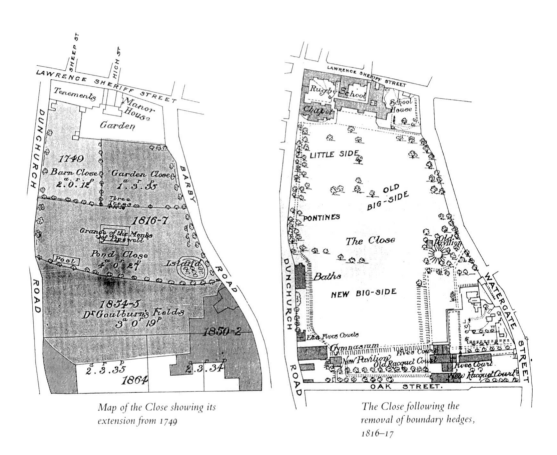

Map of the Close showing its
extension from 1749

The Close following the
removal of boundary hedges,
1816–17

from the slender information about his character is that he had considerable drive and a sufficiently forceful personality to be remembered sixty years later by men who were both senior and junior to him at school as something of a cheat, who was prepared to take advantage of his seniority to override the rules.

If Ellis had the *nerve* to challenge the customary football code, what about the opportunity? How immutable were the rules, and would he physically have been able to get very far? Contrary to widely held belief the football game played at Rugby was not a deeply entrenched tradition. Schoolboy letters and biographical reminiscences of eighteenth century Rugby are full of accounts of fishing, swimming, poaching and running, with cricket alone being mentioned as a team game. It was only after the turn of the century that football increased in popularity and a recognized code of play developed. The rules, as Bloxam said, were few and simple. They were a framework for play and made no attempt to define methods in any detail. Circumstances varied, and the game was adjusted by mutual consent to accommodate the prevailing conditions.

Two important governing factors were the available ground and the number of players. It chanced that during Ellis' time at Rugby both these elements changed substantially. In his first term, in 1816, the Trustees needed to take back the playground on the Barn Close to provide a site for a chapel. The new building programme was by now substantially complete, and the number of pupils was expanding. Football was transferred to a new playground which was created by removing the boundary hedges between the two small fields to the south, leaving a very much larger area for play. This fell naturally into two parts, more or less divided by the elm trees which had been retained when the hedges were removed. One side of this new space was poorly drained and wet, so the other, particularly in the winter, provided the better ground and was used for football. It was both wider and substantially longer than the old field, and changes in playing practices must have occurred as the game adapted to the bigger ground.

It was generally accepted that new practices could be incorporated if they were deemed advantageous to the conduct of the game. The decision lay with a loosely constituted group of the best players and praeposters, and Ellis would have first learned his football at a time when the game was settling in after the move, and would have grown up to accept modifications as a matter of routine. Indeed building works and all the associated disturbances continued on the fringes of the Close throughout his early years at school causing a constant shifting of the playground boundaries.

The second factor which altered the nature of play during the later part of Ellis' schooldays was a rapid decline in the number of pupils, particularly in the upper school. A great row in 1822 had resulted in the expulsion of a number of boys and the withdrawal of others. There had been 380 pupils under Dr Wooll in Ellis' first term, but by the time he left the roll was reduced to 143 and the numbers did not entirely recover until the appointment of Dr Arnold. For his last two years Ellis was a member of an unusually small group of senior boys. In a game where the numbers on either side were not specified, simply a rough division being made between the players available on the day, the size of the school inevitably influenced the numbers involved in football games. In his last two years Ellis faced less opposition from senior players than would have been the case a few years earlier or later. He was a good athlete with 'no lack of assurance' and he had a good brain. In any controversy about the acceptability of his method of play at football Ellis was well equipped to argue the toss. Obviously there was some argument.

Mr Harris, although too young to have been involved personally in any dispute, was perfectly clear, even seventy years later, that Ellis was at odds with other leading players. This fact had made sufficient impression to stick in his mind long after the reasons for it had faded. John Bloxam, however, was an immediate contemporary and a direct participant, far more likely to recall the point at issue.

The facts then, are these. Running with the ball was unknown at Rugby before 1821, though it was practised in a limited way after 1830. A new ground and fluctuating numbers created different conditions of play during the 1820s leading to various changes which had become established among Arnold's pupils in the 1830s. Change was not taboo provided that it was approved by a consensus of leading players. Ellis himself persisted in practices which were *not* readily acceptable and carried sufficient weight as a praeposter and fine cricketer to be able to do as he pleased. He did not, however, succeed in persuading all the other leading players to adopt his methods, and was probably regarded as unfair more for refusing to accept the custom of consensus than for attempting an innovative move. He was a pushy character with a reputation, whether deserved or not, for bending the rules both at work and at play. He was named as the boy first remembered as running with the ball in an article written by a gentle, elderly antiquarian who had no part in the rivalries between the advocates of the various forms of football which had been promoted in the 1860s. Indeed Matthew Bloxam rather disapproved of the innovations which he saw in the Rugby game, and infinitely preferred it as it was in his youth, '*football and not handball*'. In naming William Webb Ellis he intended to imply no commendation, and there is no reason to cast doubt on his reliability as a source.

The conclusions of the Old Rugbeian Committee on the subject of Webb Ellis are careful and unsensational. Their report states;

that at some date between 1820 and 1830 the innovation was introduced of running with the ball, and that this was in all probability done in the latter half of 1823 by Mr W. Webb Ellis. . . . To this we would add that the innovation was regarded as of doubtful legality for some time, and only gradually became accepted as part of the game, but obtained customary status between 1830 and 1840 and was duly legalized first in 1841–2.

All the evidence supports their finding, which appears inconspicuously placed in a privately printed pamphlet. Their main objective in publishing their report had been to correct Montague Shearman's mistake in suggesting that the Rugby game was the lone example of 'primitive' football surviving in a school. This done, the report attempts to provide some account of how the carrying game developed. In seeking corroboration for the Webb Ellis story the committee were prompted by no more sinister motive than a desire to expand their knowledge of the matter through the recollections of contemporary witnesses while there were still one or two alive to consult.

The big mistake made by the Old Rugbeian Society was in the wording of the plaque which they decided to erect on the Close in 1900 to pronounce their understandable pride in the game which had developed there. They intended to celebrate the game, but instead created a myth. As soon as they decided to mention Webb Ellis they were in trouble. He was more anti-hero than hero, and the only adjective they had to describe him was 'unfair'. In a piece of inspired rhetoric he was instead recorded as having shown 'a fine disregard for the rules of the game as played in his day', and his obstinate refusal to comply with custom was translated into a spirited and imaginative defiance of regulation. Suddenly Webb Ellis became, in the popular imagination, a rebel in a good cause.

All manner of underlying intentions have been ascribed to the Old Rugbeians on the evidence of that granite plaque in the headmaster's wall. If they had been looking for a great man in order to establish for Rugby football a history in the respectable Carlylean mould as WJ Baker has suggested, then they could have chosen a more acceptable figurehead from the many whose individual initiatives had influenced the early game. If they had been seeking to make some kind of statement about public school amateurism in football they could, indeed perhaps *should*, have inscribed the stone in celebration of the game itself. As it was they chose to record the fact that their committee had investigated and verified, that, if running with the ball was to be recognized as the single most distinctive feature of Rugby Football, then William Webb Ellis was the first boy recorded as having tried it out. They then faced the difficulty of his reputation, and came up with a formula which at the same time acknowledged and made a virtue of his flagrantly irregular behaviour. It was a brilliant piece of public relations, and captured the collective imagination as surely as the most carefully orchestrated modern advertising campaign.

The popular history of Rugby Football was written in 1900 quite literally in a tablet of stone. The report of the committee carefully noting the gradual acceptance of the carrying game was forgotten, and the 'big bang' story was born.

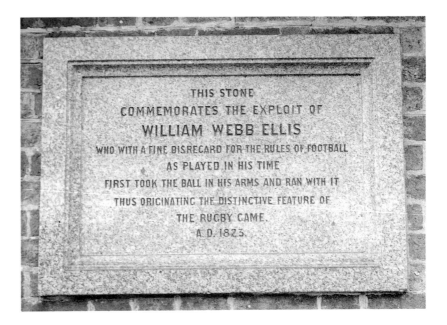

Commemorative tablet set in the Headmaster's wall on the Close

The Complete Correspondence from the Report of the Sub-committee of the Old Rugbeian Society, 1897

FROM *THE ORIGIN OF RUGBY FOOTBALL* BY HF WILSON, HE CHILD, AG GUILLEMARD, AND HL STEPHEN

Dear Sir,

Your Committee have raised an old and warmly debated question of half a century back. In my first year, 1834, running with the ball to get a try by touching down within goal was not absolutely forbidden, but a jury of Rugby boys of that day would almost certainly have found a verdict of 'justifiable homicide' if a boy had been killed in running in. The practice grew, and was tolerated more and more, and indeed became rather popular in 1838–39 from the prowess of Jem Mackie, the great 'runner in'.

Jem was very fleet of foot as well as brawny of shoulder, so that when he got hold of the ball it was very hard to stop his rush. He was a School House and Sixth Form boy, therefore on the numerically absurdly weak side in those two most exciting matches of that time. (He was M.P. for Kirkcud-brightshire in later years, and a very useful but silent member). The question remained debateable when I was Captain of Big Side in 1841–42 when we settled it (as we believed) for all time. 'Running in' was made lawful with these limitations, that the ball must be caught *on the bound*, that the catcher was not 'off his side,' that there should be no 'handing on,' but the catcher must carry the ball in and 'touch down' himself. Picking up off the ground was made absolutely illegal, as [was] running in from off your side – a ball caught by a player 'off his side' must be *at once* knocked on or the holder might be mauled; and no handing on was allowed. I am not familiar with the present rules but from looking on now and then I suppose our old settlement has been superseded; at least the game seems to me to have developed into much too much of hand-ball. I may be *laudator temporis acti*, but hold very strongly that the football of the fifties and early sixties was the finest form that football has ever attained. I don't doubt Matt. Bloxam was right that 'running in' was not known in his day. The 'Webb Ellis tradition' had not survived to my day . . .

Ever yours most truly,
Thos. Hughes.

On receipt of this letter it was thought advisable to enquire further of Judge Hughes whether the rules of which he spoke were committed to writing, and if he could name any survivors of the period between Mr. Bloxam and himself. He was good enough to reply as follows, from the same address, on 18th March, 1895:

Dear Mr. Wilson,

I don't suppose you will find any entry of the rules as to 'running in' in writing amongst the old Bigside books, if indeed these still exist, which I should doubt. Our Bigside Football 'levies,' at which such matters were settled, were held on the Island, or the little mound under the Elms, between Littleside and Bigside (I fancy it has disappeared like the moat) either before or after matches, during which sharp discussion had arisen whether such and such a goal should count, or the like. I certainly can't remember *signing* any written rules as Captain, but am quite clear about the practice having been settled, as in my last. The only living survivor of the period between Bloxam and myself, who was a good enough player to remember the rules as to 'drop-kicks,' 'running in,' 'picking up,' &c., that I remember, is H. H. Gibbs [now Lord Aldenham], the head of the big firm of Antony Gibbs and Sons, and leader of the Bimetallists. His address is St. Dunstan's, Regent's Park, and I should advise you to write to or go and see him. He was of the School House, got into the Sixth, and left (I think) in 1837.

All success to the Committee, of whose existence I am glad to know.

Ever yours,
Thos. Hughes.

This second letter afforded two additional clues which were immediately followed up. Lord Aldenham very kindly wrote at once to the following effect:

March 22, 1895.

Dear Sir,

My evidence does not carry the matter much further back than Tom Hughes's can do, seeing that my Rugby career began in October, 1832, and his in October, 1834.

I can hardly think that the practice of running with the ball was 'only gradually coming into vogue' in his day.

I well remember that it was fully recognised in mine which ended in 1836. At what time it began in those four years, if it did not begin before, I can't say, but I certainly remember no time when it was considered absolutely illegitimate.

But any one who practised it set in more active motion the legs of his opponents for the purposes both of running and 'hacking,' using the latter as upon *hostem humani generis*; but if he escaped, it was all fair. Probably from what you quote from Bloxam it must have arisen between 1820 and 1830, and very likely in the year to which he assigns it. I recommend your consulting Peregrine Birch, a zealous football-player, whose Rugby record dates from December 1831. I don't remember his address, but it is I think at no great distance from London, and you would find it in one of the Directories at your Club.

Faithfully yours,
Henry H. Gibbs.

Besides writing himself, Lord Aldenham was so good as to send the enquiry on to Mr. J. R. Lyon, who entered Rugby School on August 12th, 1830. That gentleman wrote from Elstree, Herts, on March 24th, 1895:

My dear Gibbs,

re Football

My impression is that I left Rugby in 1834. [He entered August 2, 1830, H.H.G.] At that time I am satisfied that it was allowable to pick up the ball if you could, and run with it through the adversary's lines − dodging the players as well as you could, and keeping your legs if possible in spite of hacks and collaring, and kicking a goal or touching the ball behind the post, to secure a *try* at the goal.

My brother Edward, who was at Rugby in Tom Hughes's time, agrees with me as to this, and I believe at the present time this practice is continued, but it is long since I have witnessed a Rugby game, and much longer since I played, as you may imagine . . .

Believe me, sincerely yours,
John R. Lyon.

Mr. Lushington also kindly sent the following answer:

March 24, 1895.

Dear Mr. Wilson,

Mr. Bloxam was a very painstaking antiquarian, and I should think his account was pretty sure to be accurate. Hughes's memory is probably more accurate on the point than mine, which tells pretty much the same story. It was done in my time, that is in the autumns of 1838–39, when I was coming to the front in football, but I should say not done very often. I remember trying it on myself on one occasion in particular, when I got particularly neatly hacked over for my pains. But it certainly was never objected to, as far as I remember, and therefore must have been recognised as a regular part of the game, as we were extremely strict about all off-side rules then.

Yours sincerely,
F. Lushington.

One other letter may be added to those of this first group of correspondents. It comes from Mr. J. W. Cunningham, until a short time ago, when he retired, the Secretary of King's College, London:

May, 8, 1895.

Dear Sir,

As far as I can call to mind, I should say that in my time the practice at Rugby was to catch hold of the ball if possible and to run with it as far as the enemy would let you. When the practice began, or who brought it in, I have no knowledge, but I can have no doubt the plan was in force and legal in my time.

Very truly yours,
J. W. Cunningham.

A fresh line of enquiry was opened up, in the most sportsmanlike manner, by Mr. Morris Davies, the energetic Secretary of the Old Rugbeian Society, who has all along taken a keen interest in our investigations. He kindly called on the late Mr. George Benn of Rugby, and found him most ready to put his recollection on paper. It will be seen that they do not quite tally with those of the authorities already cited; but they are extremely valuable in themselves, as Mr. Benn was perfectly clear on the points he discussed. We may also mention that he remembered Mrs. Ellis, the mother of Mr. Bloxam's hero, but does not think he ever saw the latter:

May 16, 1895.

Dear Sir,

My recollections of football at Rugby would begin about 1835, for though I entered the School [October 7] in 1830, I could not have played before 1835.

I do not remember any rules against running with the ball, but picking it up from the ground was considered decidedly wrong and not allowed. If the ball was caught on the first bound, it was quite legitimate, when there seemed to be a chance of getting through, to run with it, and, if no chance presented itself, a drop-kick was the usual custom.

I think it must have been in 1839 or 1840 that a match was made of 15 or 20 on each side chosen from those who were thought to be some of the best players, and I remember coming into collision with Mackie and getting the worst of it. Hughes would most likely remember the match: he and his brother playing in it. *Running with the ball was certainly in existence in my time*, but I do not remember any sort of plan of passing it from one to the other at that time.

There are two Old Rugbeians of my day that might tell you something, Sir Alexander John Arbuthnot and his brother Sir Charles George Arbuthnot. Both played at football in my time and could very likely give valuable information as to running, &c., &c.

I remain, yours truly,
George Chas. Benn.

Sir Alexander Arbuthnot recently replied to an enquiry by the Committee as follows:

February 1, 1897.

Dear Sir,

I am sorry that I cannot answer your question as to Rugby Football. When I went to Rugby in 1832 the practice of running with the ball was in full force, and I never heard until I read your letter this morning when or under what circumstances it had commenced. When I went from Rugby to Haileybury, then the East India College, in 1850, I found the Harrow game in vogue there. I thought it a stupid game and got a Committee appointed to devise a new game. The Committee consisted of a Harrow boy, a Woolwich boy, who had also been at Rugby, and me. We abolished running with the ball; but with this exception adopted the Rugby rules, as to off your side, etc., etc.

Yours very truly,
Alex. J. Arbuthnot.

It remained for Mr. Davies to discover a still older Rugbeian than those we have already named, in the person of the Rev. T. Harris, brother of Mr. E. Harris the Solicitor at Rugby, who have both died within the last two years. From him, through the kindness of his friend, the Rev. H. Homer, the following exceedingly interesting particulars were obtained, affording a remarkable corroboration of Mr. Bloxam's statements. We print Mr. Homer's letter first. He entered the School in October, 1828:

May 11, 1895.
Dear Mr. Davies,

Your letter of the 9th duly reached me yesterday. Of Mr. William Webb Ellis I can give you no information. I do not recollect sufficiently about the game in question to make statements for publication. I do not know that I ever saw any rules for the game. There were rules, of course, observed. As far as I recollect, *the ball was carried*, if a fellow could get hold of it; but how far this was done depended on circumstances. As Sam Weller would have said, he was tackled pretty quickly, who tried on this dodge. I am sending your letter on to Mr. Thomas Harris, who was much senior to me, and who would be likely to know something about the things you have asked information about. I should think that Mr. F. H. Deane of South Kilworth, who is constantly in Rugby, could tell you about the game as played in his day. We were contemporaries. When I hear from Mr. Harris I will write to you again.

Believe me,
Yours very truly,
Henry Homer.

Now comes Mr. Harris, who (like Mr. Bloxam) administers a deadly thrust to the a priori theorising of the Badminton volume. He entered the school in September, 1819, aged 7.

May 13, 1895.
My dear Homer,

I will try and answer the questions submitted as to Rules of Football at Rugby in my time, ending with the year 1828.

1. *Picking up and running with the ball in hand was distinctly forbidden.* If a player caught the ball on a rebound from the ground, or from a stroke of the hand, *he was allowed to take a few steps so as to give effect to a 'Drop-kick,' but no more:* subject of course to interruption from the adverse players. I remember Mr. William Webb Ellis perfectly. He was an admirable cricketer, *but was*

generally regarded as inclined to take unfair advantages at Football. I should not quote him in any way as an authority.

2. If the ball was caught in the hands from a kick, the catcher was entitled to a 'place try' at goal, retiring a sufficient distance from the place where the catch was made.

3. All laying hands upon and holding a player was strictly forbidden under any circumstances. . . .

> With kind regards,
> Yours very truly,
> T. Harris

I do not remember any other material points in connection with Football: a grand game as I used to consider it, as formerly played. I may add that my brother, John Harris, who left Rugby in 1832, and who was a devoted lover of the game, agrees with me in the particulars given above. He happens to be at this time staying with me.

> May 25, 1895.

Dear Sir,

I am afraid that I can add but little to the recollections of Rugby Football which I gave in my letter to Homer. As to Mr. W. Webb Ellis and his practices, you must observe that I was several years his junior, and had not either reasons or opportunities for closely observing his manner of play. *I am sure, however, that it was very generally regarded as unfair by the leading players of the day.* It may be that his practice of running with the ball, which Mr. Matthew Bloxam speaks of as having been invented by him, was the point objected to; but of this I cannot speak from my own observation.

I may add that in the matches played by boys in the lower part of the School, while I was myself a junior, the cry of 'Hack him over' was always raised against any player who was seen to be running with the ball in his hands.

Our Laws in those days were unwritten and traditionary, so that I can give no authority beyond custom.

Pray accept my thanks for the kind words to myself and those in which you speak of my late brother.

> Believe me, yours very truly,
> T. Harris.

It may, we think, be fairly considered to be proved from the foregoing statements, that in 1820 the form of football in vogue at Rugby was something approximating more closely to Association than to what is known as Rugby football to-day, that at some date between 1820 and 1830 the innovation was introduced of running with the ball, [and] that this was in all probability done in the latter half of 1823 by Mr. W. Webb Ellis, who is credited by Mr. Bloxam with the invention and whose 'unfair practices' were (according to Mr. Harris) the subject of general remark at the time. To this we would add that the innovation was regarded as of doubtful legality for some time, and only gradually became accepted as part of the game, but obtained a customary status between 1830 and 1840, and was duly legalized first by Bigside Levee in 1841–42 (as stated by Judge Hughes) and finally by the Rules of 1846 (Appendix A).

We append a few other letters received from Old Rugbeians which are of interest in connection with the game. For the two first we are indebted to the research of Mr. H. L. Stephen.

Nov. 11, 1895.

Dear Mr. Stephen,

I am afraid I cannot throw any light that will be much use in your enquiry about the Rugby Football. I was playing that game pretty constantly from about 1830 to 1833, but as to carrying the ball, though I remember it was an occasional practice to do so, I cannot recall that there was any law on the subject. My impression is that it used to be carried until an opponent came so near as to be within what might be called kicking distance, say two or three feet, when it had to be thrown down between the two. This was the practice, I am pretty sure, but I do not think that there was any printed or written code to refer to. I am sorry that I cannot contribute any further information on the subject.

I remain,
Yours very truly,
H. G. Allen.

Mr. Allen, however, sent on the enquiry to a contemporary of his own, the Stipendiary Magistrate of Swansea, Mr. John Coke Fowler (entered the School September 1830), who replied as follows:

Nov. 12, 1895.

My dear Allen,

As to football, my recollection of a great many games at Rugby is quite in accord with yours. Many a time I have caught and run with the ball in the way you describe, and rushed towards the goal to try a drop-kick. But one was usually intercepted and obliged to put the ball down, before one's kick could send it over the bar. I have, however, no knowledge of the practice before 1830, or of the rules which governed you and me and Co. . . .

Yours sincerely,
John Coke Fowler.

Another source of information suggested by Judge Hughes was Mr. Peregrine Birch, (entered the School December 1831,) whose son sent the following letter:

6th June, 1895.

Dear Sir,

I ought to have written to you before to tell you that my father's recollection of the exact Rugby game in his time is not very good, but he seems pretty clear upon the fact that when he was at Rugby the ball could not be 'picked up,' but that, if caught, it could be carried as long as, physically speaking, the carrier was allowed to do so. I tried to learn whether the ball had to be caught before it touched the ground, or whether it might have been caught on first bounce; and I fancy from what he said the first bounce would have done; but my father was not very certain about this. I have no doubt that my father did carry the ball very effectively, for within my memory he was an extraordinary drop-kick. . . .

Yours truly,
R. W. Peregrine Birch.

Mr. Samuel Garratt (entered the School September, 1831) wrote from Rocheberie, Blackwater Road, Eastbourne, on 23rd May, 1895:

Dear Sir,

I have been hunting through my papers for a small book of Rules on the Rugby game of football, or should have replied to yours of the 16th earlier. The practice of running with the ball and being hacked down by the pursuers was in vogue when I entered the School. I enclose the copy of Rules referred to, which please return.

Yours faithfully,
Saml. Garratt.

Canon Nevill of Norwich has sent the following letter:

May 4, 1897.

My dear Wilson,

I have put down my recollections of the custom prevailing in my time 1830–40, with regard to running with the ball.

If the ball were fairly caught before touching the ground, it was lawful to run as far as possible, and any kick, punt or drop, was allowed.

If the ball had touched the ground and was then caught on the bound, it was lawful to run, but only a drop kick was allowed.

If the ball were *thrown by hand*, especially from the trees, the ball must be thrown down, no punt or drop, or running was counted fair.

If however it were *kicked out* from 'touch,' it was treated as in other cases; if caught in the air or on the first bound, running if possible was allowed.

But in no case and under no circumstances was it fair to take up the ball from the ground and run: whether still or rolling it might only be kicked as it was found.

Yours very sincerely,
H. R. Nevill.

The Committee received the following communication, through Mr. Davies, from the Rector of South Kilworth, mentioned above by Mr. Homer:

Dear Sir,

I entered the School in 1830 and left in 1839. During that period there were no backs, half-backs, or forwards selected before the matches commenced, as is now done: it was very much 'please yourself:' but certain celebrated kickers and fast runners somehow or another used to stay behind, waiting outside the scrummages to seize the opportunity of making a drop, etc. (I infer the captains arranged all this just before commencing.) I believe that running with the ball in the arms, taken on the bound, prevailed in my time; but as a rule a mark was made from fair catches, and the player making the mark retired towards his own goal and took a drop or a punt. A successful drop could score a goal, but a punt could not. If the player made his mark within a reasonable distance of the goal posts, the ball was placed and a try attempted.

I feel sure when a ball was thrown out of touch at right angles, that a player to whom it came might knock it on in the direction of the goal he was making for.

Yours very truly,
Francis Hugh Deane, D.D.

CHAPTER 6   *THE SINGLE ACT*

The words of the plaque have been adopted as the starting point for nearly every investigation since made into the origins of Rugby football. Articles are regularly written and programmes broadcast which claim to have exposed the Webb Ellis 'myth'. Most are content to quote selectively from the evidence collected by the Old Rugbeian Committee about William Webb Ellis. Few trouble to read the rest of the document in which it is made perfectly clear that running with the ball was introduced, though not established, in the decade between 1820 and 1830. This fact does not depend upon the probability or otherwise of Webb Ellis being the innovator, but is supported by all the available sources. Assuming the generally accepted premise that the single most significant difference between Rugby and Association football is the rule which allows the ball to be carried, then it is fair to say that modern rugby football can trace its ancestry in a direct line to the game invented on the Close at Rugby.

In his chapter on Rugby Union in *Sport in Britain: A Social History*, Gareth Williams perceptively remarks that the 'commemorative tablet erected at Rugby School . . . tells us more about the late-Victorian mind than it does about the early nineteenth-century beginnings of rugby football'. He might usefully have applied the same judgement to the arguments expressed in *Gentlemen, Barbarians and Players* which he goes on to endorse. The authors, E. Dunning and K. Sheard, are sociologists who allow their twentieth century preconceptions to intrude upon their evaluation of the historical facts. In dismissing the Webb Ellis story they argue that 'it is just not sociologically plausible that a deeply entrenched traditional game could have been changed fundamentally by a single act, particularly that of a low-status individual such as Webb Ellis is reputed to have been'. It couldn't have happened, they are saying, because Webb Ellis was a day-boy and therefore of no consequence. Yet Bloxam is at pains to point out that if he had not been a praeposter and high up in the school Webb Ellis would not have got away with it. There was never any suggestion that his contemporaries *approved* of his play, but they appear to have been unable to prevent it.

A single act, say Dunning and Sheard, would not have been effective in establishing a new practice. Quite right. But it is equally unlikely that any *single* act would have been sufficient to earn Webb Ellis a reputation for unfairness. Rules were, and are, often broken, but it is a regular habit of misbehaviour that gives a player a bad name. Ellis was a clever boy, and since promotion through the school in those days depended entirely upon academic ability, once he had reached the Sixth Form he had automatically become a praeposter. Dunning and Sheard appear to think that before Dr Arnold's arrival at Rugby 'prefects had been selected by virtually autonomous competition between the boys'. This was not the case, though had their assumption been correct, the sociological argument that Webb Ellis was a 'low status individual' would hardly have squared with the fact that he had become a praeposter in 1823 at a relatively young age. He had a full three football seasons in the Sixth Form, and therefore had plenty of opportunity to persist in his breach of the rules if he so wished. There were no referees to prevent him, only the weight of opinion of the other leading players. Furthermore the expulsion or withdrawal of many of his contemporaries following a rebellion in 1822 had significantly reduced the numbers in his peer group and thereby diminished any opposition he might have encountered.

The possibility for change was generally acknowledged in a scheme of play which outlined a few straightforward rules and left the particulars open to discussion. Flexibility was then, and remained for the next fifty years, a notable feature of the Rugby game. It was this willingness to adapt to prevailing conditions which allowed the game to adjust and ultimately to survive. In that sense it was not, as Dunning and Sheard believed, 'a deeply entrenched traditional game'. Nor was it 'uncivilized'. Indeed Bloxam and others who played the non-carrying game recall it as being well organized, with little of the 'struggling' which characterised the succeeding decades.

Barbarians, Gentlemen and Players continues with the even more curious proposition that the boys at Rugby were motivated to make deliberate changes in the structure of their football to realise 'the desire of the Rugby personnel to get it accepted as a leading school'. The argument is based upon the assumption that Rugbeians believed themselves to be of a lower social standing than members of the 'older' public schools. The evidence for this supposition is taken in part from a story which appears in public school folklore in many variations, but is here quoted as the reply of the captain of cricket at Eton to his Rugby counterpart who had requested a match: 'Rugby, Rugby. . . . well, we'll think about it if you can tell me where it is' – a joke which is perpetuated today by Southerners who profess to have no knowledge of England beyond the north London suburb of Watford. There was, of course, and indeed there still is rivalry between schools, but this is not a phenomenon confined to the public schools, and usually occurs between institutions of more or less equal status.

Not only is it suggested that Rugby was anxious to improve 'the comparatively low standing of its personnel' by asserting its individuality, but Rugbeians are further purported to have been 'constrained to divest themselves of socially "contaminating" attributes, to abandon activities with lower-class connotation'. These were the motives to which Dunning and Sheard ascribe the invention of Rugby's distinctive version of football. They ascribe the H-shaped goal, the oval ball and the practice of running in partly to 'a desire to draw attention to the school', and partly to 'an attempt to develop a game-form radically different from that played by the lower classes; that is a type of football devoid of the socially contaminating lower class associations and therefore appropriate as a game for gentlemen'.

If Rugbeians had indeed entertained the conscious social ambitions attributed to them it is curious that they should have allowed their own game to grow away from those played in the schools they were so desirous to emulate. As we have seen the popular games which survived into the mid-nineteenth century generally allowed both kicking and carrying, and included a great deal of effective scrummaging. Rugby had, if anything, moved towards these alleged 'contaminating lower-class' games, and not away from them.

Dr Thomas Arnold,
Headmaster of Rugby School,
1828–42 (T Phillips)

Dunning and Sheard see the introduction of written rules at Rugby in 1845 as a necessary measure 'to reduce the possibility of disruption and to minimise the chances that matches which started out as playful competition would be transformed into "serious" fighting'. It is their interpretation that the rules relating to physical force were made 'more stringent' in 1845, though there are no previous written laws on which to base their comparison. As we shall see later, the rules were drawn up with such speed and such absence of dissent that it is probably safe to assume that they simply confirmed and clarified the *status quo*. The in-built constraints were based upon precedents which had been agreed by common consent as the game developed. In their imaginative look at these first printed rules the sociologists go so far as to suggest that as 'it was stipulated that players were to use only their persons for controlling and propelling the ball, this suggests that, prior to 1845 bats and sticks had sometimes been used'. It would be just as valid to conjecture that before Mrs Beeton consigned her first recipe for beef stew to paper she had been in the occasional habit of using ostrich meat!

Barbarians, Gentlemen and Players is frequently cited as an historical account of the early years of modern Rugby football, but it should be remembered that it is a study presenting a sociological interpretation of the events in terms of a series of class struggles. It is not a history.

Arnold is generally acknowledged to have been a great reforming Headmaster. He did not, as Dunning and Sheard assume, 'settle on a compromise position' between the conflicting pressures of his own middle-class origins and the values of the 'established classes' who, as Trustees, had been responsible for his appointment. Nor was he responding to the market demands of an energetic and ambitious new wealthy middle class. When he was appointed to Rugby in 1828 he inherited an established public school, so successful that it had been completely rebuilt to accommodate a steadily increasing demand for places from the country squires, landowning gentry and churchmen whose sons represented the majority of pupils. Academically the school was in good shape. Morally, in Arnold's view, it was not. This he set out to reform. His motivation was a strong conviction that Christian values could and should be applied to every aspect of daily life, and he believed that he had a duty to send out into society men who would propagate those values. Just before he went to Rugby he expressed in a letter to John Tucker 'a most sincere desire to make it a place of Christian education. At the same time my object will be, if possible, to form Christian men, for Christian boys I can scarcely hope to make'. Had he been Headmaster of any other school, regardless of the social status of his pupils he would have pursued the same course and achieved the same success.

During his Headmastership and afterwards Rugby certainly attracted a greater number of entries from the prosperous industrial families than the other traditional public schools. Arnold's reputation was an important factor, but the geographical location of the school also played a significant part. The building of the railways in the 1830s put Rugby on the map. Routes designed to link the manufacturing heartlands of the Midlands and the North-west with the capital passed within a mile of the school and, along the railways built to transport their goods, the factory owners in significant numbers sent their sons on the train to the most easily accessible of the public schools. Certainly they were seeking to enhance the social standing of themselves and their sons, but these first generation meritocrats were shrewd enough to recognize the value of a first rate education, and were a good deal more concerned to choose a school which would offer their sons the opportunity of academic success than to see that they played a socially acceptable brand of football. Parental concern about their children's achievement on the games field is not generally evident until the last thirty years of the nineteenth century. By then a generation of parents who had themselves taken part in competitive team games at school began to take an interest in the sporting prowess of their sons, and the modern cult of athleticism took off. Football remained a domestic affair in Arnold's Rugby, and few parents would have had much knowledge of how it was played. It is precisely this lack of adult interference which allowed the boys to perfect for themselves a tailor-made sport ideally suited to their own needs. It required no more complex provision than a grass field, goals and a ball, and provided occupation and exercise for any number of participants. In due course the majority of the newer schools which had no traditional games were to appreciate its excellence as a schoolboy game and to adopt it as their own.

SOURCE 6 *Dr Arnold and his Præposters*

FROM *THE LIFE OF DR ARNOLD* BY AP STANLEY

Whilst he made the Præpostors rely upon his support in all just use of their authority, as well as on his severe judgment of all abuse of it, he endeavoured also to make them feel that they were actually fellow-workers with him for the highest good of the school, upon the highest principles and motives – that they had, with him, a moral responsibility and a deep interest in the real welfare of the place. Occasionally during his whole stay, and regularly at the beginning or end of every half-year during his later years, he used to make short addresses to them on their duties, or on the general state of the school, one of which, as an illustration of his general mode of speaking and acting with them, it has been thought worth while to give, as nearly as his pupils could remember it, in the very words he used. After making a few remarks to them on their work in the lessons: 'I will now,' he proceeded, 'say a few words to you as I promised. Speaking to you, as to young men who can enter into what I say, I wish you to feel that you have another duty to perform, holding the situation that you do in the school; of the importance of this I wish you all to feel sensible, and of the enormous influence you possess, in ways in which we cannot, for good or for evil, on all below you; and I wish you to see fully how many and great are the opportunities offered to you here of doing good – good, too, of lasting benefit to yourselves as well as to others; there is no place where you will find better opportunities for some time to come, and you will then have reason to look back to your life here with the greatest pleasure. You will soon find, when you change your life here for that at the Universities, how very few in comparison they are there, however willing you may then be, – at any rate during the first part of your life there. That there is good, working in the school, I most fully believe, and we cannot feel too thankful for it; in many individual instances, in different parts of the school, I have seen the change from evil to good – to mention instances would of course be wrong. The state of the school is a subject of congratulation to us all, but only so far as to encourage us to increased exertions; and I am sure we ought all to feel it a subject of most sincere thankfulness to God; but we must not stop here; we must exert ourselves with earnest prayer to God for its continuance. And what I have often said before I repeat now: what we must look for here is, firstly, religious and moral principles; secondly, gentlemanly conduct; thirdly, intellectual ability'.

CHAPTER 7

THE HOMERIC STRUGGLE

Thomas Arnold was Headmaster of Rugby from 1828 until his sudden death in 1842 on the day before his 47th birthday. He is generally supposed to have been responsible for the introduction of the idea of muscular Christianity into the British educational system and is frequently cited as the originator of organized games. He would have been amazed. It was no part of his intention that the reforms he made at Rugby should promote sport into a central role in school life.

When he arrived at Rugby, Arnold found a system in place 'not unlike to the administration of a conquered state. The Head Master was an autocrat . . . he and his colleagues were looked upon as the natural enemies of boyhood'. The boys in their turn had a private organization of their own in which the strong ruled the weak. Among themselves they adopted a strict code of honour, but beyond their own society the general standard of behaviour was often dreadful. It was Arnold's genius that instead of trying to destroy this schoolboy mafia system he chose to employ it for his own purposes.

The idea of a formal hierarchy among the pupils had been introduced by Dr James when he was appointed Headmaster in 1778. He brought with him from Eton the scheme of appointing senior boys as praeposters and using them to govern the younger ones. He saw this as an important part of the administrative structure which he outlined in meticulous detail and put into operation at a rapidly expanding Rugby. Unusually for a headmaster of that time he concerned himself

Dr James's monument

not only with the education of his senior pupils, but he showed considerable imagination in trying to improve the minds of younger boys. In a memorial tribute to him Samuel Butler, who was his star pupil and became Headmaster of Shrewsbury School, remembers that James, 'thinking according to the Comenian system that pictures are the most intelligible books to children, painted the planets on the garden wall bounding the play close.' And so no opportunity was lost, even in the playground, to reach out to the minds of idle boys.

> *E'en on the wall, that they may read who run,*
> *At distance due the planets watch the sun,*
> *And many an idler first acknowledged there*
> *His moon-blest earth, and every world a sphere.*

Doubtless the planets made excellent targets in the private games of the bored small boys sent to keep goal during football, but what better way to impress upon them the science of the skies.

Dr James' great skills lay more in organization and in scholarship than in reform. He preferred to legislate against unacceptable behaviour rather than to make much attempt to improve it, and was more concerned to repair damage than to prevent it – one of his rules commanded that boys in boarding houses should repair any windows broken in neighbouring properties *at the end of each week*. Generally they clubbed together to pay the endless glazier's bills, and an offender would only expect to pay for his own damage if he was discovered by the authorities. Such was the schoolboy code which prevailed, and, as may be expected, protection was paid for with penalties. Differences between equals were settled by organized fights surrounded by 'all the ceremonies of the fistic art', and junior boys were completely at the mercy of the senior boys whose natural authority was endorsed by Dr James through his appointment of praeposters.

Out of this system had grown the expectation that the fags would be at the beck and call of the praeposters with little control from the masters. The arrangement had been in operation for 50 years before Arnold came on the scene, and he was far too wise to the conservative ways of boys to seek to abolish it. Instead he tried to reform it by expecting his praeposters to accept that responsibility went hand in hand with authority. The senior boys continued to govern the school, but were taught that they did so as a duty and not as a right.

Some of the more barbarous of the customs perpetrated in the boys' sub-culture had already been phased out by Dr Wooll in 1814. The rites of passage from one form to another, which involved running the gauntlet between lines of boys wielding knotted hand-kerchiefs or hurling clods of clay had been stopped, and the gentler penalty was substituted of providing a treat or 'guttle' for the boys in the next form. However Dr Wooll did nothing to limit the autocratic rule of the praeposters, and by 1822 the fags had had enough. Following some injustice they defied both praeposters and masters in a prolonged episode which resulted in the expulsion of some and the withdrawal of many more. These boys were, of course the contemporaries of Webb Ellis, and their departure considerably reduced the weight of competition in his immediate peer group.

By Arnold's day some of the old terrors were being remembered with nostalgia, and the *Rugby Magazine* of 1836 positively lamented the passing of tougher times;

> *In the days when twenty fellows*
> *Drank out of one large mug,*
> *And pewter were the dishes,*
> *And a tin can was the jug;*
> *In the days when shoes and boots*
> *Were three times a week japanned,*
> *And we sat on stools, not sofas,*
> *There were giants in the land!*

When new boys on the pump were set
To pelt at and to sing,
Or sent from the Close to Pendred's
For a pennyworth of string,
In the days when fags a long hour
In the passage had to stand,
In the days of happy night fags
There were giants in the land.

When Sixth and Fifth form fellows
Had all been duly chaired,
And he who told a falsehood
Was cobbed and never spared,
And we walked around the School-field
With our breakfast in our hand,
Ere the days of tea and coffee, –
There were giants in the land.

By the time these verses were written it is apparent that Arnold's reforms had taken root. The boy mafia, with many of its attendant customs and barbarisms, had been sufficiently reduced for the boys themselves to acknowledge its passing. There were some regrets. There is an implication that Rugby had lost as well as gained by Arnold's changes, and that it was in danger of becoming soft. Sofas and tea were replacing stools and beer, and academic promotion was no longer accompanied by ritualistic rites of passage to higher forms. The law of the jungle had been tamed to a large extent by the moral and religious pressures brought to bear on the ruling boys by Arnold, but he had wisely made no attempt to control the organization of their games. This was left entirely to the pupils themselves.

Major decisions, such as when cricket should give way to football in the autumn, were made by a democratic meeting of the whole school. Early in September the canvassing began, 'the question becomes a murmur, the murmur becomes a growl, and growls are always listened to, if loud enough'. Finally a 'Levee of Big-Side' was arranged, and the whole school assembled to hear the motion proposed that football should be introduced. Supporters would turn up wearing two or three overcoats just to stress that the cold weather had come in, while the cricketers in their shirt sleeves argued for a precious week or two longer for their sport. Others occasionally proposed a compromise, half the Close for football and half for cricket, but 'good healthy excitement never likes your moderate people much', and they never prevailed. Discussion was kept to a minimum, most of the voters having made up their minds beforehand, and a show of hands, with a division if called for, decided the issue. Immediately footballs were purchased and brought into play and the first puntabout began.

The introduction of these formal procedures into the boys' conduct of their own affairs was a hall-mark of Arnold's headmastership. Sport, debating and discipline were each governed by a strictly observed code. The opportunity was inbuilt for dissenting voices to be heard, and this principle applied as much in football as elsewhere.

In his letters to the Old Rugbeian enquiry Thomas Hughes tells of settling disputes over points of play in 'levies' held on the Island, or on the little mound under the elms. The Captain of Big Side and a group of senior players would gather either before or *after* matches and 'sharp discussion' took place about the legality of points of play. If any dissenting voices had been raised they would decide after the day's play whether goals should count or not. Throughout the 1830s policy was discussed and rules decided by this touchline cabinet, and from it emerged an acknowledged formula for football play.

At one such gathering in 1841–2 Hughes recalls the question of running with the ball was settled 'as we believed, for all time.' He and others are sure that running with the ball to get a try by touching down within goal 'was not absolutely forbidden' in the early 1830s. Lord Aldenham & JR Lyon who entered in 1830 and 1832 respectively, were both certain that running was allowable in their day, though both add that anyone trying it might expect to face a concerted barrage of hacking and collaring. Indeed the experience of trying to reach the goal line closely reflected the ceremonial run-in to a higher class which had by now passed out of practice but not out of memory. A player running in knew that he would face intense opposition. The difference was that he *chose* to take the risk, and it was in recognition not only of his physical achievement but of his courage that in the rare cases when he succeeded he was rewarded by securing a try at goal.

These individual displays of bravado, regarded with suspicion in Webb Ellis' day, gained respectability in the 1830s when the old scratch matches between teams 'chosen in' on the day were replaced by matches between particular groups bound together by other loyalties. The School House, the biggest single house in the school, began to play matches against the rest of the school. The House side was substantially smaller than the opposition, but it made up in organization and motivation what it lacked in numbers. The circumstances were ripe for the making of heroes. The great kicker and the brave runner were no longer performing for themselves but for their sides, and they came to be regarded not as exhibitionists but as warriors. Football at Rugby was elevated by its classically educated players from a playground game to a Homeric struggle in which strength alone did not necessarily win the day.

The Match

FROM *TOM BROWN'S SCHOOLDAYS* BY THOMAS HUGHES [set in the 1830s]

'But why do you wear white trousers in November?' said Tom. He had been struck by this peculiarity in the costume of almost all the School-house boys.

'Why, bless us, don't you know? – No, I forgot. Why, to-day's the School-house match. Our house plays the whole of the School at football. And we all wear white trousers, to show 'em we don't care for hacks. You're in luck to come to-day. You just will see a match; and Brooke's going to let me play in quarters. That's more than he'll do for any other lower-school boy, except James, and he's fourteen.'

'Who's Brooke?'

'Why, that big fellow who called over at dinner, to be sure. He's cock of the School, and head of the School-house side, and the best kick and charger in Rugby.'

'Oh, but do show me where they play. And tell me about it. I love football so, and have played all my life. Won't Brooke let me play?'

'Not he,' said East, with some indignation; 'why, you don't know the rules – you'll be a month learning them. And then it's no joke playing-up in a match, I can tell you. Quite another thing from your private school games. Why, there's been two collar-bones broken this half, and a dozen fellows lamed. And last year a fellow had his leg broken.'

Tom listened with the profoundest respect to this chapter of accidents, and followed East across the level ground till they came to a sort of gigantic gallows to two poles eighteen feet high, fixed upright in the ground some fourteen feet apart, with a cross bar running from one to the other at the height of ten feet or thereabouts.

'This is one of the goals,' said East, 'and you see the other, across there, right opposite, under the Doctor's wall. Well, the match is for the best of three goals; whichever side kicks two goals wins: and it won't do, you see, just to kick the ball through these posts, it must go over the cross bar; any height'll do, so long as it's between the posts. You'll have to stay in goal to touch the ball when it rolls behind the posts, because if the other side touch it they have a try at goal. Then we fellows in quarters, we play just about in front of goal here, and have to turn the ball and kick it back before the big fellows on the other side can follow it up. And in front of us all the big fellows play, and that's where the scrummages are mostly.'

Tom's respect increased as he struggled to make out his friend's technicalities, and the other set to work to explain the mysteries of 'off your side,' 'drop-kicks,' 'punts,' 'places,' and the other intricacies of the great science of football.

'But how do you keep the ball between the goals?' said he; 'I can't see why it mightn't go right down to the chapel.'

'Why, that's out of play,' answered East. 'You see this gravel-walk running down all along this side of the playing-ground, and the line of elms opposite on the other? Well, they're the bounds. As soon as the ball gets past them, it's in touch, and out of play. And then whoever first touches it, has to knock it straight out amongst the players-up, who make two lines with a space between them, every fellow going on his own side. Ain't there just fine scrummages then! and the three trees you see there which come out into the play, that's a tremendous place when the ball hangs there, for you get thrown against the trees, and that's worse than any hack.'

Tom wondered within himself, as they strolled back again towards the fives' court, whether the matches were really such break-neck affairs as East represented, and whether, if they were, he should ever get to like them and play-up well.

He hadn't long to wonder, however, for next minute East cried out, 'Hurra! here's the punt-about, – come along and try your hand at a kick.' The punt-about is the practice ball, which is just brought out and kicked about anyhow from one boy to another before callings-over and dinner, and at other odd times. They joined the boys who brought it out, all small School-house fellows, friends of East; and Tom had the pleasure of trying his skill, and performed very creditably, after first driving his foot three inches into the ground, and then nearly kicking his leg into the air, in vigorous efforts to accomplish a drop-kick after the manner of East.

Presently more boys and bigger came out, and boys from other houses on their way to calling-over, and more balls were sent for. The crowd thickened as three o'clock approached; and when the hour struck, one hundred and fifty boys were hard at work. Then the balls were held, the master of the week came down in cap and gown to calling-over, and the whole school of three hundred boys swept into the big school to answer to their names.

'I may come in, mayn't I?' said Tom, catching East by the arm and longing to feel one of them.

'Yes, come along, nobody'll say anything. You won't be so eager to get into calling-over after a month,' replied his friend; and they marched into the big school together, and up to the further end, where that illustrious form, the lower fourth, which had the honour of East's patronage for the time being, stood.

The master mounted into the high desk by the door, and one of the præpostors of the week stood by him on the steps, the other three marching up and down the middle of the school with their canes, calling out 'Silence, silence!' The sixth form stood close by the door on the left, some thirty in number, mostly great big grown men, as Tom thought, surveying them from a distance with awe. The fifth form behind them, twice their number, and not quite so big. These on the left; and on the right the lower fifth, shell, and all the junior forms in order; while up the middle marched the three præpostors.

Then the præposter who stands by the master calls out the names, beginning with the sixth form; and as he calls, each boy answers 'here' to his name, and walks out. Some of the sixth stop at the door to turn the whole string of boys into the close; it is a great match day, and every boy in the School, will-he, nill-he, must be there. The rest of the sixth go forwards into the close, to see that no one escapes by any of the side gates.

To-day, however, being the School-house match, none of the School-house præposters stay by the door to watch for truants of their side; there is *carte blanche* to the School-house fags to go where they like: 'They trust to our honour,' as East proudly informs Tom; 'they know very well that no School-house boy would cut the match. If he did, we'd very soon cut him, I can tell you.'

The master of the week being short-sighted, and the præpostors of the week small, and not well up to their work, the lower school boys employ the ten minutes which elapse before their names are called, in pelting one another vigorously with acorns, which fly about in all directions. The small præpostors dash in every now and then, and generally chastise some quiet, timid boy, who is equally afraid of acorns and canes, while the principal performers get dexterously out of the way; and so calling-over rolls on somehow, much like the big world, punishments lighting on wrong shoulders, and matters going generally in a queer, cross-grained way, but the end coming somehow, which is after all the great point. And now the master of the week has finished, and locked up the big school; and the præpostors of the week come out, sweeping the last remnant of the School fags – who had been loafing about the corners by the fives' court, in hopes of a chance of bolting – before them into the close.

'Hold the punt-about!' 'To the goals!' are the cries, and all stray balls are impounded by the authorities; and the whole mass of boys move up towards the two goals, dividing as they go into three bodies. That little band on the left, consisting of from fifteen to twenty boys, Tom amongst them, who are making for the goal under the School-house wall, are the School-house boys who are not to play-up, and have to stay in goal. The larger body moving to the island goal are the School boys in a like predicament. The great mass in the middle are the players-up, both sides mingled together; they are hanging their jackets, and all who mean real work, their hats, waistcoats, neck-handkerchiefs, and braces, on the railings round the small trees; and there they go by twos and threes up to their respective grounds. There is none of the colour and tastiness of get-up, you will perceive, which lends such a life to the present game at Rugby, making the dullest and worst fought match a pretty sight. Now each house has its own uniform of cap and jersey, of some lively colour: but at the time we are speaking of, plush caps have not yet come in, or uniforms of any sort, except the School-house white trousers, which are abominably cold to-day: let us get to work, bare-headed and girded with our plain leather straps – but we mean business, gentlemen.

And now that the two sides have fairly sundered, and each occupies its own ground, and we get a good look at them, what absurdity is this? You don't mean to say that those fifty or sixty boys in white trousers, many of them quite small, are going to play that huge mass opposite? Indeed I do, gentlemen; they're going to try at any rate, and won't make such a bad fight of it either, mark my word; for hasn't old Brooke won the toss, with his lucky halfpenny, and got choice of goals and kick-off? The new ball you may see lie there quite by itself, in the middle, pointing towards the School or island goal; in another minute it will be well on its way there. Use that minute in remarking how the School-house side is drilled. You will see, in the first place, that the sixth-form boy who has the charge of goal has spread his force (the goal-keepers) so as to occupy the whole space behind the goal-posts, at distances of about five yards apart; a safe and well-kept goal is the foundation of all good play. Old Brooke is talking to the captain of quarters; and now he moves away. See how that youngster spreads his men (the light brigade) carefully over the ground, half-way between their own goal and the body of their own players-up (the heavy brigade). These again play in several bodies; there is young Brooke and the bull-dogs – mark them well – they are the 'fighting brigade,' the 'die-hards,' larking about at leap-frog to keep themselves warm, and playing tricks on one another. And on each side of old Brooke, who is now standing in the middle of the ground and just going to kick-off, you see a separate wing of players-up, each with a boy of acknowledged prowess to look to – here Warner, and there Hedge; but over all is old Brooke, absolute as he of Russia, but wisely and bravely ruling over willing and worshipping subjects, a true football king. His face is earnest and careful as he glances a last time over his array, but full of pluck and hope, the sort of look I hope to see in my general when I go out to fight.

The School side is not organized in the same way. The goal-keepers are all in lumps, any-how and no-how; you can't distinguish between the players-up and the boys in quarters, and there is divided leadership; but with such odds in strength and weight it must take more than that to hinder them from winning; and so their leaders seem to think, for they let the players-up manage themselves.

But now look, there is a slight move forward of the School-house wings; a shout of 'Are you ready?' and loud affirmative reply. Old Brooke takes half-a-dozen quick steps, and away goes the ball spinning towards the School goal; seventy yards before it touches ground, and at no point above twelve or fifteen feet high, a model kick-off; and the School-house cheer and rush on; the ball is returned, and they meet it and drive it back amongst the masses of the School already in motion. Then the two sides close, and you can see nothing for minutes but a swaying crowd of boys, at one point violently agitated. That is where the ball is, and there are the keen players to be met, and the glory and the hard knocks to be got: you hear the dull thud thud of the ball, and the shouts of 'Off your side,' 'Down with him,' 'Put him over,' 'Bravo.' This is what we call 'a scrummage,' gentlemen, and the first scrummage in a School-house match was no joke in the consulship of Plancus.

But see! it has broken; the ball is driven out on the School-house side, and a rush of the School carries it past the School-house players-up. 'Look out in quarters,' Brooke's and twenty other voices ring out. No need to call though: the School-house captain of quarters has caught it on the bound, dodges the foremost School boys who are heading the rush, and sends it back with a good drop-kick well into the enemy's country. And then follows rush upon rush, and scrummage upon scrummage, the ball now driven through into the School-house quarters, and now into the School goal; for the School-house have not lost the advantage which the kick-off and a slight wind gave them at the outset, and are slightly 'penning' their adversaries. You say, you don't see much in it all; nothing but a struggling mass of boys, and a leather ball, which seems to excite them all to great fury, as a red rag does a bull. My dear sir, a battle would look much the same to you, except that the boys would be men, and the balls iron; but a battle would be worth your looking at for all that, and so is a football match. You can't be expected to appreciate the delicate strokes of play, the turns by which a game is lost and won, – it takes an old player to do that, but the broad philosophy of football you can understand if you will. Come along with me a little nearer, and let us consider it together.

The ball has just fallen again where the two sides are thickest, and they close rapidly around it in a scrummage; it must be driven through now by force or skill, till it flies out on one side or the other. Look how differently the boys face it! Here come two of the bull-dogs, bursting through the outsiders; in they go, straight to the heart of the scrummage, bent on driving the ball out on the opposite side. That is what they mean to do. My sons, my sons! you are too hot; you have gone past the ball, and must struggle now right through the scrummage, and get round and back again to your own side, before you can be of any further use. Here comes young Brooke; he goes in as straight as you, but keeps his head, and backs and bends, holding himself still behind the ball, and driving it furiously when he gets the chance. Take a leaf out of his book, you young chargers. Here come Speedicut, and Flashman the School-house bully, with shouts and great action. Won't you two come up to young Brooke, after locking-up, by the School-house fire, with 'Old fellow, wasn't that just a splendid scrummage by the three trees!' But he knows you, and so do we. You don't really want to drive that ball through that scrummage, chancing all hurt for the glory of the School-house –but to make us think that's what you want – a vastly different thing; and fellows of your kidney will never go through more than the skirts of a scrummage, where it's all push and no kicking. We respect boys who keep out of it, and don't sham going in; but you – we had rather not say what we think of you.

Then the boys who are bending and watching on the outside, mark them – they are most useful players, the dodgers; who seize on the ball the moment it rolls out from amongst the chargers, and away with it across to the opposite goal; they seldom go into the scrummage, but must have more coolness than the chargers: as endless as are boys' characters, so are their ways of facing or not facing a scrummage at football.

Three-quarters of an hour are gone; first winds are failing, and weight and numbers beginning to tell. Yard by yard the School-house have been driven back, contesting every inch of ground. The bull-dogs are the colour of mother earth from shoulder to ankle, except young Brooke, who has a marvellous knack of keeping his legs. The School-house are being penned in their turn, and now the ball is behind their goal, under the Doctor's wall. The Doctor and some of his family are there looking on, and seem as anxious as any boy for the success of the School-house. We get a minute's breathing time before old Brooke kicks out, and he gives the word to play strongly for touch, by the three trees. Away goes the ball, and the bull-dogs after it, and in another minute there is shout of 'In touch,' 'Our ball.' Now's your time, old Brooke, while your men are still fresh. He stands with the ball in his hand, while the two sides form in deep lines opposite one another: he must strike it straight out between them. The lines are thickest close to him, but young Brooke and two or three of his men are shifting up further, where the opposite line is weak. Old Brooke strikes it out straight and strong, and it falls opposite his brother. Hurra! that rush has taken it right through the School line, and away past the three trees, far into their quarters, and young Brooke and the bull-dogs are close upon it. The School leaders rush back, shouting 'Look out in goal,' and strain every nerve to catch him, but they are after the fleetest foot in Rugby. There they go straight for the School goal-posts, quarters scattering before them. One after another the bull-dogs go down, but young Brooke holds on. 'He is down.' No! a long stagger, but the danger is past; that was the shock of Crew, the most dangerous of dodgers. And now he is close to the School goal, the ball not three yards before him. There is a hurried rush of the School fags to the spot, but no one throws himself on the ball, the only chance, and young Brooke has touched it right under the School goal-posts.

The School leaders come up furious, and administer toco to the wretched fags nearest at hand; they may well be angry, for it is all Lombard-street to a china orange that the School-house kick a goal with the ball touched in such a good place. Old Brooke of course will kick it out, but who shall catch and place it? Call Crab Jones. Here he comes, sauntering along with a straw in his mouth, the queerest, coolest fish in Rugby: if he were tumbled into the moon this minute, he would just pick himself up without taking his hands out of his pockets or turning a hair. But it is a moment when the boldest charger's heart beats quick. Old Brooke stands with the ball under his arm motioning the School back; he will not kick-out till they are all in goal, behind the posts; they are all edging forwards, inch by inch, to get nearer for the rush at Crab Jones, who stands there in front of old Brooke to catch the ball. If they can reach and destroy him before he catches, the danger is over; and with one and the same rush they will carry it right away to the School-house goal. Fond hope! it is kicked out and caught beautifully. Crab strikes his heel into the ground, to mark the spot where the ball was caught, beyond which the School line may not advance; but there they stand, five deep, ready to rush the moment the ball touches the ground. Take plenty of room! don't give the rush a chance of reaching you! place it true and steady! Trust Crab Jones – he has made a small hole with his heel for the ball to lie on, by which he is resting on one knee, with his eye on old Brooke. 'Now!' Crab places the ball at the word, old Brooke kicks, and it rises slowly and truly as the School rush forward.

Then a moment's pause, while both sides look up at the spinning ball. There it flies, straight between the two posts, some five feet above the cross-bar, an unquestioned goal; and a shout of real genuine joy rings out from the School-house players-up, and a faint echo of it comes over the close from the goal-keepers under the Doctor's wall. A goal in the first hour – such a thing hasn't been done in the School-house match these five years.

'Over!' is the cry: the two sides change goals, and the School-house goal-keepers come threading their way across through the masses of the School; the most openly triumphant of them, amongst whom is Tom, a School-house boy of two hours' standing, getting their ears boxed in the transit. Tom indeed is excited beyond measure, and it is all the sixth-form boy, kindest and safest of goal-keepers, has been able to do, to keep him from rushing out whenever the ball has been near their goal. So he holds him by his side, and instructs him in the science of touching.

At this moment Griffith, the itinerant vendor of oranges from Hill Morton, enters the close with his heavy baskets; there is a rush of small boys upon the little pale-faced man, the two sides mingling together, subdued by the great Goddess Thirst, like the English and French by the streams in the Pyrenees. The leaders are past oranges and apples, but some of them visit their coats, and apply innocent-looking ginger-beer bottles to their mouths. It is no ginger-beer though, I fear, and will do you no good. One short mad rush, and then a stitch in the side, and no more honest play; that's what comes of those bottles.

But now Griffith's baskets are empty, the ball is placed again midway, and the School are going to kick off. Their leaders have sent their lumber into goal, and rated the rest soundly, and one hundred and twenty picked players-up are there, bent on retrieving the game. They are to keep the ball in front of the School-house goal, and then to drive it in by sheer strength and weight. They mean heavy play and no mistake, and so old Brooke sees; and places Crab Jones in quarters just before the goal, with four or five picked players, who are to keep the ball away to the sides, where a try at goal, if obtained, will be less dangerous than in front. He himself, and Warner and Hedge, who have saved themselves still now, will lead the charges.

'Are you ready?' 'Yes.' And away comes the ball kicked high in the air, to give the School time to rush on and catch it as it falls. And here they are amongst us. Meet them like Englishmen, you School-house boys, and charge them home. Now is the time to show what mettle is in you – and there shall be a warm seat by the hall fire, and honour, and lots of bottled beer to-night, for him who does his duty in the next half-hour. And they are well met. Again and again the cloud of their players-up gathers before our goal, and comes threatening on, and Warner or Hedge, with young Brooke and the relics of the bull-dogs, break through and carry the ball back: and old Brooke ranges the field like Job's war-horse; the thickest scrummage parts asunder before his rush, like the waves before a clipper's bows; his cheery voice rings over the field, and his eye is everywhere. And if these miss the ball, and it rolls dangerously in front of our goal, Crab Jones and his men have seized it and sent it away towards the sides with the unerring drop-kick. This is worth living for; the whole sum of school-boy existence gathered up into one straining, struggling half-hour, a half-hour worth a year of common life.

The quarter to five has struck, and the play slackens for a minute before goal; but there is Crew, the artful dodger, driving the ball in behind our goal, on the island side, where our quarters are weakest. Is there no one to meet him? Yes! look at little East! the ball is just at equal distances between the two, and they rush together, the young man of seventeen and the boy of twelve, and kick it at the same moment. Crew passes on without a stagger; East is hurled forward by the shock, and plunges on his shoulder, as if he would bury himself in the ground; but the ball rises straight into the air, and falls behind Crew's back, while the 'bravos' of the School-house attest the pluckiest charge of all that hard-fought day. Warner picks East up lame and half stunned, and he hobbles back into goal, conscious of having played the man.

And now the last minutes are come, and the School gather for their last rush every boy of the hundred and twenty who has a run left in him. Reckless of the defence of their own goal, on they come across the level big-side ground, the ball well down amongst them, straight for our goal, like the column of the Old Guard up the slope at Waterloo. All former charges have been child's play to this. Warner and Hedge have met them, but still on they come. The bull-dogs rush in for the last time; they are hurled over or carried back, striving hand, foot, and eyelids. Old Brooke comes sweeping round the skirts of the play, and, turning short round, picks out the very heart of the scrummage, and plunges in. It wavers for a moment – he has the ball! No, it has passed him, and his voice rings out clear over the advancing tide, 'Look out in goal.' Crab Jones catches it for a moment; but before he can kick, the rush is upon him and passes over him; and he picks himself up behind them with his straw in his mouth, a little dirtier, but as cool as ever.

The ball rolls slowly in behind the School-house goal not three yards in front of a dozen of the biggest School players-up.

There stand the School-house præpostor, safest of goal-keepers, and Tom Brown by his side, who has learned his trade by this time. Now is your time, Tom. The blood of all the Browns is up, and the two rush in together, and throw themselves on the ball, under the very feet of the advancing column; the præpostor on his hands and knees arching his back, and Tom all along on his face. Over them topple the leaders of the rush, shooting over the back of the præpostor, but falling flat on Tom, and knocking all the wind out of his small carcase. 'Our ball,' says the præpostor, rising with his prize, 'but get up there, there's a little fellow under you.' They are hauled and roll off him, and Tom is discovered a motionless body.

Old Brooke picks him up. 'Stand back, give him air,' he says; and then feeling his limbs, adds, 'No bones broken. How do you feel, young un?' 'Hah-hah,' gasps Tom as his wind comes back, 'pretty well, thank you – all right.'

'Who is he?' says Brooke. 'Oh, it's Brown, he's a new boy; I know him,' says East, coming up. 'Well, he is a plucky youngster, and will make a player,' says Brooke.

And five o'clock strikes. 'No side' is called, and the first day of the School-house match is over.

CHAPTER 8   *THE WILL TO WIN*

Once the idea of competition between groups had entered into football the modern game began to take shape. The need for agreed rules immediately became apparent, and judgements made by the 'levees' on the island were recorded to be consulted when precedents were needed. For a decade or more this method of adjudication was good enough. In a relatively small community word of mouth was sufficient to ensure that the current laws were understood. This was acknowledged in the preface to the 1846 printed rule book:

The following book of Rules is to be regarded rather as a set of Decisions on certain disputed points in Football, than as containing all the Laws of the Game, which are too well known to render any explanation necessary to Rugbeians.

By the time the rules were committed to paper in 1845 the principle was already well established that innovation was not only permissible but necessary to allow play to adapt to changing circumstances. Thereafter the rules were reviewed annually and adjusted where needed.

The organization of football became quite a complex affair. Puntabout was regulated so that chaos did not reign as boys practised, and

Little Side games were arranged for the junior boys for whom play with bigger players would be dangerous. Dr. Arnold, in another reforming move, had gradually phased out the old lodging houses in the town where all boarders who could not be accommodated in the School House had previously lived. During his reign masters were encouraged to set up boarding houses, which quickly came to challenge one another in sport, thus establishing a framework for competition in school games which survives strongly to this day. At first these house matches were relatively insignificant affairs, the real excitement being reserved for the Big Side Matches. These were the backbone of Rugby Football in the middle decades of the nineteenth century.

The formula appears to have been developed uniquely at Rugby, and produced a game with a distinctive character. In the early days matches were played between sides drawn up in a variety of ways. The boys who came from North played those from the South, those with names beginning with the letters of the first half of the alphabet played those beginning N–Z, and so on. However the matches which created the most excitement were those played between socially identifiable groups within the school. The two great matches were between the Sixth Form and the School and the School House and the School. Later a third important match against the Old Rugbeians was introduced.

These alignments made for interesting matches because there was no attempt, as there is today, to compete under equal conditions. To begin with the sides were never numerically balanced. The School House fielded about sixty boys of all ages to take on the combined forces of the rest of the school, while the Sixth probably mustered about 40 players representing the top brains though by no means necessarily the best athletes, to meet the challenge of the rest. The teams were unpredictable up to the last minute because any Old Rugbeian who turned up on the day was entitled to play for the side he had belonged to when at school. Naturally it tended to be only the keen players who volunteered their services, and with their superior size and skill they made a substantial contribution to the game.

The smaller sides needed to recognize and make use of every attribute they had. Good players were deployed to take the best advantage of their speed, strength or kicking skills, while the rest formed a disciplined force well-known to one another and efficiently directed by a single leader. The opposition enjoyed no such organization or authority.

In *Tom Brown's Schooldays* Thomas Hughes wrote the classic account of one of these early Big Side matches. He was at pains to stress 'how the School House side was drilled' by Old Brooke who had assigned specific tasks to distinct groups of players, each with its own leader. The opposition, on the other hand was 'any-how and no-how', with divided leadership and no distinguishable organization on the field. The overwhelming attribute of the School House was the will to win. Even Tom Brown, the youngest new boy, was as

Thomas Hughes, author of Tom Brown's Schooldays

eager as anyone else to take part. The fags for the opposition, on the other hand, were 'looking for a chance of bolting', and had no sense of team loyalty. Even so the School side had an overwhelming advantage in numbers, and there were plenty of good individual players keen to prove their worth.

The field of play reflected many of the variables of the battlefield, and it is unsurprising that Hughes, who published *Tom Brown's Schooldays* in 1858 shortly after the Crimean War and during the Indian Mutiny, should have used military terminology to describe the match. 'A battle' he said, 'would have looked much the same to you, except that the boys would be men, and the balls iron.' He saw in Old Brooke 'the sort of look I hope to see in my general when I go out to fight', and equated the divisions of players with the light and heavy brigades at Balaclava. There was glory to be got in the battle, even for the youngest players, and both Tom Brown and his young friend East won their spurs for their bravery that day.

It was in this generation, during the 1830s, that the football field was established as the chief forum in which boys could prove their

After the match in School House

courage and fitness to their fellows and so earn themselves recognition. The qualities they respected in one another were leadership, athletic ability, guts and loyalty, and the game they created allowed both individuals and teams to develop these attributes to the full. The comradeship crossing all the barriers of hierarchy which prevailed in the School House following success in one of these Big Side contests was an experience which most of the participants would never forget. Hughes rightly devoted a whole chapter to the celebrations after the match, which were not only a reward for victory in the game just finished, but an inspiration for future encounters. Because every single member of the House had taken part and had been given the opportunity to make whatever contribution he could, even the youngest and least athletic could enjoy the euphoria to the full. Newcomers were immediately included and their ambitions channelled by the example of their elders. The fellowship of the School House Hall, the beer and singing, the discussions and recollections were as important to the whole ethos of the game as the play itself. This sense of comradeship became part of a tradition which is echoed today in club houses all over the world. Rugby football has always been a players' game first and foremost.

The sense of belonging was strengthened by ritual ceremonies, at least one of which survives to the present. When the School House is victorious the names of the players are placed in a box kept behind the wainscoting above the fireplace in the old hall, and no strangers are allowed to be present while this is done. A new generation is thus admitted to the elite, to become, its turn, part of history. This desire to record just about everything that happened in the school erupted in the early 1840s, when every meeting was formally minuted, House Annals were begun and budding lawyers and politicians imposed a new efficiency and organization upon most of the free time boys had previously filled for themselves.

The Arnoldian Rugbeians represented a new social mix. The squirearchy were still sending their sons, but in not quite such numbers since Arnold's liberalism had alarmed them a little. There were more military families taking advantage of the free schooling for local residents and renting houses in the town, and the clergy favoured the new moral tone. But these groups really only shifted the balance. The new element came from the industrial middle classes emerging from the manufacturing areas. These boys belonged to no establishment, and for the most part lived in or close to industrial towns. They were not brought up to the traditional country pastimes from early childhood, and were better able to excel on the playing field than at field sports. Football, cricket and running were more to their taste than hunting and fishing, and much easier to arrange. Arnold, who believed in the importance of personal fitness and felt that physical recreation relaxed and refreshed the mind, made no objection to his pupils organizing football games, though he never sought to bring sport under the control of the masters, nor did he ever suggest that it should form any official part of the curriculum.

The boys in their turn invested in football much of the philosophy which governed their own lifestyle. Youngsters had to serve their time as goalkeepers and prove their worth before being allowed to 'follow up' in matches. The right to participate fully in the game admitted them to membership of an elite group and was an important milestone in a boy's school career. The passage through adolescence to manhood has been marked in all societies by the conferring privilege to mark seniority and achievement. Big Side football at Rugby, including as it did every member of the school, provided a common ground where strength and courage could be demonstrated and publicly acknowledged.

Cross-country running at
Rugby School
(Godefroy Durand, 1897)

The Sixth Match

FROM AN ARTICLE BY WD ARNOLD, SON OF DR ARNOLD, CO-AUTHOR
OF THE FIRST FOOTBALL RULES, 1846

Drawn up before the Island goal is the Sixth Form, a little band, some forty
in number – some huge, strong, massive; others light, smart, active; all
eager, courageous, zealous. It is with them as with the warriors of old: not
the weight, not the mass, but each man's individual prowess must gain the
victory. How well is each acquainted with his particular post and duty!
These are to play forward, these to lead the sudden rush, or by their vast
bodies check the threatening scrummage, or turn the direction of a
tumultuous 'run in'. These, again, are to play back or forward as occasion
offers, the tirailleurs or light infantry of the tiny army; to change the aspect
of the moment by a happy drop, and turn the tide of victory from the Island
to the white gate. Lastly, there are those who feel that keeping goal,
defending the very crown of conquest, is no mean or unworthy task, since
beneath those very bars were given to immortality the names of Clough and
Harry Thorpe. Nor do the adversaries present a less magnificent and orderly
appearance; but alas, it is a host as that of the Philistines. Of four hundred
and sixty adversaries two hundred stand forth to battle, leaving the countless
multitude to guard the camp. There they stand, those two hundred – the
scarlet and gold of the Schoolhouse; the green and gold of Cotton's; the
purple and silver star of Mayor's; the flushing red and crescent of Arnold's;
the orange and silver of Price's; the crossed black of Anstey's, all stand in
terrible array against the devoted band. It is the contest of age and weight
against numbers; and numbers are no small help; and weight in the Fifth and
Twenty begins to be painfully respectable. But now all is silent. Far from
each other lie the opposing hosts. Between, in a line with the three trees,
reposes the yet intact ball. All is hushed – still! Suddenly, from some
stentorian lungs amid the two hundred, comes a shout, 'Are you ready?' A
moment's pause, a hurried glance all round – and again the silence is broken,
and the Sixth leader answers with a solitary emphatic 'Yes!' Once more
perfect stillness. A single chosen champion of the Fifth steps forth between
the two lines, rushes at the quiescent ball. Shouts of 'Well kicked!' 'Catch it!'
and then adieu to words. Those stationary bands, as by a magician's wand,
are transformed into one restless, moving, thronging mass. The ball, soon
stopped in its aerial career, is lost in the gathering crowd, and the Sixth
Match is begun; and when once begun, who shall describe its progress?
Surely no one ungifted with Homeric vision can do it justice; yet for want of
a worthier bard will we ambitiously essay the arduous task.

The ball is caught; again it rises in the air; but this time caught no more, for
he who vainly stood forth to meet it just touches the ball, and at the same

time falls prostrate before the weight of the advancing foe. Onward it goes through the trees; but lo! one adroit, active, cunning, has caught it on the bound, with slippery wiles eludes countless adversaries, and with one successful drop sends it far over the heads of the advancing party. Thus is the tide of war changed with a vengeance. Onward rush the gallant Fifth, and just as the ball is within a hundred yards of the goal it is caught by some stalwart champion of the Twenty, put under his arm, and suddenly 'Maul him!' 'Well done!' 'Go it!' re-echoes from three hundred lungs, and every member of either side is thronging to the conflict. Then comes the tug of war. The hapless and too adventurous hero who first grasped the ball, and he who first dared to stay his course by his rough embrace, both roll on the ground, locked in each other's arms, the foundation of a pyramid of human flesh, giving vent to screams, yells, and groans unutterable. But no soldier ever grasped his colours more strenuously on the field of battle than does this gallant member of the Twenty the no less precious ball. Stifling, suffocating, crushing backwards and forwards heaves the thickest mass. At last numbers will tell: the goal is passed: the gallant holder of the ball, disdaining to speak before, hears the cry 'In, In!' And collecting what breath is left in his exhausted lungs, gasps out – 'My ball.' A side glance – all eyes to the left – and the fact is indisputable: the ball is in goal. Instantly every one gets or is dragged up; stray caps are picked up and restored, and the struggling mass dissolved. These, exulting, retire some twenty-five yards; those, mournful, lean against goal posts, or otherwise ease their weary limbs.

At last suspense is over; a try – a failure; no exultation, though deep joy. Slowly and deliberately the ball is kicked out; not, however, without something of military tactic. 'Kick towards the three trees, we always do better there, we can keep together; and kick high, so that we may charge up before they catch it' – so counsels some venerable and athletic Nestor; and true to the word up goes the ball, and before it descends, the heavy sons of the Upper Bench are upon it, and with one shout of triumph the three trees – the Thermopylae of the Close – are gained, and the ball is hastening towards the school goal. In touch. A dead silence, both parties preparing for a struggle. Out comes the ball; some giant hand strikes it yards on towards the school goal, and, like bloodhounds on the scent, the Sixth close in. 'Look out in goal!' Vain cry! Is not a fight going on by the schoolhouse wall, and what discipline shall break the ring? Vain cry! Already has the leader of the Sixth side, the champion of hare and hounds, got the ball under his arm, and who may hope to stop him? There is a sudden cessation of motion; it is evident that the ball is in goal; but who has touched it? Ah, that is the question. 'Whose ball?' pant the laggers as they run up. 'Theirs,' is the sullen answer in the huge host. 'Ours,' the thrilling response from and for the Forty. But it is a long way out, close to the path by the white gate. 'Who'll kick it out?' Grave question! Awful responsibility! At last a man is found; the long line of fellows who can place are drawn up to catch; perfect silence! – the man who is to kick it out walks in and takes up the ball quite quietly – as if more than kingdoms did not depend on his skill! Nay, to prove his coolness, he looks round and requests the opposite party to 'go in.' At last he kicks – the ball is in the air; forth rush the opposing host as a wave of the sea; but even as the mad wave dashes impotently upon the gallant breakwater, so fruitlessly rush they upon that single man, who, short, sturdy, smiling, has already caught, and like an imprisoned angel hugs the ball. It is caught and well before too. Now another silence. Who is to kick? Pass over the bashfulness, the reasonable agitation, at length the doomed man, doomed to glory or to bitter disappointment, steps forth between two anxious lines. Those who could not tremble in the scrummage or the charge are gasping and shaking now; the enemy with eye and foot alert, prompt for the charge. At length the following short and pithy conversation, always the forerunner of action: 'Place it low.' 'As low as that?' 'Yes – but, stop a minute – don't put it down till I give the word – NOW! ! !' Like a cannon ball on rushes he, and on rush the charging host; – but baffled are their attempts; too truly has the placer done his work; – the ball is high in the air, and all eyes are staring from their sockets as they watch its course. 'Yes – No – Yes, a goal, a decided goal, – by Jove, it's a goal.' Yes, it is a goal, and there is the cry of 'Over.'

CHAPTER 9   *CRIMSON VELVET CAPS*

Dress customarily offered some indication of a boy's status. He would progress from skirts to trousers as he left the nursery, from buttoned-on jackets to the bobtail coats of adolescence, and finally to the cut-away coat and waistcoat of a young manhood. This was the style of the society in which he lived, and not a peculiarity of school. However these clothes were not particularly practical on the games field, and the first indications of special dress for football occurred in the early part of Arnold's Headmastership when the School House boarders started to wear white duck trousers. The textile mills in Lancashire were by then producing cotton material at prices sufficiently low to make special clothing for sport a practical proposition. From the players' point of view cotton, though excellent for cricket in the summer, was not ideal on cold winter days, and it was too thin to offer protection against the shinning and hacking which were part and parcel of football at that time. The probability is that they were introduced as a practical measure to keep day-wear clean. They were light and easier to launder in white, since they could be boiled. Perhaps the practical Mrs Arnold, herself the mother of school-aged sons, suggested that their use might ease the lot of the matron in charge of keeping the clothes of sixty boys presentable.

78

White trousers soon came into universal use, and by the end of the 1830s the appearance of a match was greatly enhanced by,

the use of a peculiar dress, consisting of velvet caps and Jerseys. The latter are of various colours and patterns, and wrought with many curious devices, which on their first introduction were accompanied by mottoes, some of which were very appropriate, others quite the reverse; as for instance the high sounding one, 'Cave Adsum' (Beware, Here I am), was occasionally worn by a boy who was generally to be found lurking on the outside of a scrummage, or who, during the course of a game, did not once kick the ball, and may therefore be reasonably supposed not to be a *very* fierce player, as his vaunting motto would imply.

Football costume of the 1840s

Writing about the 1847 season CH Newmarch goes on to say,

These vanities have, as far as we could judge from a match at which we were present a few months ago, now gone out, leaving, however, the many-coloured caps and Jerseys to contrast with the white trowsers, and give a very lively and pleasing appearance to the game.

They had not altogether vanished, but the personal decoration on jerseys had been replaced in about 1844 by house emblems designed by Henry Crealock, who later became a Lieutenant-General and distinguished war artist of the Indian Mutiny and China Campaigns. The skull and crossbones which is still the emblem of School House is a survivor of the 'vaunting' mottoes sported by individuals, and may well have been inspired by the jersey of a leading School House player of the day. The first formal resolution passed about match dress declared in 1846 that, 'the parties at matches should be distinguished by the colours of their jerseys, the one party wearing white, the other striped jerseys'. This ruling neatly allowed for house colours and emblems to be worn, while at the same time providing distinguishing uniforms for contestants in the variously aligned Big Side matches. When the first International match was played a quarter of a century later with no fewer than 10 Rugbeians in the England side, the white trousers and jerseys they adopted were derived from the Rugby School dress. Rumour has it that for many years the Captain of

House football dress (Henry Fellows, 1858)

England used to ask the permission of the Captain of the School to allow England to use the all-white strip, but this is probably no more than a schoolboy conceit.

The cap is the best known item of football dress to derive from the school. The velvet caps sported in the late 1830s were shaped variously like smoking caps and jockey caps and were worn by those boys sufficiently senior to be allowed to 'play up' in the main body of the match. They were originally brought in as a more practical form of headgear than the top hats which were the ordinary dress and suffered expensively when lost and trampled on the field of play. In the autumn of 1839 Queen Adelaide, the widow of William IV, paid a visit to Rugby School. As a compliment to Her Majesty the boys of School House lined the quadrangle wearing caps in the royal colours of crimson velvet with gold tassels. The Queen later asked to see football played since she had heard it was a pretty spectacle, and the boys immediately obliged regardless of their best dress. The School House played the School, still wearing their royal caps, and so, for the first time a team uniform was worn for football. In his autobiography Sir Alexander Arbuthnot recalls that he 'once had the honour of kicking off in a football match before Queen Adelaide'. His football career included introducing the Rugby rules to Haileybury, with the exception that 'we abolished running with the ball', and kicking two goals in a match in Madras when a Member of the Council. However he found it 'rather too hot for that sort of fun' and turned his attention instead to founding the Madras Cricket Club in 1846. Here again he was a party to innovative sporting headgear, but this time it did not catch on. 'In my youth,' he said, 'cricketers always played in tall black beaver hats, and I wore a similar top-hat, made of white felt, in India.'

The match watched by Queen Adelaide is confirmed as the first occasion on which uniform team caps were worn by Mr JG Holloway in a letter quoted by Sydney Selfe;

We *did* wear red plush caps as the distinctive mark of the School House players, and we *did* run with the ball *if while on your own side you* could pick it up or catch it in front of goal.

His contemporary, Revd. Samuel Sandes also remembered the crimson velvet caps, but he was the first to point out their true usefulness to players.

We all wore crimson velvet caps. The custom with the big boys was at the beginning of the football season to send a pair of boots to the shoemaker's in order to have thick soles put on them bevelled at the toes (like a man o' war's bows) so as to cut the shins of the enemy. Often have I seen boys thus lamed sitting on the seats under the elm trees, disabled for further playing, so *to distinguish ourselves in a scrummage* we wore crimson caps.

The boots Sandes describes were known as *navvies*, and, though they continued to be worn, the evil practice of sharpening the soles, together with other dangers such as metal studs, were abolished by the boys themselves.

In the match that I refer to, I, being a fast runner, and like a little rat, harder to get at by the dog than a big rat by the dog, was put on the outside by the road. The ball came to me, I caught it up and ran for dear life to the enemy's goal, where unhurt I touched down. I walked out, kicked up with my heel the sod in the most approved fashion, and placed the ball at the proper angle for Tom Hughes, who kicked our second goal beautifully high. So we won both goals that day, and I felt proud of it, for Arnold and Queen Adelaide were looking on.

Queen Adelaide, Dr Arnold and Matthew Arnold watching football (Jane Arnold, 1839)

Not long after the 1839 match coloured velvet caps were adopted by all the houses, but became a mark of distinction which could only be worn at the invitation of the Head of House. Jerseys were used to distinguish one side from another, while caps denoted players whose performance in lesser games had been good enough to entitle them to 'Follow up' in Big Side Matches. In this way the cap first entered football as a mark of excellence, and in all branches of the sport the pinnacle of a player's career is still to be 'capped' for his country. At Rugby School in contrast, there is no XV cap, and chosen players are still invited by the Captain to *follow up* for the school. Good players, not exclusively members of the 1st XV, are awarded caps, and these continue to be in the player's own house colours, made of velvet and trimmed in gold or silver just as they were in the beginning.

One form of embellishment which seems not to have survived

much beyond the end of the First World War is the embroidered record of the owner's football career carefully worked on the silk lining inside the cap. Each major match in which he played, either at school or afterwards, is included, giving the date, the names of the competing sides and the score, with the owner's name in the centre. These caps became prized possessions, and were often passed down through families.

In an article written in 1923 on the occasion of the match played on the Close to celebrate the centenary of the game, Arthur A Pearson remembered the day when he was awarded his cap:

To get one's cap was the great ambition of all football enthusiasts. . . . I can well remember, as the proudest morning of my life, when one morning in the Sixth Form a piece of paper was passed round to me signed by the Head of School, Arthur Godley, now Lord Kilbracken, with the welcome words upon it, *You may wear your cap for the Sixth Match*. That cap is now hanging up in the room in which I write, with the date in it of the day when I first won it – October 7th, 1865.

It is interesting to see that in the England team photograph taken to commemorate the first International against Scotland, many of the players are wearing the following-up caps they had earned at school. By this time the fashion for velvet football caps had spread to other schools and clubs, and until about 1880 Rugby tradesmen had a monopoly in their manufacture similar to that enjoyed by the makers of footballs.

An article in the *New Rugbeian* written in the autumn of 1859 describes the dress considered suitable for football by the thirty-two Old Rugbeians who had returned to Rugby to challenge the school. The author is clearly unimpressed by their haphazard appearance. There were sixty players on the School side, immaculate in white, and on this occasion supported by the traditional crowd of goal-keepers whose presence was still obligatory for the three 'great' matches of the season. However the goalkeepers were wearing their greatcoats and sheltering against the rain behind umbrellas 'staring as only fellows in goal can stare' and making it perfectly plain that they had no intention of taking any active part in the play.

Here come the old Rugbeians in every conceivable form of dress; flannels are common enough, but after that there is very little that savours of football at Rugby; gorgeous smoking caps, or common black velvet caps are the most popular form of head-dress; some few appear with pieces of velvet on their heads, which you in vain endeavour to appropriate to any particular house, so much has time done to render them unintelligible. Then in the way of jerseys, instead of the striped jersey which is their legal costume, most of them have flannel shirts of every conceivable hue; and a very few have ordinary white shirts; but they are very old Rugbeians probably, who have forgotten the destructive effect of football on calico and linen.

As the century progressed trousers were tucked into socks, were replaced by knee-breeches, and eventually shorts were worn by all players. Flannel replaced cotton for trousers during the American Civil War when cotton was in scarce supply. It was greatly preferred by the players, since it was thicker and therefore offered greater warmth and more protection. Flannel trousers were then introduced as a mark of distinction for players allowed to 'play up' but who had not yet been awarded caps. The jerseys and caps have altered little except in details of styling since their introduction in the 1840s. The advantages of an easily identifiable team uniform were apparent, and soon became the norm for all sports.

I Told Them They May 'Take Their Caps'

FROM AN ARTICLE BY A SCHOOLBOY IN THE *NEW RUGBEIAN* VOL II, 1859/60

Then follows the blissful moment when they march down to Cosby's, and solemnly order all 'the pomp and circumstance of war', – the badge of dignity and all its minor accessories. (I think it was a surpassingly grand idea – that of working up the football costume to such a perfection of loveliness; I feel sure it has a great deal to do with the respect for, and love of, the game. Like the scarlet uniform of the soldier it seems to inspire the wearer with an unknown power.) Nor do they feel satisfied till they have given precise and lengthy directions; how the ribbon is to be neither too long nor too short, but just to hit off the *aurea mediocritas*; how the cap is to be sufficiently loose to admit of a facile abstraction, so that by a judicious immersion in the mud of the slope it may assume an antiquated appearance wholly irreconcileable with the period of its days; and how the flannel should be duly fitted by an assiduous preparation to resist any untimely deprivation of its beauty and elegance beneath the relentless hands of the implacable washerwoman.

SOURCE 10   *Laws of Football Played at Rugby School, 28 August 1845* [first written rules]

RESOLUTIONS

That only in cases of extreme emergency, and only by the permission of the heads of the sides, shall any one be permitted to leave the Close, after calling over, till the game be finished, and consequently, that all dressing take place before that time.

That the punishment for absenting oneself from a match, without any real and well-grounded reason, be left to the discretion of any Praepostor.

That whenever a match is going to be played, the School shall be informed of it by the Head of the School in such manner as he shall think fit, some time before dinner on the day in question.

That no unnecessary delay take place in the commencement of the matches, but as soon as calling over be finished, the game be commenced.

That the old custom, that no more than two matches take place in the same week be strictly adhered to, of which, one must always take place on Saturday, without some strong cause to the contrary.

That all fellows not following up be strictly prohibited from playing any game in goal, or otherwise conducting themselves in any way which shall be deemed prejudicial to the interests of their side.

That in consequence of the great abuse in the system of giving notes to excuse fagging, &c. and otherwise exempt fellows from attendance at the matches, no notes shall be received which are not signed by one of the Medical Officers of the School, and countersigned by the Head of the House, or by a Master when the case specified is not illness.

That all fellows at Tutor during calling over, or otherwise absent, shall be obliged to attend as soon after as possible.

That the Head of the School take care that these resolutions be generally known among the School, and as far as the case may be they shall apply equally to the big sides.

That Old Rugbaeans shall be allowed to play at the matches of Football, not without the consent, however, of the two heads of the sides.

RULES

i. FAIR CATCH, is a catch direct from the foot.

ii. OFF SIDE. A player is off his side if the ball has touched one of his own side behind him, until the other side touch it.

iii. FIRST OF HIS SIDE, is the player nearest the ball *on his side*.

iv. A KNOCK ON, as distinguished from a *throw on*, consists in striking the ball on with the arm or hand.

v. TRY AT GOAL. A ball touched between the goalposts may be brought up to either of them, but not between. The ball when *punted* must be within, when caught without the line of goal: the ball must be place-kicked and not dropped, even though it touch[ed] two hands, and it must go over the bar and between the posts without having touched the dress or person of any player. No goal may be kicked from touch.

vi. KICK OFF FROM MIDDLE must be a place.

vii. KICK OUT must not be from more than ten yards out of goal if a place-kick, not more then twenty-five yards, if a punt, drop, or knock on.

viii. RUNNING IN is allowed to any player on his side, provided he does not take the ball off the ground, or take it through touch.

87

ix. CHARGING is fair, in case of a place-kick, as soon as a ball has touched the ground; in case of a kick from a catch, as soon as the player's foot has left the ground, and not before.

x. OFF SIDE. No player being off his side shall kick the ball in any case whatever.

xi. No player being off his side shall hack, charge, run in, touch the ball in goal, or interrupt a catch.

xii. A player when off his side having a fair catch is entitled to a fair *knock on*, and in no other case.

xiii. A player being off his side shall not touch the ball on the ground, except in touch.

xiv. A player being off his side cannot put *on his side* himself, or any other player, by knocking or throwing on the ball.

xv. TOUCH. A player may not in any case run with the ball in or through touch.

Touch 'standing up'.
First illustration of a line-out
(Charles Harcourt Chambers,
1845)

xvi. A player standing up to another may hold one arm only, but may hack him or knock the ball out of his hand if he attempts to kick it, or go beyond the line of touch.

xvii. No agreement between two players to send the ball *straight out* shall be allowed on big side.

xviii. A player having touched the ball straight for a tree, and touched the tree with it, may drop from either side if he can, but the opposite side may oblige him to go to his own side of the tree.

xix. A player touching the ball off his side must *throw* it *straight out*.

xx. All matches are drawn after five days, but after three if no goal has been kicked.

xxi. Two big side balls must always be in the Close during a match or big-side.

xxii. The discretion of sending into goals rests with the heads of sides or houses.[1]

xxiii. No football shall be played between the goals till the Sixth match.

xxiv. Heads of sides, or two deputies appointed by them, are the sole arbiters of all disputes.

xxv. No strangers, in any match, may have a place kick at goal.

xxvi. No hacking with the heel, or above the knee, is fair.

xxvii. No player but the first on his side, may be hacked, except in a *scrummage*.

...rummages were upright and ...e ball worked out by hacking ...harles Harcourt Chambers, ...45)

xxviii. No player may wear projecting nails or iron plates on the heels or soles of his shoes or boots.

xxix. No player may take the ball out of the Close.

xxx. No player may stop the ball with anything but his own person.

xxxi. Nobody may wear cap or jersey without leave from the head of his house.

---

[1] Deputies may be allowed to act by the head of the School side, at the Sixth match.

xxxii. At a big-side, the two players highest in the School shall toss up.

xxxiii. The Island is all in goal.

xxxiv. At little sides the goals shall be four paces wide, and in kicking a goal the ball must pass out of the reach of any player present.

xxxv. Three Praepostors constitute a big-side.

xxxvi. If a player take a punt when he is not entitled to it, the opposite side may take a punt or drop, without running if the ball has not touched two hands.

xxxvii. No player may be held, unless he is himself holding the ball.

CHAPTER 10

THE BOOK OF RULES

```
FOOTBALL RULES
─────────────
THE FOLLOWING
𝕽𝖚𝖑𝖊𝖘
WERE SANCTIONED BY A LEVEE
OF THE SIXTH,

On the 28th of August, 1845,

As the

LAWS OF FOOTBALL

PLAYED

At Rugby School

─────────────

RUGBY:
J. S. CROSSLEY, PRINTER.
```

The Arnold era at Rugby had been a time of energy and innovation. Football had progressed from a pastime at the beginning of the decade to a passion at the end. *Ad hoc* games had given way to annual contests no longer to be afterwards 'consigned to the limbo of oblivion' as they were in Webb Ellis' day, but events to be savoured, discussed and remembered. The numerically unequal encounters, which contrasted with the evenly divided sides of the previous generation, provided opportunities for boys to furnish proof of their courage and endurance. Once again there were 'giants in the land'.

Arnold's death was very sudden. He was a vigorous man of almost 47, and on the last day of the summer term, just when the emotions of schoolboys are at their height, he suffered chest pains on waking, and shortly afterwards died. The shock to Rugby was profound. Inevitably the reaction of the boys and many of the staff in the following year or so was to try to create at Rugby some kind of living shrine to Arnold. In many areas of school life matters which had previously been handed on by word of mouth were meticulously recorded. Minute books were started to note the decisions of the Sixth Form law-makers, and the first of a long series of autobiographical articles and novels about life under Arnold appeared in print.

We probably owe the Webb Ellis story to this Arnold fugue, for Matthew Bloxam was *not* an Arnold man, and, to counter the tide, over the years he produced a series of talks and articles about his own youth under Dr Wooll, for whom he had great affection.

Bloxam was not alone in feeling some dismay at this outburst of nostalgia which threatened to bring all progress to a halt. The authors of the *Rugby Miscellany*, a school magazine published in 1845–6, include a number of articles warning against clinging unselectively to tradition. With tongue in cheek they write,

How fruitful with legends are the annals of football, in the glorious days of yore when a half holiday came not without a broken leg, or at least a compound fracture of the arm. Alas! what would our ancestors have said; could they have known the time would come, when years should pass without one single leg being broken, that even sprained ancles and fractured collar bones should be exciting events of rare occurrence; that Rugbeians should let football, their own game, fall into decline!

In another article the Editors complain that the 'carcase, as it were, of a dead Rugbeian lay in our path wherever we turned, and prevented us advancing a single step'. They claimed 'kindred fellowship of spirit with the Railway Kings and Cotton Lords, being equally with them the creation of modern, burning, life-like energy.' They were content to acknowledge the redoubtable chieftains of football's recent past, but protested vigorously that their own contemporaries did not deserve the gloomy verdict of degeneracy passed upon them by Old Rugbeians now at the universities.

For be it remembered that football as played by five hundred, differs materially from football as played by three hundred people, and that for some few to carry the tide of war by the force of their own weight, and the strength of their good arm, or more properly, perhaps, their good leg, was an easier matter when the mass of opponents was so very considerably smaller than it is at present; we mean smaller to apply both to quantity and quality, for we believe firmly . . . that the average size is bigger than it used to be rather than smaller.

The increasing numbers in the school not only altered the nature of the game, but rendered impractical the old scheme of communicating adjudication on the rules by word of mouth. In 1844 the Head of School appointed a committee of eight to set out regulations for 'the better observance of football', and the following year, in August, a Levee of the praeposters enacted 'that a committee of three be chosen by votes to draw up written Rules for Football, to be afterwards submitted to a Levee of the Sixth'.

They elected William Delafield Arnold, the seventeen year-old fourth son of the late Headmaster who later became Director of Public Education in the Punjab. He wrote *The Sixth Match*, one of the great descriptions of Big Side football in its heyday. He died in Gibralter on his way back to England in 1859. Next on the list was WW Shirley, who is depicted in one of the first illustrations ever made of football play. He was only sixteen when he joined the trio asked to draw up the rules. He was a first class mathematician, and became Regius Professor of Ecclesiastical History at Oxford. The third member of the committee was Frederick Hutchins, chosen, perhaps, for his legal bent. He qualified as a solicitor in 1851 and practised in London.

They received their instructions on 25 August, 1845, and submitted their thirty-seven rules to the Sixth Levee on 28 August. These were immediately passed, and on the same day it was agreed they should be printed. A tiny rule book was published, so small that it could easily be carried, even on the field of play, and with a minimum of fuss the laws of the game were circulated.

On 20 October the rules were again up for revision, but it was agreed that they should continue for the remainder of the season, and that the following year boys below the Sixth who were good players should be included in the review team. There was obviously no intention that the written rules should amount to much more than a set of current guidelines, and no feeling that the trio had drafted a final, immutable version.

In the event, though they were regularly updated over the years, these early laws provided the substance and much of the terminology for the first set of rules approved by the Rugby Football Union (RFU). In 1846 and 1847 a larger committee, this time consisting of Big Side players as well as the Sixth Form, tidied up the order and amplified one or two points, but made no significant changes. The ledgers of Lawrence the printer record that Thomas Bloxam, author of the letter recording Webb Ellis' problems with the Latin Prize, ordered fifty copies of the 1847 rules, presumably for distribution outside the school, but there is no indication of where he might have used them. They may have been for his own private pupils, or possibly some copies may have been destined for his old University, Oxford. Wherever they went these small rulebooks represented the earliest positive indication of Rugby rules being disseminated on any scale beyond the school itself.

It was not until 1862 that the rule book deliberately took on a wider purpose. For the first time there is evidence that outside pressure was being brought upon the school to clarify the laws. Old Rugbeians with experience of club and university play requested changes which were, according to a report in the *New Rugbeian*, favourably considered.

In consequence of the urgent representations of many old Rugbeians, a committee was appointed by Big Side *levee* to amend the rules of football with regard to the prevalence of mauling, and of taking up the ball without due attention to the distinction between *rolling* and *bounding*. The Committee subsequently brought the following motions before Big Side:

'That, in addition to the present rule for taking the ball out of touch, any player getting the ball in touch be at liberty to carry the ball out himself, from five to fifteen yards, at his own discretion, and to put it down.'

Also, 'that when a maul in goal is on the ground, no player not already in the maul may take part in it, and when any player has been pulled out of the maul off his side, he may not re-enter it.'

These rules, it is hoped, will go far to diminish mauling. As to taking up, it is obvious that no amendment of the present rule would be satisfactory. The fact is that it must be *public opinion*, and not a printed rule that will really improve the present practice. And we hope and firmly believe that public opinion is strongly set against all unfair taking up.

On the printed copy of the revised 1862 rule book which he later presented to the Old Rugbeian Committee, FO Kitchener noted on the cover; *The first attempt to codify the customs*. The Rugby School rules were now written for the benefit of *all* players of the game whether at Rugby or elsewhere, and no customary knowledge was presumed. Kitchener had returned to Rugby in 1862 as a master. He had been up at Cambridge where he must have been involved in the arguments over football practices which led to the drafting of the *Cambridge Rules* of 1863 on which the Football Association code was based. When he got back to Rugby who better to advise the boy legislators on the points which needed clarification for non-Rugbeians? Demand for the Rugby rules was coming by now not only from the universities but from the emerging clubs. Liverpool, Manchester, Richmond and

Sale were all founded between 1857 and 1861. Other schools too were adopting the game. Marlborough and Cheltenham had been playing for some time, but in 1862 Clifton College, Wellington and Haileybury were also playing to the Rugby rules. The new edition produced at Rugby did an admirable job. It began with a plan of the field, and continued with an excellent resume of how the game operates. A brief definition of terms followed, and finally the rules were set out, still adhering very closely in content to the earlier versions. Before the section on rules a note is inserted pointing out that certain items 'are of course, intended solely for Rugbeians.' For the first time there is open acknowledgement that the game had a substantial following beyond the network of Old Rugbeians who knew the rules 'too well to render any explanation necessary', and the school assumed the mantle of lawmaker for the game at large.

There is no better account of the technicalities of the Big Side game than the introduction to this 1862 rulebook.

SOURCE 11   *Plan and Text from 1862 Rulebook*

PLAN OF THE FIELD

This Plan does not represent the shape, but only the arrangement of the ground; it is better to have it an oblong than a square.

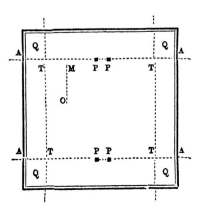

Plan of the field (1862 Rules)

AA. AA. Lines of Goal.
PP. PP. Goal Posts.
TT. TT. Lines of Touch.
M. Imaginary place where mark is made after a touch down in goal.
O. Imaginary place whence kicked.
Q,Q,Q,Q, Touch in Goal.

INTRODUCTION

Football is played on a large level field or piece of ground, near either end of which is erected a goal, composed of two upright posts eighteen feet high, with a crossbar placed ten feet from the ground. From each goal a line is cut, called the *line of goal*, to the edge of the field; all the part behind this line is *in goal*, the part between the goals being the field of action. The sides are marked off by lines similar to the lines of goal, and all the edge of the field outside them is said to be *in touch*. [The part behind the goal line and also behind the touch line is called *Touch-in-goal* (see Plan).]

If the field in which the football is played is larger than the part on which the game is played, the touch lines and goal lines are considered as indefinitely produced. Thus much about the field.

The game is commenced by one side kicking off from the middle of the field, to do which a player good at place-kicking is chosen (see Rule 1).

The object of the game is to kick the ball over the adversary's goal, which can be done either by *dropping a goal* or *placing a goal*: the former in the course of the game, and by any player of the opposite side who may happen to have the ball in his hands: the latter only after a *touch down in goal* (or by a 'fair catch,' see Rule 3). The touch down is accomplished in the following manner: any player who catches the ball, either fair or on the bound (provided he be not *off his side*) may run with it if he can, till he gets behind the line of goal of the opposite side, where he will touch it down as near as he can to the goal, if possible between the posts. This feat is called *running in*. If the touch down be too far from the goal posts to try a goal, one of the side who touched it down takes it up and makes a mark with his heel, and retires a little, and then 'punts' it out slantwise towards his own side, who spread out to catch it. The moment it is punted the opposite side, who are along the line of goal (as in the case of a touch down), may charge, but if any of the other side have caught it and made his mark they are obliged to stop charging, and not go beyond the mark made by the catcher. He who has caught it then proceeds to place it for another to kick, as hereafter described in case of a fair catch. If the touch down be near enough to try a goal, then two of his side are commissioned by the head of the side to take it out, one of them, who is to kick it, being naturally chosen for his expertness in place kicking. Then he who is going to kick it takes it up, brings it to the line of goal, and touches it down in a line with the place at which the person who ran in touched it down. If the runner-in touched it between the posts, he touches it down at one of the posts (all this is to be done *behind* the line of goal). He then makes a mark with his heel on the spot, taking care to keep all the time within the line of goal. The players of the opposite side may then come as far as the mark, but no farther, and may stretch forward with the view of 'mauling' (see *infra*) the two who are taking it out, if they do not succeed in the following action: the player who is to place-kick goes just out of the reach of the opposite side who are stretching forward. He then, still standing within the goal-line, kicks the ball gently off his toes into the hands of the other, who is standing just outside the goal line to receive it. The moment it is in his hands he makes a mark with his heel outside the line (of course as far as he can stretch in the direction of the goal post). The moment he has it in his hands the opposite side may charge, and try to get the ball away from him (called '*mauling*'.) This however they cannot do when he has made his mark, so that only in cases where he fails in making his mark directly, or if he makes it inside the goal line, or if he touches the ball before it is off the toe of the other, do they succeed in mauling him. When he has made his mark, he carries the ball out in a line with the mark, until it is at a suitable distance from the goal to kick; he then makes a small nick in the ground with his heel, for the ball to rest upon, and places it therein. The kicker then takes a short run and kicks it. The moment the ball is on the ground, the other side may charge from the goal line, or rather from on a level with the mark made by the player who took it out. If the ball goes over the cross-bar (whether it touches or not) at whatever height, it is a goal. If it rises directly over the end of one of the posts it is called a *poster*, and is no goal. If it touches any body but the kicker, before it has gone over the bar, it is no goal. If the ball be touched, when once outside the goal line, by anybody but him who is taking it out, the other side may charge and maul. Whenever a fair catch (see Rule 3) is made, the catcher makes his mark. At that mark, and on a level with it, the opposite side may stand, but not before it, and the catcher may either drop it himself, or place it for another to place-kick it. The rules about charging are the same as when it is touched down in goal.

When the ball goes outside the line of touch, the first player who touches it down, takes it and walks with it to the touch line, and throws it out at right angles to the line of touch, or bounds it outside the line of touch, (i.e. in the field) and catches it again, and runs with it, or drop-kicks it himself. (See Rule 32.)

When the ball goes into touch in goal it is considered as out of the field, and is taken out by the side whose goal it is, as if they had touched it down in their own goal.

Whenever the ball rolls into either goal, either it is touched down by one of the opposite side, (in which case it is proceeded with as in the case of a running in), or it is touched down by one of the side whose goal it is; or, if the ball be bounding, one of the side whose goal it is takes it up, and runs with it out of goal, if he can. In the second case, when it is touched down by one of the side whose goal it is, they act as follows: the opposing side retire, and one of the side who touched it down, takes it out, but not further than twenty-five yards, and 'drops' it; accordingly it is advisable to place posts on the touch line to mark the twenty-five yards.

When any body has the ball in his hands, any of the opposite side may maul him; if he cannot get free of them, or give the ball to some other of his own side (not in front of him) who can run with it, he cries 'have it down;' he then puts it down and kicks it, and all who have closed round him (the two sides must, however, be on their respective sides of the ball, or else they are off their side, in which case they cannot 'hack,') begin kicking at the ball, and often encounter each others' shins. When any body is running with the ball, any of the opposite side may either maul him and pull him over, or get the ball from him, or else 'hack' him over, but he may neither hold and hack him simultaneously, nor may he hold him after the ball is gone. When players are off the sides, they are made on their sides again: first, if the ball strike any body of the opposite side; secondly, in the case of Rule 8.

Generally, three or four of the swiftest runners, and most expert at dropping, keep some distance behind the rest, and are called back players; some, too, who are clever at 'dodging,' play half-back, i.e. midway between the back players and the rest.

DEFINITIONS

A DROP KICK or DROP is accomplished by letting the ball drop from your hands on to the ground, and kicking it with your toe on *the very instant* it rises.

A PLACE KICK is kicking a ball after it has been placed on the ground, in a small nick, made by the heel of the placer.

A PUNT is a kick straight off the toe, without letting the ball touch the ground.

A SCRUMMAGE is that event previously described, after the ball is down.

RULES

N.B. – Rules 32, 33, 36, 37, 40–45, and the notes to Rules 32 and 37, are, of course, intended solely for Rugbeians.

1. KICK OFF FROM MIDDLE must be a place-kick.

2. KICK OUT must not be from more than twenty-five yards out of goal.

3. FAIR CATCH is a catch direct from the foot, or a knock on from the HAND of the opposite side.

4. CHARGING is fair, in case of a place kick, as soon as the ball has touched the ground; in case of a kick from a catch, as soon as the player offers to kick, but he may always draw back, unless he has actually touched the ball with his foot.

5. OFF SIDE. A player is off his side when the ball has been kicked, or thrown, or knocked on, or is being run with by any one of his own side behind him.

6. A player entering a scrummage on the wrong side, is OFF his side.

7. A player is OFF his side even when a player on his own side has kicked the ball from behind him and then run before him.

8. ON SIDE. A player is on side when the ball has been kicked, thrown, or knocked on, or run with (five yards) by any of the opposite side, or when it has touched the body of any player on the opposite side before him, i.e. in advance of him.

9. A player being off his side is to consider himself as out of the game, and is not to touch the ball in any case whatever (either in or out of touch); or in any way to interrupt the play, and is of course incapable of holding the ball.

10. A catch from a throw on is not a *Fair* Catch.

11. KNOCKING ON, as distinguished from throwing on, is altogether disallowed under any circumstances whatsoever. In case of this rule being

broken, a catch from such a knock on, shall be equivalent to a fair catch.

12. If however the ball be hit by the arm, and not by the hand, the catch from such a knock on, shall not be considered equivalent to a fair catch.

13. It is not lawful to take the ball off the ground, except in touch, or after it has been touched down in goal to take it out, for *any* purpose whatever.

14. It is not lawful to take up the ball when *rolling* as distinguished from *bounding*.

15. In a scrummage succeeding a maul, it is not lawful to touch the ball with the hand, except in the event of a Fair Catch.

16. FIRST OF HIS SIDE is the player nearest the ball *on his side*.

17. RUNNING IN is allowed to any player on his side, provided he does *not take the ball off the ground*, or through touch.

18. RUNNING IN. If in case of a run in, the ball be held in a maul, it shall be lawful for a player on the same side to take it from the runner in, provided he has entered the maul behind the runner in.

19. No player out of a maul may be held, or pulled over, unless he is himself holding the ball.

20. Though it is lawful to hold any player in a maul, this holding does not include attempts to throttle, or strangle, which are totally opposed to all the principles of the game.

21. That any player obtaining a ball in a maul, do have it down as soon as possible when outside the twenty-five yard posts at either end.

22. No player may be hacked and held at the same time.

23. Hacking with the heel is unfair.

24. Hacking above, or on the knee is unfair.

25. No one wearing projecting nails, iron plates, or gutta percha, on the soles or heels of his boots or shoes, shall be allowed to play.

26. TRY AT GOAL. A ball touched between the goal posts may be brought up to either of them, but not between them.

27. The ball when punted must be within, and when caught, without the line of goal.

28. The ball must be place-kicked and not dropped; and if it touches two hands the try will be lost.

29. A goal may be dropped by any player *on his side*, if the ball has not been touched down in goal.

30. It shall be a goal if the ball goes over the bar (whether it touches or not) without having touched the dress or person of any player; but no player may stand on the goal bar to interrupt it going over.

31. No goal may be kicked from touch.

32. TOUCH. A ball in touch is dead; consequently the first player on his side must in any case touch it down, bring it to the edge of touch, and throw it straight out, but may take it himself if he can.[1]

33. No player may take the ball out of the close, i.e. behind the line of trees beyond the goal.

34. No player may stop the ball with anything but his own person.

35. If a player take a punt when he is not entitled to it, the opposite side may take a punt or drop, without running, (after touching the ball on the ground) if the ball has not touched two hands, but such a drop may not be a goal.

36. The part of the Island which is in front of the line of goal is in touch, that behind it in goal.

37. The discretion of sending into goal rests with heads of sides, or their deputies.[2]

38. Heads of sides, or two deputies appointed by them, are the sole arbiters of all disputes.

39. All matches are drawn after five days, or after three days if no goal has been kicked.

40. Two big side balls must always be in the close during a match or big side.

41. No football shall be played between the goals till the Sixth match.

42. Three Præpostors constitute a big side.

43. At a big side the two players highest in the School shall toss up.

44. Old Rugbeians shall be allowed to play at the matches of football, not however, without the consent of the two heads of the side; but no stranger may have a place kick at goal.

45. The walk in front of the Headmaster's House, leading to the Barby Road is in goal.

---

[1] The ditch round the Island is in touch, except that part behind the line of goal, (which is in goal).
[2] No player who has not had leave to follow up before may get a Cap or Jersey, without leave from the head of his house.

CHAPTER 11 *A GOOD OVAL BALL*

Big Side Ball

Match and Puntabout Ball

The distinctive shape of the modern Rugby football is an instantly recognizable feature of the sport. In the early days it was rounder and larger, the shape and size being determined by the pig's bladder from which it was made. Bladders had been blown up and used as footballs from time immemorial, and had to be encased in leather for special games otherwise they would have been too easily punctured.

These leather casings were made by shoemakers whose skills and equipment fitted them for the task, and there were several in Rugby who supplied footballs to the schoolboys. It was a lucrative business, for footballs were not cheap and quite a large number were needed for 'puntabout' or practice sessions. Talking of the early 1840s W. D. Arnold, co-author of the first written rules, recalls that once football had been voted in for the season 'all join in rushing down to Gilbert's or Jenson's, and in a short time two, three or four Puntabouts are flying behind the chapel'. Discussions about the use of practice grounds indicate that once the season got going far more balls were produced, the property of both individuals and houses, and constant attempts were made to limit the numbers in use at one time.

These puntabout balls were half an inch or so smaller in all dimensions than the balls used for Big Side games. It is not entirely clear why this should have been the case, but presumably since puntabouts were used by boys of all ages the smaller size was found to be more suitable. Big Side balls must also have been considerably more expensive, requiring as they did not only a monumental bladder from a very large pig, but larger sections of the high quality leather needed to make good footballs.

The best known of the old football manufacturers is Gilberts, whose products are still made and distributed worldwide. William Gilbert was the founder of the firm and according to his obituary in the local paper, 'like most of the old Rugby shoemakers, his materials and workmanship were noted for their general excellence'. Where he differed from the other excellent shoemakers was in his business acumen. By the time he died in 1877 his footballs were not only on sale in London, but were already being exported all over the world. It

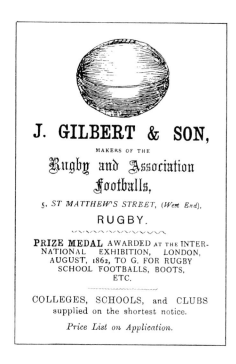

An advertisement for Gilbert's Footballs (1880)

J. GILBERT & SON,
MAKERS OF THE
Rugby and Association
Footballs,
5, ST MATTHEW'S STREET, (West End),
RUGBY.

PRIZE MEDAL AWARDED AT THE INTER-NATIONAL EXHIBITION, LONDON, AUGUST, 1862, TO G. FOR RUGBY SCHOOL FOOTBALLS, BOOTS, ETC.

COLLEGES, SCHOOLS, and CLUBS supplied on the shortest notice.

Price List on Application.

may be that John Lillywhite, who had been employed by the boys in 1850 as the first cricket professional at Rugby, had something to do with Gilbert's success by offering an outlet in London to supply footballs to the burgeoning London clubs of the 1860s. At any rate it is interesting to conjecture that in his lifetime old William Gilbert, who was born in 1799, *could* have made footballs both for William Webb Ellis in 1823 and for the first International match in 1871.

William Gilbert moved to a small shop in St Matthew's Street, Rugby, in 1842. He had previously been in the High Street, but his new premises, literally a stone's throw from the old practice ground behind the chapel, must have helped his business. Boys needing a football or a pair of boots will, all other things being equal, choose the nearest supplier, and this move was evidence of Gilbert's understanding that convenience was all-important in a competitive situation.

William was a bachelor, and it was his nephew James who joined him in the business and eventually succeeded him. James was popular with the boys, and an affectionate portrait of him was drawn by EFT Bennett who entered Rugby School in 1862. Writing in 1930 shortly before he died, Bennett told James Gilbert the younger,

Your Grandfather was a delightful man and a friend to us (very wild and naughty boys I suppose) and a great tweaker maker. He was a wonder of lung strength and, before the pump came in, blew even the big match balls up tight. . . . Jim did anything we asked him to do, and I never can remember him being put off by our rough rushes into his shop. [Tweakers were catapults, generally purchased by boys for the purpose of hunting rooks. They were unpopular with the authorities and no doubt responsible for many broken windows.]

The ability to blow a ball up tight was of great importance, and neither a pleasant nor an easy task. The stem of a clay pipe was fastened to the opening to avoid direct contact with the untreated bladder, but this precaution failed to provide sufficient protection for the wife of Richard Lindon, the chief rival to the Gilbert family in the manufacture of footballs from about 1850. She contracted a lung disease, thought to have come from years of blowing up pigs' bladders, and her husband not unnaturally sought a safer way to inflate footballs.

His great inspiration was to make an artificial bladder out of rubber. It was an invention which, coupled with his discovery of an inflator, revolutionized the manufacture of footballs. Lindon made his breakthrough in 1862 but unfortunately he failed to patent it, a fact which cost him lasting fame and fortune.

Lindon's failure to capitalize on his invention echoed the disappointment of Charles Goodyear, the American inventor of the process of vulcanization which had made India-rubber a commercially viable product. Stickiness, particularly when heated, had initially proved a major drawback to rubber as a useful substance. Goodyear had bought a process of treating the rubber with sulphur which cured this disadvantage, and in 1839 accidentally discovered vulcanization by dropping some of this product on a hot stove. In 1851 he had exhibited at the Great Exhibition in London. It was a tremendous event for which the Crystal Palace was built, intended to display to visitors from home and abroad the achievements of the

An advertisement from the 1890 Rules

British Empire and the new industrial age. Items utilising vulcanised rubber were displayed to a wide public, and for a while the patents Goodyear had taken out held good in England, but there were difficulties in France and elsewhere. Others profited by his process, but by 1855 Goodyear himself was in prison for debt. No such severe fate overtook Lindon, but it was the Gilberts who had the acumen to make the widest use of the discovery he had made.

Like Goodyear, William Gilbert had been at the Great Exhibition of 1851. Exhibit No. 187 was a Rugby School Football 'of leather dressed expressly for the purpose', and officially classified as an *Educational Appliance*. He had gone to great pains with his display stand made to a design by Matthew Bloxam, Gilbert's near neighbour, and which made a great impression on a schoolboy who wrote home to his mother describing it so that she might recognize it on her visit to the Crystal Palace:

It is a house . . . built entirely of leather, at least you can see nothing but leather. The house is a sort of open shed, only shut in at the back and open at the front and sides, four wooden posts support the roof which are all covered with ornamented hand-cut leather. The structure on the inside is meant to represent our football goals (which are in reality of this form [here he draws a diagram], as I daresay you will remember,) from which depend two foot-balls both of real size. The one quite plain only very much finished off and well blown up with *Rugby School Match* on one side and *School Match* on the other. The other one is embroidered [sic] with blue (they are both made with common leather only of course more prepared, and rather lighter in colour than ours) silk markings all done with hand and he says that this one alone cost him 2 gns to make.

This stand is still in Gilbert's old shop in St Matthew's Street, now a football museum. Mr James Gilbert the younger remembered when the original ball displayed at the 1851 Exhibition was still in the family's possession, and in his booklet *The Gilbert Story* he said that he could vouch that 'the shape of the ball then was much the same as shown in Mr Bennett's sketches.'

These drawings illustrated an article in the *Badminton Magazine* which EFT Bennett had written about football in the 1860s. They made balls from four pieces of cowhide stitched together, taking their slightly oval shape from the bladder. Bearing in mind that the use of natural materials ensured that no two balls were ever exactly the same, there is reason to suppose that the balls of the 1820s and 1830s were very similar to those sketched by Bennett. In *Tom Brown's Schooldays* the passage is often quoted in which the new ball at the beginning of the School House match is placed in the middle, *pointing* towards the school or the island goal, so demonstrating that in the early 1830s it was not spherical. Later in the same passage Crab Jones is carefully described in his skilful placing of the ball for a kick at goal by old Brooke.(The real Crab Jones was Edmund Smyth, later a Colonel in the Indian Army and a distinguished Himalayan and Alpine climber.)

Place it true and steady! Trust Crab Jones – he has made a small hole with his heel for the ball to lie on, by which he is resting on one knee, with his eye on old Brooke.

Such meticulous attention to exact placing would scarcely have been necessary with a round ball. Opinion seems to be generally agreed that these balls were ideally suited for the place kicks from which most of the goals were scored. Bennett seems to be saying that the larger balls offered even more advantage in this respect.

The Big Side Balls were half an inch larger than the ordinary ball (and this is a very vast difference); the ends were well rounded, and seventy yards was not at all an impossible kick: how few now think of trying a goal even from thirty yards!

There are numerous tales of stupendous kicks using the older style of ball, but one of the most able and famous players of them all was CS Dakyns, whose ability to drop kick with either foot was extraordinary. The Reverend F Marshall said in his book *Football: The Rugby Union Game,*

Many a time have I seen him drop a goal from a distance of fifty or sixty yards, when an opponent has had a firm hold on one of his arms, but failed to get possession of the ball; which, held by the string, Dakyns would let fall from his unencumbered hand in front of an unerring foot.

Dakyns was equally renowned for his running, dodging and tackling when at Rugby and as a founding member of Richmond, where he played from 1861–8 while a student at King's College, London. He later emigrated to America and settled in Portland, Oregon. In Marshall's opinion 'Pup Dakyns was the best all-round football player who ever donned a jersey'.

The four Dakyns brothers were all footballers; one was a master at Clifton College from its foundation until 1890, and another was said to have enjoyed playing the game so much that he stayed at school until he was twenty, and eventually had to be asked to leave! Pup Dakyns was the youngest of the four who were all day-boys, and was probably brought up with a ball in his hand, as was young Edmund Bowden Smith, the son of one of the masters, who was photographed with his family in about 1862 proudly holding his football by its string. This is one of the earliest photographs of a rugby ball, gleaming and lovingly cared for by its small owner.

The best balls are made from selected English split-hide which is tight in the fibre and strong in the grain. These hides are roughly measured into panels, soaked, shaped, dried, rolled and finally cut into accurate panel shapes before they are greased with dubbin, which is a mixture of cod-oil and tallow. The panels are stitched together by hand and the seams rubbed down to flatten them. The whole then has to be turned inside out through the three inch hole left for the mouthpiece. This task alone is almost impossible for anyone but an expert. Finally the outer seams are rubbed down, the opening sewn and the bladder inserted and inflated. In a first rate ball the leather will have been carefully chosen and dressed, and the panels matched from

*The Bowden-Smith family,
shown with a football (1862)*

the tightest part of the hide. The invention of the rubber bladder made possible a ball of more regular shape and size, and obviated the need for each case to be tailor made. From 1871 Gilberts have patterns showing less rounded ends than were common a decade earlier, but in general terms the process of manufacture changed little.

The skill of the Rugby football makers was fiercely, and very properly defended by Arthur Guillemard against JC Thring who had made a scathing attack on the oval ball in a letter to *The Field* on 26 February, 1863.

Was the oval shape an accident [Thring asked] from want of skill in the worker in leather at Rugby, who, like the tailors, then persuaded his victims that it was the true artistic shape? Or was it designed for the sole benefit of the place-kicker, for I have never yet heard that it was supposed to be better for the general game, and I can witness to its untrue rebound.

I beg to differ with him [replied Guillemard] for I am pretty sure that no-one after having played with a good oval ball will discard it for the round. All the balls made at Rugby are oval, more or less; and I think that, as the makers there gained medals at both the Great Exhibitions of 1851 and 1862, they are entitled to some respect as knowing how to work in leather. They send footballs to Marlborough, Wellington College, and Winchester, and several other schools, and to London, as well as to Australia and New

Zealand, where many people would deem the science of football quite unknown. . . . I beg to inform him that the makers at Rugby can make a ball in any possible shape, and, even more, they can produce one to vie with – I think I might say beat – any one in England. The round ball is perhaps better for the use of some clubs who forbid carrying the ball; but I am sure that Rugbeians will never use round balls when they can get oval.

Indeed demand grew for a ball even more pronounced in its oval shape, but it was 1892 before the RFU fixed standard dimensions requiring the ball to be oval in shape and as far as possible to measure between 25.5 and 26 inches in width circumference, and 30–31 inches in length circumference. In 1931 the width was reduced in answer to the demands of players. New Zealand has traditionally preferred a ball half an inch less in circumference than the ball used in the Home Countries. Similarly there were local preferences in the number of panels used to make up a ball, and four, six or eight may be used. New Zealand favoured four, where South Africa liked eight. As club football proliferated and the number of players was limited to fifteen, new tactics developed in response to the reduced size of the sides. The change in shape towards a narrower ball answered to the need generated by the carrying and passing game which gradually replaced the predominantly kicking game of earlier years.

RUGBY FOOTBALL CENTENARY

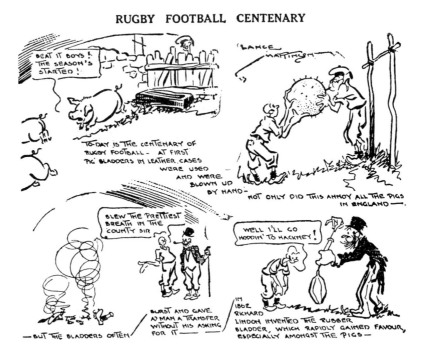

A cartoon from the Daily Herald *(1923)*

SOURCE 12

A Senior Boy Looks Forward to the Day When he can Enjoy Reminiscing about his Football Experiences, Gently Mocking the Conceits of Old Rugbeians

AN ARTICLE WRITTEN BY A SENIOR PUPIL IN THE *NEW RUGBEIAN* 1859

'My first Big Side!' what delightful recollections are called up by those thrilling words, 'My first Big Side!' What footballer (for it is of football, not of cricket, that I am speaking at present), what footballer does not remember with proud feelings that important era in his Rugby existence? while in future years he discourses before wondering New Caps of 'my first Sixth Match,' of the gigantic swells (now only known by name or tradition) whom he pluckily tackled, or still more pluckily (in his own eyes at least) hacked over as they were running in; of the terrible scrummages, those bugbears of youthful footballers; 'good gracious! my dear fellow, talk of scrummages now-a-days! why, you should just have seen the scrummages in the Sixth Match two years ago; those were the sort of things to make your hair stand on end. Fellows did not care a fig for the ball then except inasmuch as it gave them a decent pretext for hacking. I remember a scrummage down by the touch line near the pavillion. By Jove! that was something like a scrummage! Why, we'd been hacking for five minutes already, and hadn't had half enough, in fact, the swells had only just begun to warm to their work, when a bystander (confound his impudence!) kindly (?) informed us that the ball was waiting our convenience on the top of the island. Poor beggar! he didn't try that trick on a second time. Those were the days too, when fellows used to roll the ball out of touch, like sensible Christians as they then were, and bowl over the fellow who stood next them with a stunning good place kick; one had none of these horrid long mauls, in which you get the wind knocked out of you for nothing, and then have the consolation of hearing that 'the ball's gone!' And then there was Hookey Walker the swell hack on the Sixth side; my eye! didn't he walk into the School! only shut up ten fellows for the season, and sent half a dozen home for the rest of the half. There was a report (I don't know if it was true or no, but I should think it was just as likely as not), that merely to see him come through a scrummage was the signal for all the ladies to shriek and faint. Bless you, my dear fellow, they enjoy looking on at a scrummage of all things now – more shame to us. And there was none of that underhand shuffling play with the ball then that there is now; no passing it along from one to the other; all was manly and straightforward. Why, to let the ball go after you had once got into a scrummage was considered to be as flagrant a transgression of the rules of football as to take it up when you were off your side. Nor did you see any of that shirking outside scrummages that's always going on now-a-days. No one thought you worth your salt if you weren't the colour of your mother earth from head to toe ten minutes after the match had begun. But, dash my buttons! you haven't a chance of getting a decent fall in the present day; and no wonder either when you see young dandies 'got up regardless of expense', mincing across Big Side, and looking just as if their delicate frames wouldn't survive any violent contact with the ball. Hang the young puppies! we shall have fellows playing in dress boots and lavender-coloured kid gloves before long. But take my word for it, all you youngsters, if you just watch a fellow of the old school playing, and take a leaf out of his book you'll get on a long sight better than if you take up any of the fiddle-faddle humbug of the present day. My maxim is hack the ball on when you see it near you, and when you don't, why then hack the fellow next you.'

CHAPTER 12 *A TRY AT GOAL*

The H shaped goal posts are as characteristic of rugby football as is the oval ball; the two complement each other. The nature of goals in traditional games was as various as the territory over which they were played. Rivers, trees, doorways and holes in rocks were all used in these cross country matches, with the goals often being quite different at each end. In games played in restricted fields or yards the goal was sometimes a line at either end of the pitch, and the target was simply to get the ball over it. Other similar games would have markers placed on the ground, or poles stuck into the earth to represent goals, the width between them varying substantially from a few feet to the full width of the playing area. Cross bars were rare, the most usual means of scoring being to pass the ball between the posts at any height. At Rugby a combination of the goal line and goal post systems was in operation, giving rise to the now immortal scheme of 'tries'.

The first goalposts of which there is any record at Rugby were erected in the Barn Close. They would have closely resembled those admired by Tom Brown on his first day at school, though it is unlikely that the uprights were at that time quite so tall as Hughes, in Tom's words, described as, a sort of gigantic gallows of two poles eighteen feet high, fixed upright in the ground some fourteen feet apart, with a cross bar running from one to the other at the height of ten feet or thereabouts.

The illustrations of the 1840s and early 1850s consistently show the H shape, but with much shorter uprights than this, though they must still have seemed enormous to a small boy.

East was at pains to explain that to score a goal the ball must go over the cross bar – 'any height'll do so long as it's between the posts'. The numerous goalkeepers were expressly forbidden to climb onto the crossbar to try to intercept, but they did have a job to do in the early games. They were the guardians of the goal *line*, and as such were responsible for making sure that loose balls were touched down before the enemy could get to them. The goalkeepers were also useful when the scrummage approached the goal line, at which point they were allowed to join in *en masse* to push it back. Occasionally some heroic youngster sought fame and fortune through trying to stop a run in, but in doing this he certainly exceeded the call of duty.

Running with the ball only gained real significance in football play when it was linked to the opportunity to score. There is considerable confusion between the practice of running with the ball and the more specific matter of *running in*. Without exception players writing of the period from 1828 onwards recall that running with the ball was tolerated, if not wholly approved. They were also unanimous in the view that any player trying it was in for a rough time. It was a red rag to a bull, and instantly provoked the opposition into particularly vigorous attack. Hacking and collaring were employed against the runner, and he had little chance of getting far. Until the late 1830s a successful run was rarely achieved, but could occasionally lead to a dropped goal.

Running in on the other hand is mentioned by only two of the correspondents quoted in *The Origin of Rugby Football*. JR Lyon, who was at the school from 1830–4, remembered that it was allowable, if you could run through the adversaries lines, to touch the ball behind the posts 'to secure a try at the goal'. Thomas Hughes confirms that in his first year, 1834, 'running with the ball to get a try by touching down within goal was not absolutely forbidden'. Nevertheless he would have expected a jury of Rugby boys to have returned a verdict of justifiable homicide had any player been killed running in!

It was worth risking life and limb to touch down behind the goal line because, by a slight manipulation of the existing rules, the opportunity could be created to try a place-kick at goal. It is clear from East's instruction to Tom Brown concerning the duties of a goal-keeper that the traditional and unwritten laws allowed the ball to be punted out from behind the goal line by whichever side touched it down. 'You'll have to stay in goal to touch the ball when it rolls behind the posts,' Tom is told, 'because if the other side touch it they have a try at goal.

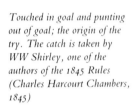

Touched in goal and punting out of goal; the origin of the try. The catch is taken by WW Shirley, one of the authors of the 1845 Rules (Charles Harcourt Chambers, 1845)

The means by which a try was secured were ingenious. The official outcome of touching the ball down was the right to punt the ball out, and a defending player would do just this. The privilege of punting out being given to the goalkeeper who touched it down was probably introduced in the first place to avoid dispute among the multitude of small boys in goal, whose opportunities to participate were otherwise minimal. A player who had touched down in the enemy goal, how-ever, would stand immediately behind the goal line, and punt the ball very gently out into the hands of a player on his own side who stood facing him a short distance away. That player could then claim he had made a fair catch and make his mark. This in turn allowed the ball to be carried back as far as was necessary for a place kick to be made at goal. The manoeuvre is well illustrated in one of CH Chambers' drawings.

In this way a device originally intended simply to move the ball out of goal and back into play was manipulated so that it eventually developed into that high point of the modern game – the try. The elaborate procedure in bringing the ball out for the goal kick continued to be observed until 1883–4, when the ritual was abolished and replaced by the straightforward recognition in the modern game that the touch down results directly in a try at goal.

The great practitioner of running in was a player called Jem Mackie, a lad of considerable strength and speed who made frequent use of the ploy during the 1838–9 season. He was elected Member of Parliament for his home constituency of Kirkcudbrightshire, and became, in Thomas Hughes' words, 'a very useful but silent member'. Hughes would undoubtedly have preferred to see Mackie named as the true originator of the carrying game rather than Webb Ellis, who was never, by any stretch of the imagination, 'a giant in the land'. Indeed Hughes rather coldly remarked that, 'The "Webb Ellis Tradition" had not survived to my day'. Hughes himself might also have made a valid claim to the title of Originator of the modern game, for he was the Captain of Big Side who, in 1841–2, finally sanctioned the legality of running in.

Scoring in the early days was by means of goals only. Big Side Matches continued for three, five or seven afternoons, or until three goals had been scored. If no goal had been kicked after three days a match would be abandoned. At the end of these titanic struggles no one was content with a draw, so accounts of the matches would invariably conclude with the comment that one side or the other had the advantage of the play. Posters, touch-downs and dead balls were recorded as a measure of such advantage, but they carried no value in deciding the game.

Up to 1875 a match could not be won unless a goal had been scored. It was then decided that if no goal had been kicked, or the score was equal a match could be decided by a majority of tries, but that a single goal should count for more than any number of tries.

Cheltenham College was the first to work out a system to quantify the advantages in play which had not until then been formally acknowledged. The scheme of points developed at Cheltenham was adopted by the RFU in 1886, allowing three points for a goal and one for a try, though the try was discounted if it was converted. Thus for a while three tries equalled one goal, which limited the power of the goal but did not entirely solve the problem of providing a scoring system which would fairly reflect the balance of play.

In 1891 tries were increased in value, the points awarded being two for a try, three for a penalty, five for a goal from a try, and four for any other goal. A further point was added for a try in 1893, and the revised scheme adopted by the International Board in 1894. More changes were made in 1905 and 1948, but it was not until the present values were introduced in September, 1971 that the try scored more than any kind of goal kick. For the first time in Rugby football the touch down over the line reigns supreme and the goal, once the sole objective, takes second place. Over the years the changes in scoring methods have reflected changing playing practices, and particularly, in the case of the value of the try, the influence of the passing game. When the run in had to be made by the player in possession far fewer tries were possible, and kicking skills were much more important.

The laws in Rugby football have always tended to follow developments in play rather than to impose playing practices from above. This pragmatic approach has allowed the game to adapt and to grow as it has spread worldwide, and it could well be due to the resistance of Rugbeians to the *imposition* as opposed to the development of new ideas in the early days that its great character has emerged.

SOURCE 13   *Football as Played at Rugby in the 'Sixties*
FROM AN ARTICLE BY ARTHUR A PEARSON IN *RUGBY FOOTBALL*,
3 NOVEMBER, 1923

On the 1st of November, 1923, a Rugby football match between England and Wales on the one side, and Scotland and Ireland on the other, was played in the Rugby School Close to celebrate the centenary of the year when William Webb Ellis, a boy at the School, in utter disregard of existing rules, on catching the ball, rushed forward with it in his hands towards the opposite goal, and so laid the foundation of the present Rugby game. During the years which have elapsed since Ellis's illegal action was duly adopted and recognized, while the distinctive features of the game have remained the same, considerable modification has been introduced from time to time, and it may therefore be of interest to give some reminiscences of Rugby football as played at Rugby in the 'Sixties.

The football season then usually began with House games, called 'little-sides,' as distinguished from the 'big-side' games described later. At these 'little-side' games all the boys of a House played together, and I recall to my mind, one day in the autumn of 1861, regarding with feelings of joyful if perhaps rather fearful expectation, a notice on the notice-board of my house, that there would be a 'little-side' that afternoon, and that 'all must come,' for these 'little-sides' were usually compulsory for all below the sixth form, unless a boy were specially exempted on medical grounds.

Most important were the school 'big-side' games, confined to the best players in the school, numbering about sixty, who were known as the 'caps,' being entitled to wear distinctive caps of velvet with gilt or silver tassles, each house having a cap of its own, with its distinctive house badge. Then there were the house matches played twenty-a-side, not fifteen as now, to determine which should be the two cock houses to play the rest of the school at the end of the autumn term. Besides these there were 'little-sides' and house-matches 'below-caps,' that is, among the boys not playing on 'big-side,' and occasionally second twenty house matches.

And now to mention some of the features of the game as played in the early 'Sixties, which have since undergone change:

(1) The ball might not be picked up unless it were on the bound, so that in the case of a rolling or stationary ball it was necessary to give it a little kick to make it bound before picking it up to run with it.

(2) If a boy running with the ball, when tackled, hung on to the ball, forcible persuasion might be resorted to to compel him to put the ball down on to the ground, when the scrummage could form round it, and it might not be picked up again, and shouts might sometimes be heard of 'wring his neck off,' should the one holding the ball prove obdurate.

(3) Punting was not in vogue in those days, the drop kick being the rule, and this was assiduously practised at what was rather inconsistently called 'punt-about,' the general ambition being to be able to drop kick equally well with either foot.

(4) Goals could be drop-kicked as now by catching the ball and making one's mark; and upon this, I imagine, was founded the elaborate ceremony then observed in the case of a 'try.' After a run in, one boy bringing the ball up to the goal-line, making his mark beyond which the other side might not come, and then retiring to a safe distance along the goal-line, when he would punt the ball into the hands of another boy of his own side, who would again make his mark just outside the goal-line, beyond which the other side might not come till the ball had been placed on the ground for the 'try,' as now.

(5) When a scrummage crossed the goal-line anyone who was not actually touching the ball had to come out, and the others rolled about on the ground till one of them should succeed in touching the ball down, or until perhaps, they got again outside the goal-line, when the rest of the scrummage might once more join in.

And now I come to one notable feature of Rugby football in the early 'Sixties, viz., hacking and hacking over; and first, a word or two regarding hacking over, which was resorted to as an alternative to tackling any one running with the ball, while the 'first-on-side,' i.e. the one nearest the ball on the opposite side might also be hacked over or charged, but not tackled. Hacking over was not necessarily a violent proceeding, it might be scientific, consisting of a gentle kick given to the runner's back leg when in the air, so as to knock it behind the other leg, with the result of at once bringing the runner to the ground; but it might consist of a violent hack at either leg, and this form of hacking over never recommended itself to me, requiring as it did, less pluck or skill than tackling, while occasionally it might be applied rather brutally.

It was a pretty sight, however, to see a good runner, with the ball tucked under one arm, fending off would-be tacklers with the other arm, and neatly jumping over the hacks aimed at his legs.

The passing tactics of the modern game are no doubt more scientific, but they offer fewer opportunities for running with the ball, while the low tackling which is universally adopted at the present time, but was only partially in vogue in the Sixties, also tends to make long runs more difficult, since it is much easier to fend off a tackler who aims at your shoulders than one who stoops to seize you round the legs.

Hacking in the scrummage was theoretically supposed to be only round the ball, but I have seen a boy come through a scrummage in an exciting match, hacking wildly into the air unconscious of the futility of the performance! While hacking and hacking-over were permissible on 'Big-side,' and in all house matches, they were never allowed in 'Little-sides,' nor was there necessarily any hacking on 'Big-side.' I remember one football term when there was practically no hacking on 'Big-side' until near the end of the term when one day one of the bigger boys on one side called out to a boy on the other side, 'let us have some fun to-day,' and forthwith hacking commenced.

The damage done to shins by hacking in a loose scrummage was usually trifling, since, when hacking oneself, hacks glanced off one's shins more or less; but I recollect once being wedged tight in a scrummage so that I could not move hand or foot, when one of the bigger boys on the other side, thinking to open out the scrummage, let fly; he was rather a friend of mine and had not, I feel sure, the least intention of going for me, and was no doubt quite unconscious of doing so; three times, however, in succession, the toe of his boot descended upon the same place in any unlucky shin, my leg being fixed so that there was no give, and then the scrummage opened out and I limped away with a shin that took a week to heal up.

But as a rule, one's hacks, of which one used to be rather proud, healed up very rapidly; though I remember once, my shins being in a more or less tender condition after some somewhat fierce house matches, my rather welcoming a strained back which rendered me *hors de combat* for a week, and so allowed my shins time to recover. Many years later I happened to graze one of my shins which for six weeks refused to heal, and when I expostulated with my doctor on the subject, referring to my old Rugby experiences, he replied with a smile, *Tempora mutantur: nos et mutamur in illis.*

After leaving Rugby, I helped with some other old Rugbeians and Marlburians to start 'The Wimbledon Hornets,' one of the earlier Rugby football clubs in the neighbourhood of London, and I recollect well the discussion which we had as to whether to have hacking or not; in the end, we referred the question to the Richmond club, which had then only recently been formed and, on learning from them that they had decided against hacking, we followed suit. It was certainly obvious that, whatever might be admissible among boys, hacking was eminently unsuitable for men in professions or business who might as a result have to limp to their offices on a Monday morning!

At school, it was different, but it was an unnecessary adjunct to the game, and was very wisely done away with; it had, moreover, the disadvantage of preventing our having any 'foreign' matches against other schools, as it was feared that the intense excitement of such matches might lead to hacking of a serious character, so that in my time there was no school twenty.

There is one other circumstance connected with hacking in the scrummage which may be of interest. Fights of the type recorded in *Tom Brown's Schooldays* were almost unknown in the 'Sixties, and I can only recollect one such fight in the five years I was at Rugby; but differences during the football season were occasionally ventilated on 'Big-side,' when the two parties were playing on opposite sides, and a rumour might get about that 'So-and-So' were going to 'have-it-down' that afternoon, 'it' being the theoretical ball supposed to be between them; it would, however, be only possible for them to carry out their intentions when they happened to meet each other in a scrummage afforded them a legitimate opportunity for indulging in the pleasure of kicking each other's shins.

Another feature of the modern game which was then the exception rather than the rule was 'heeling out,' and I particularly remember this because of its fatal effect when resorted to on one occasion against my own house. In 1865, in the house matches which had taken place to determine which were to be the two cock houses, while the School house was indisputably first, the trials for the second place had resulted in the following complication, Blake's had beaten Arnold's, Arnold's had beaten Evan's, and Evan's had beaten Blake's, so that each of the three might claim to have directly or indirectly beaten the other two.

A 'Big-side' levée, which consisted of all the upper school, was accordingly summoned to consider the knotty point, and it was eventually decided that each of the three houses should play against the School house, and that which ever did best should be second house. Now my house (Arnold's), had already played against the School house, and had made a very good game of it, but in this first match the School house had realised that our strength lay mainly in our half-backs, and in our second match against them to prevent the ball falling into the hands of our half-backs, they resorted to heeling out more systematically than had ever to my recollection been practised before, with disastrous results for our chances of being second house.

The more usual play in those days was to take the ball through the scrummage, and, following hard up, kick it past the half-backs; and in this I had some advantage, since, being one of the smallest 'Caps' on Big-side, I was able to see what was going on, so to speak, below the general level, and I used to aim at getting the ball between my feet and waiting quietly till I could push my way, or be pushed through the scrummage, and then making a dash to get the ball past the half-backs and following it up for all I was worth. Such a plan of action would, of course, be impossible now with the much smaller and looser scrummages of the modern game. And here I may mention that in a Twenty of those days there were usually two, or sometimes three, half-backs and two or three full-backs, with very occasionally a three-quarter back.

While House matches were played twenty a side, the number of 'Caps' playing on Big-side were, as I have said, about sixty, and to these might be added an occasional Old Rugbeian, or one of the Masters, and among the latter I can remember in particular my old mathematical master and friend, Canon Wilson, who is still with us. In these games there were, therefore, usually about thirty a side, while in the three great matches of the Sixth against the School, the School against the Old Rugbeians, and the Two Cock Houses against the rest of the School, the numbers were very much larger, sometimes as many as sixty a side, and one might almost go to sleep in a scrummage till the wagging of heads in one's neighbourhood showed that the ball was coming near one's own part of the scrummage.

Another peculiar feature of the first two of these matches was that all the School below the Fifth Form had, on these occasions, to keep goal, in ordinary clothes of course, and to remain behind the School goal line, and if during the game the scrummage should be pushed near the goal line, then all the goal-keepers might join in to push out, such an opportunity being heartily welcomed to relieve the monotony of idleness.

As regards football dress, this consisted of jerseys and flannel trousers for all in their House Twenties, but those below were condemned to wear white ducks, hardly the most suitable dress for football, but after all boys have not, I think, been more foolish in the matter of dress than their elders have often been.

While the Big-side games were always played in the afternoon, House matches were usually played in the morning, and, though Big-sides were not compulsory, it was rather a point of honour to 'follow up' in the afternoon after playing a House Match in the morning, to show that one was not done up with the morning's exertions.

With respect to accidents, these were few in number, and I can only recollect during my five years at Rugby one broken leg, one broken collar-bone, and the case of one boy who received injuries to his back, from which, however, he completely recovered.

There is one other feature of the Rugby game as played at Rugby in the Sixties which may be worth mentioning, viz., that we had no umpires or referees, and yet got on very well without them!

To get one's cap was the great ambition of all football enthusiasts, and permission to take one's cap was given, if I remember right, by the Head of the House Twenty to those in his House not in the Sixth Form, and by the Head of the School to those in the Sixth; in any case I can well remember, as the proudest moment of my life, when one morning in the sixth Form a piece of paper was passed round to me signed by the Head of the School, Arthur Godley, now Lord Kilbracken, with the welcome words on it, 'You may wear your cap for the Sixth Match.' That cap is now hanging up in the room in which I write, with the date in it of the day when I first won it – 7 October, 1865. But I was a football enthusiast, and I can recollect feeling in a critical House Match that I would willingly be smashed up if only our House could win the match.

The old game was no doubt unscientific compared with the game of the present day, but it was a glorious game, and I look back upon my last football term as one of the happiest times of my life, when I remember wondering sometimes to myself as, sitting, it may have been, over my

Study fire after a hard fought and successful House Match, if life could ever be so delightful again.

The match on 1 November was played in the Old School Close, where so many have played the old game who have now passed away, as also have famous 'Three Trees' of the old days, against whose trunks we were sometimes squeezed more tightly than was pleasant, but which were a great feature of the Close in the past; and if the old game has somewhat changed since those days, the old spirit of it still goes on, and long may it be so.

CHAPTER 13 *NEVER, SHORT OF MANSLAUGHTER*

The independent attitude of Rugbeians towards the management of their games was inbred. As boys they had always fiercely guarded their right to organize their own sports, and as men they saw no reason to change. By the same token there is no evidence that they sought to impose their version of football on others, though they seemed happy enough to welcome outsiders into it, and made no secret of their own preference.

For most of the nineteenth century the authorities at Rugby were happy to endorse sport as a beneficial pastime and to provide space and time for play, but the rest was up to the boys. To begin with the Head of School and the Sixth Form made all the arrangements, but as time went on responsibilities were delegated or shared in response to the demands of the good *players* who rightly felt they had a contribution to make.

The boys were responsible for everything. They arranged for the maintenance of the Close, rented further fields when they needed them, purchased footballs, cricket nets, goal posts and any other necessary equipment, and even employed their own cricket professional. All this was paid for by subscriptions raised from members of the school and stringent accounts were kept, often involving substantial sums of money.

In addition matches were arranged, practice grounds regulated, rules laid down and records kept of all the major sports. Disputes were settled by arbitration, and any necessary umpiring on the field of play was arranged between the heads of sides. In Big Side football matches where particularly large numbers were involved a captain could be required to appoint as many as six deputies to act on his behalf in different parts of the field. In the vast scrummages of those days only players involved were in a position to tell what was happening. The whereabouts of the ball in a scrummage could only be determined by seeking a particularly vigorous area of activity among the players. It was therefore practical to use players rather than umpires to adjudicate. All versions of the rule book contain the statement that 'Heads of sides or two deputies appointed by them are the sole arbiters of all disputes'. The only sanction they seem to have had was the power to send a player into goal to join the younger boys, but it is not clear whether this demotion was permanent or temporary. Later attempts to bolster the authority of umpires with a half-crown fine seem to have met with limited success, and by and large it was public opinion which enforced fair play.

The RFU addressed the question of referees and umpires in 1885, and produced a set of regulations for their guidance the following year. As may be expected regular updates were produced thereafter, but 1886 goes down in history as the year when the whistle and flag were brought into play as reliable means of signalling to players. The Union had developed a scheme of free kick penalties to control infringements, particularly of the off-side rule, and in 1888 it was decided that goals might be obtained from such free kicks. The umpires were also empowered to send a player off the field for rough play, echoing the school sanction of 'sending in to goal'.

The headmasters at Rugby showed admirable restraint in leaving their pupils alone to administer their own games. Arnold, as Housemaster of the School House, turned out on occasion to watch them play, and with sons of his own taking part he doubtless knew a good deal about football. He approved, but never interfered. The first headmaster to intervene successfully in the conduct of games was Dr Frederick Temple, later Archbishop of Canterbury. In 1858, his first year, Temple abolished the practice of standing in goal. He felt, with good reason, that it was a wholly unproductive way for younger boys to spend their time, and they were so bored by it that they were even

Dr Frederick Temple,
Headmaster of Rugby School
and later Archbishop of
Canterbury

whiling away their time trying to attach fire-crackers to the players' clothes. There was an outcry from the Old Rugbeians, so he was persuaded to allow compulsory standing in goal only in the three great matches. There was great rejoicing among the fags, and when at a stroke they were liberated the game suffered no ill effects whatsoever. Their usefulness had long since diminished, and there was no longer any need to use goalkeeping as a form of apprenticeship. By Temple's day there were written rules to teach the laws, and far more opportunities for younger boys to participate in games of their own. Seven grounds were now available, and house competitions at junior level, as well as 'little-sides' in which all the boys of a house played together ensured that, in the absence of any adult coaching, younger boys were taught the game. Nevertheless the Old Rugbeians were incensed, although it was probably the fact that Temple had interfered rather than the abolition of goalkeeping which had really upset them.

The lesson was not lost on Temple, who well understood the value of games in developing character as well as fitness. The Sixth remained in charge of the Close and the games played upon it, though Temple did insist that he should approve any taxes levied by them for expenses. The Head of School was still, as he had always been, also the Captain of Football. The Select Committee investigating the Public Schools in the 1860s expressed their approval of this arrangement, which, they thought, prevented games 'swells' from rivalling the eminence of the intellectuals. The first football captain who was not the Head of School was WH Bolton in 1871–2, in whose favour the Head of School had resigned. He later captained Oxford.

Once Temple was asked by a visitor who was alarmed by the apparent roughness of the play they had been watching whether he ever stopped a match. 'Never,' replied Temple emphatically, 'short of manslaughter'. He understood the need to let the boys regulate their own games, but even so made one further incursion into their territory when he demanded that intentional hacking should be stopped.

Hacking was always one of the most controversial aspects of the Rugby School game. Just as *running with the ball* and *running in* are often confused, so are *hacking* and *hacking over*. Hacking originated in the huge scrums of the Big Side games when no one had much idea where the ball was until he felt it with his feet. Forwards stood upright and simply hacked their way forwards with (or more often without) the ball. Sometimes one player would act as *post*, his duty being to get the ball between his feet and stand bolt upright allowing the forwards to propel him through the melee. As WHD Rowse remarked in his *History of Rugby School*,

What with these immense sides, in a match which might last through four afternoons in succession, and what with the hacking (even though hob nails and iron plates were not allowed), Rugby football was not then a game for tender-hearted parents to look on with equanimity.

These scrummages provided an excellent opportunity for boys to pay off old scores, or to join forces in a deliberate attack on an unpopular rival. While this practice had the effect of curbing the worst excesses of any bullying or overweeningly despotic senior boys, such attacks could be barbarous, and it was hacking employed for this purpose which Temple quite rightly banned. The heroes of a Rugby novel by AG Butler, declare unambiguously before a match that 'for them the one interest in the game, the one object in the field, was to lame Potter', a praeposter who had misused his authority:

Football on Big Side,
1851 – the earliest photograph
of footballers at Rugby School

Certain big Fifth Form fellows of the class commonly called 'good hacks', who, though they did little else in the game, were good in giving and receiving hacks, vowed to give it him. 'Fight neither with small or great, fight only with the King of Israel', was their plan of action, and as Potter had lots of pluck, and was also famous among other things as a good hack, bloody shins on both sides were certain to follow. Those were the times, happily long past, when a rule had to be made that you might not hack and hold a fellow at the same time. No penalty attended the violation of this rule, but public opinion fairly well enforced it.

Holding may have been forbidden, but it was possible to get well and truly trapped in the scrummages and to be quite helpless to protect yourself. 'I recollect once being wedged so tight in a scrummage that I could not move hand or foot, when one of the bigger boys on the other side, thinking to open out the scrummage, let fly . . . three times in succession the toe of his boot descended upon the same place in my unlucky shin, my leg being fixed so that there was no give.' In this instance no animosity was intended and Pearson bore no grudge, though his injuries were painful.

After one Cock House match the forwards of the losing side were said to have been so badly injured that their housemaster 'sat down on the grass and wept like a child'. In retelling the tale WHD Rowse remarks that perhaps not too much should be made of this, 'for the gentleman in question evidently had the gift of tears, and used to

'Old Vecq', the French Master (DH Bolton)

weep over a Greek play in form'. Perhaps it was these boys that G. C. Vecqueray, later an Oxford Blue, tried to take into the School House, to which he belonged, to have their injuries treated. The old School House butler showed his disapproval of such weakness by forbidding them entry with the stern words 'let *them* bury their *own* dead'.

Vecqueray's father, known to boys for four decades as 'Old Vecq', was brought over to Rugby from Bruges in 1859 as a French master. Now it was the custom at Rugby that masters or Old Rugbeians could join in games if they so wished, and Old Vecq was quite determined to take an active part – even in football. He joined in the littleside games organised by the houses, but unfortunately chose to wear elastic sided boots to play in. The temptation to kick the ankles of a new 'Froggy French' master overcame the young Rugbeians, and one of GC Vecqueray's earliest recollections is of his mother cutting off his father's boots every Saturday evening as he sat before the fire after his weekly game of rugger with his ankles so swollen that they could not be removed any other way. Old Vecq stuck it out until the boys desisted out of respect for his courage and determination, and since boys are not too particular about the exactitudes of nationality, he probably influenced the view of generations of Rugbeians about the sporting abilities of the French! Another Frenchman, WH Waddington, had also been a footballer of distinction when at Rugby, and confirmed his athletic credibility at Oxford by rowing in the Boat Race, but although he briefly became Prime Minister of France and was a distinguished French Ambassador in London, he was in fact half English and undoubtedly regarded by Rugbeians as an honorary

Englishman. Old Vecq, so far as Rugby lads were concerned, was probably a much better ambassador.

So much for hacking in the scrummage. It was a brutal business, painful when inflicted by boys, but positively dangerous in adult games. Insistence that hacking should be retained nearly cost the game its very survival in the 1860s as non-Rugbeians refused to countenance it in clubs and universities. For Old Rugbeians hacking represented a test of character and fortitude, a rite of passage into positions of leadership and the proof of their own courage. Outsiders had no such sentimental preconceptions and regarded it with horror.

At the school itself the justification for hacking as a necessary means to drive the ball through the packed scrummages of the traditional Big Side games was fast disappearing. 'An excessive devotion to House matches' was remarked upon in the school magazine, and these twenty aside games with their looser scrummages came strongly to the fore during the 1860s. New means were devised to extract the ball from the scrummage, notably the practice of heeling out, which emerged as a systematic move in 1865.

Thus hacking in the scrummage succumbed not only to the protests of the humanitarians, but to the threat of natural redundancy. But hacking *over* was more vigorously defended. This was the original means of stopping a player who was running with the ball by tripping him as an alternative to collaring him. A skilful player could apply a gentle, glancing kick to the oncoming opponent which, if it caught him in the right place, (on the shin about three inches above the ankle), and at the right time, (just as he was changing his balance to avoid the challenger), would bring him down on his face 'like a shot rabbit'. Scientifically performed this manoeuvre was both useful and efficient. It could also be used against the opposition player nearest to the ball, who could be charged or hacked over, but not tackled. Needless to say not all players were expert, and hacking over when mis-timed or mis-used was brutal.

Possibly it was an art best learned young, and certainly best practised upon boys who fell less heavily. AN Hornby, Captain of the Lancashire County Cricket XI and a well known three-quarter back at football was prevented from scoring a try when playing in a match against the school by being neatly hacked over behind the goal line on the gravel path by the headmaster's garden wall. He unfortunately fell hard and was knocked unconscious, and thereafter spoke very strongly against hacking over and the methods of play employed at Rugby School.

One of the most delightful defences of hacking over as a triumph of science over strength is the tale of TH Case, who, as an elderly man, took on a formidable opponent with great success:

It happened thus: Tommy Case was a very musical man. He asked a party to the first full performance of Wagner's *Ring* at Covent Garden Opera House. That performance lasted the whole day (10 a.m.–11 p.m. or thereabouts). We were all let out at about 6.30 p.m. to get some food. There was an enormously big (and rather 'moist') Covent Garden Market Porter outside who found it amusing to barge into all the ladies and gentlemen on the pavement. He barged into our party and fell heavily – flat on his nose, with an amazed expression as soon as he did so. Tommy Case was then talking about Baconian Philosophy, and beaming through his glasses as usual. When we had got about 5 yards past the intoxicated and prostrate 15 stone porter, he said, 'That is an instance of *lumen siccum* (a Baconian Philosophical phrase meaning *dry light*). I hacked that man over rather neatly, didn't I?'.

It seems that the knack of hacking over was rather akin to riding a bicycle – once learnt never forgotten. In his youth Case played cricket for Oxford for three years in succession, and later became Professor of Moral Philosophy at Oxford, and President of Corpus Christi until 1924.

Excellent though the credentials were of its supporters, hacking clearly had to go if the game was to gain acceptance as a sport for adults as well as boys, and it was not accepted by the RFU in 1871. At about the same time it died a natural death at the school, and was formally abolished there in 1876.

The Match

FROM *THE THREE FRIENDS: A STORY OF RUGBY IN THE FORTIES* BY AG BUTLER

That afternoon was no ordinary match. The Sixth had made itself unpopular of late through the over-zeal and roughness of some of its members: and on this day, as hacking was then the rule, many old scores of vengeance, or antipathy, were to be paid. Above all, Potter was singled out for punishment. He was one who gloried in unpopularity, saying that 'as he could not be a jolly fellow, he would be a brute'; and, as such, he pushed his rights as a Preposter to extremes, and caned fellows for the merest trifles. Consequently, there was a conspiracy on foot to pay him off. And certain big Fifth form fellows of the class commonly called 'good hacks,' who, though they did little else in the game, were good in giving and receiving hacks, vowed to give it him. 'Fight neither with small nor great, fight only with the King of Israel,' was their plan of action, and, as Potter had lots of pluck, and was also famous among other things as 'a good hack,' bloody shins on both sides were certain to follow. Those were the times, happily long past, when a rule had to be made (was it not written in a little blue book called 'the Rules of Football'?) that you might not hack and hold a fellow at the same time. No penalty attended the violation of this rule, but public opinion fairly well enforced it. The proscribed practice probably dated from prehistoric times, remotely connected with savage ancestors, and, though it had little real football in it, was long supposed to be one chief glory of the Rugby game.

Now I am not going to describe a football match *in toto*, or attempt to vie with Tom Brown's immortal School-house match. Under the 'windy' elms of the classic Rugby close, did the fatal Three, careless of all meaner ends, pursue their hated victim Potter. The Sixth might win, the School be licked into a cocked hat: but for them the one interest in the game, the one object in the field, was to lame Potter.

It was a close game. The School, having reduced the number of their side till it was about a third more than their opponents, had also to some extent imitated their tactics. Beside the usual full-backs – the Triarii of old – were light skirmishers, answering to the present half-backs, who had to seize the ball when issuing from a scrimmage, and do with it the best they could. Among these Fleming had a place found him, being attached, as a squire to a knight, to Twining, the best half-back on the School side.

And then came that weary waiting-time before kick-off, when the keen player, conscious of a great gap in the region of the waist, shivers with excitement, not with fear, not with cold, not with anxiety as to the result, but with that strange fever of the nerves which seems to pinch him in the centre, so that the leathern waistband has to be taken in several holes. Wasps, the great fighters of the insect world, have discovered this, and in the course of ages have reduced their waists, the emotional centre of the wasp tribe, to a minimum. Without this they would be tortured by that sense of central hollowness, of which Fleming was now conscious. 'When will they begin?' is always the thought of the young player of fifteen. Till then, however calm outwardly, his nerves are all on fire within. 'When will they end?' is oftener the feeling of his older captain, who sees the forces of his side exhausted, so that, as the evening closes in, they can hardly stay the ball from crossing the line.

At last! The kick is made, the ball is off, and the great scrimmage under the Three Elm Trees, which is to last (in these rude ancient times) for ten minutes, is begun.

Potter, the chief forward of the Sixth, led on his side well. With his short, sturdy, thick-set figure, like a dwarfed Hercules, he wedged his way through his opponents, always on the ball, so long as he could find it; or, if he lost it, forcing a path through to the other side, and returning back to recover it. Little they then thought of tactics, or screwing, or heeling out, or suchlike miserable devices of these scientific days. It was one long, dense, determined shove of breast to breast, and shoulder to shoulder, while well-shod boots were dealing savage hacks upon defenceless shins. And above all rose, in the clear frosty air, a human steam, acceptable, it is to be hoped, to the powers who watch over football, over the breathless contest of youthful pluck and endurance in the well-fought field. And still the scrimmage went on. In such a *mêlée* it was not easy, as may be imagined, for the Three to find out Potter, nor for Potter to be conscious of the fell purpose of the Three. When he did so he did not flinch. Once he came upon their outside member, and, feeling his assault, returned it with a kick – as the other described it afterwards – like that of a mad bullock, and passed on unheeding. One to one, he was more than a match for them. But at last, when in the thickest of the press he met them full in front, then ensued a conflict which we will not describe particularly. Enough to say that all thought of the game, as a game, was forgotten, and the private vendetta was fought out to the bitter end. Even after the scrimmage was over, the fight still continued. And if the wrong done to Fleming was avenged, yet the avengers carried away marks which, however honourable as scars, were none the less painful and disabling. Some of the scars of football, it is said, men carry to their graves.

But to return to the game. To be a good half-back there is needed a quick eye, a light foot, and a lithe body, dissolving as it were into vapour as you meet an opponent's charge, and forming again, with the old onward impetus, on the other side. All these Fleming had in perfection, and, though still too young for any great feats, he again and again executed short runs or neat kicks into 'touch' ('passing' was then unknown), which earned him the applause of Twining, his immediate superior; once, even a nod and grunt of approval from the head of his side. Then at last came his opportunity. The Sixth that year was weak: most of their old champions had passed away to Oxford and Cambridge; and Potter, though still game and dauntless as ever, had lost much of his first dash and deadly onset owing to his late encounter. Slowly the ball was driven back past the Three Trees, along the touch line, towards the Island goal, until at last a good 'throw out' landed it just at the feet of Twining, who seized it and made a dash for the Sixth goal, closely followed by Fleming. The distance was not great, and shouts of 'Collar him!' 'Strangle him!' 'Hack him over!' rose like a scream, or yell, from the Sixth side, while all their swiftest runners were upon him in an instance. In vain his writhing, in vain his struggles, in vain his wrestling tricks, against the octopus clutch of his pursuers! The goal was not for him. Gripped round the waist by one, throttled round the neck by another, while a third tightly clasped his legs and ankles, he was thrown down, half choked and strangled, on the grass, letting the ball escape him as he fell, which, as it bounded, was snatched up by Fleming, who, after a short swift course of wondrous twists and dodges, like a hunted hare, under the arms, almost through the legs of his opponents, lodged it safely across 'the line.' Then arose – there were no umpires in those days – the usual roar of voices: 'Our ball!' 'Off side!' 'Yah!' 'Bah!' on this side, and on that, like a pack of hounds fighting over a quartered fox, until the strife was promptly quelled by the Head of the School, a tall dignified person in whiskers, who had a conscience, and a 'try' was awarded to 'the School.' This was, as we now say 'converted,' and, amid wild tumult of enthusiasm, conquerors and conquered changed sides, scowling as they went.

Then occurred an incident of rare mark even in the annals of Rugby. On the Sixth side was a player belonging to the School-house, who, like the Black Knight in *Ivanhoe*, had hitherto taken little part in the game. His cap was new, his jersey untorn, his white trousers unblemished by a stain. He had been into no scrimmage, and made none of those brilliant rushes which are the admiration of lookers on. Standing apart, near to the backs but not one of them, he had often seemed about to get the ball, but, from want of quickness or ill-luck, he had always seen it fall into the hands of another. Nothing as yet had been done by him to justify his House-name of 'the Switcher.' But now at last, when the School, encouraged by success, were pressing the Sixth hard, and seemed near upon a second goal, fortune suddenly favoured him. The ball passing from the scrimmage near to the Barby entrance, by the Headmaster's garden, was kicked by some one (why did he not run with it?) straight for the Sixth goal, where 'the Switcher' was standing. He caught it up, tucked it under his arm, and, starting into sudden life, was off with the speed of lightning. 'He's off!' 'Look out!' 'Stop him!' the School leaders shouted. They knew their danger. Once give 'the Switcher' his chance, and you might as well try to stop a winner of the Derby. In a moment, running round all obstacles, he had reached the Three

Trees; and, though Twining, followed by Fleming, running close behind, clutched him by the jersey, he tore himself from his grasp; and, parrying the attack of the back-player by a push from his long arm, he went through 'small fry' of the School side, like a hot knife through a pat of butter, and placed the ball between the goal-posts. It was all over in a few seconds, a splendid sprint of over a hundred yards; and when he returned, with head thrown back, fierce look, and proud impatient twitching of the shoulders, he was greeted with acclamations by his own side:

> And even the ranks of Tuscany
> Could scarce forbear to cheer.

They had simply watched him, as he ran, in stupid amazement. He was indeed 'the Switcher'. And that run in, the really splendid feature of Rugby football, became proverbial. It had covered the whole distance from goal to goal.

CHAPTER 14 *ARNOLD'S MEN*

R ugbeians found it hard to accept the limitations placed upon them by the spread of their game beyond their immediate control. Their closed environment had allowed changes to be made to the rules as and when popular usage had demanded. Between 1820 and 1860 enormous alteration had taken place in both the style of play and its organization. Football had needed to adapt not only to changing physical circumstances, but to a whole new ethos in education and in society at large. The Rugby game had been left almost entirely in the hands of the players, with minimal intervention from above. The changes they introduced were 'demand led' and quickly implemented. The objective was to create the best possible game to meet the needs of a particular group of schoolboys. They wanted excitement, competition, and the chance to perfect and display athletic skills such as kicking and running. They also needed the sense of fellowship and the incentive to prove their courage, endurance and loyalty. The folklore which quickly grew around the game allowed boys to measure their own achievements against those of their predecessors and at the same time to aspire to immortality themselves.

In the strongly academic schools of the nineteenth century, where promotion was based exclusively on success in examinations, there was an undoubted need for some area for the less academic pupils to excel. The games field took on this role, and football matches, which were frequently described with all the terminology of battle, encouraged public acclaim for the 'manly' virtues which were held in high regard by society at large.

The football game which had evolved at Rugby was widely regarded as satisfying the ideal requirements for a game for boys. Its spread into other schools was almost inevitable. One of the first schools to adopt Rugby School rules was Marlborough. GEL Cotton, characterized as 'The Young Master' in *Tom Brown's Schooldays*, went there from Rugby to become Headmaster in 1852. He inherited a school where the boys were accustomed to run wild in the countryside in their free time and he needed to introduce controls. He had seen at Rugby the way in which football and other games had to a large extent diverted boys from poaching and other illicit pursuits, and made a conscious decision to develop organized sports at Marlborough to this end. He appointed to his staff four or five young Rugbeians who successfully reformed the games, particularly football, which they naturally promoted along Rugby lines. There was no question of Marlborough slavishly adopting the Rugby game in every detail. The same independence of spirit applied there as at Rugby, and hacking, for instance, was never recognized. A system of awarding caps to accomplished players reflected the Rugby scheme, but did not copy it. In a sense Cotton took a short cut by using his staff to impose a pattern of games at Marlborough which resembled as closely as possible the organization which had been evolved at Rugby by the boys. It is interesting to note that Thomas Hughes, who wrote *Tom Brown's Schooldays* as an introduction to school life for his own children and nephews, in fact sent his son to Marlborough where he thought that under his old Rugby friend Dr Bradley the boy would be more directly brought up in the Arnold tradition than he would have been at Rugby. The links between the two schools were strong, and a shared enthusiasm for their style of football prompted old boys of both schools to promote it actively in the universities and beyond.

As Cheltenham College had similarly close links with Rugby, much the same type of game was played. Henry Highton, who had been both a pupil and master under Dr Arnold, took over the school, though rather briefly, in 1859. His mind was probably on higher things than football and schoolmastering, since he won a medal from the Society of Arts for 'discoveries with reference to electric telegraphs' which he had tested at Rugby by linking his boarding house across the street to the main school in the early 1850s. TW Jex-Blake was another Principal of Cheltenham from Rugby, and in his time the College formally adopted the Union rules. Jex-Blake himself was an athlete of repute, and as a boy at Rugby had been a member of an energetic and businesslike generation who had, among other things, appointed the first cricket professional, hired the first additional playing fields, and defrayed the expense of printing the updated football rules by making a charge of two pence for each copy, which 'paid exceedingly well'. Jex-Blake was one of the committee which was formed 'to consult about the building of a Pavilion'. The pavilion in question, erected in 1851, is believed to be one of the oldest surviving buildings of its kind. When Jex-Blake returned to Rugby as Headmaster he presided over a rather more ambitious building programme which gave the school its present architectural character.

Jex-Blake's contemporary at Rugby was AG Butler, another noted athlete, who became Headmaster of Haileybury in 1862. He is generally thought to have introduced the Rugby game there, though AJ Arbuthnot claimed to have brought in something based upon it in 1840. Arbuthnot's game abolished running with the ball, which must have substantially altered the nature of the play, but it was intended otherwise to reproduce the Rugby game. Butler was a great man for leaping, and had a reputation at school for his feats in cross country runs. His most famous achievement was a prodigious leap from a very short run over a river at a point which became known as Butler's Leap. His name now graces an industrial estate on the site. He was a footballer and cricketer of renown, and was succeeded at Haileybury by another keen player, EH Bradby. Apart from their headmasters the three schools, Rugby, Cheltenham and Haileybury, had strong social links through their associations with India. It was not for lack of enthusiasm that Rugby football did not take on in India, but the climate and hard ground defeated all attempts to establish it, and common sense channelled sporting activity into cricket and polo. The demise of the Calcutta Football Club in 1877, and the desire of the remaining members to 'do some lasting good for the Cause of Rugby Football' gave the game its best known trophy. The club's remaining funds were devoted to the purchase of the magnificent Calcutta Cup, which the RFU wisely elected should be of Indian workmanship.

The immediate connections through headmasterships between Rugby and other schools which adopted the Rugby game are numerous. John Percival, the founding Headmaster of Clifton and some of his staff were from Rugby, and the game was played there from the beginning. One of the earliest inter-school fixtures was between Clifton and Marlborough in the mid 1860s, but it took more than twenty years for tempers to cool thereafter and the challenge was not repeated until 1891! When Percival returned to Rugby as Headmaster in 1887 he was appalled to find that the football shorts worn by the boys exposed their knees. He immediately ordered that they should be lengthened in the cause of decency, and the tailors of the town experienced an unexpected boost to their business with several hundred pairs of shorts requiring their attention. It did not work, of course, for the long, flapping shorts were hopeless to play in, and the boys simply rolled them up. Not to be defeated Percival demanded that elastic should be inserted, but his preferment to a Bishopric denied the tailors a further bonanza.

Another cleric destined for high ecclesiastical office, EW Benson, left Rugby in 1858 to become the first head of Wellington College. He allowed representatives to attend the meeting on 26 January, 1871 at which the RFU was founded. Wellington unequivocally adopted the Rugby School rules, and the Head of School declared in 1860 that disputes arising during a match should be settled by reference to them. Wellington was particularly influential in the spread of the game because so many pupils went into the armed services. In 1875 the Captains of RMA Woolwich, RMC Sandhurst and the Royal Naval College were all Wellington men. As they travelled the world in their regiments and crews the army and navy were able to field teams or arrange games wherever they happened to be. They were in a position actually to demonstrate the game, and provided a tremendous boost (as they still do) to isolated overseas clubs. The Calcutta Club had played one of its first matches against HMS *Galatia* in 1871, and was sustained by the presence of the 3rd Battalion of the Buffs for the remainder of its existence. The services valued football not only as a means of keeping men fit, but as a means of promoting fellowship. As early as the 1870s the Secretary of State for War authorised the donation of ground at Portsmouth to be used as United Services grounds 'in order that the two Services should be brought into closer contact'.

At the original meeting of the RFU the only school other than Wellington which sent representatives was St Paul's. They were presumably able to attend the term-time rendezvous because the school was in London. FW Walker, a Rugbeian, was High Master in 1876 having previously been at Manchester School. The two Bedford Schools were among other schools to come under Rugby headmasters and to produce good players in the early years. Last, but by no means least AW Potts went from Rugby to Fettes in 1870. The Edinburgh schools were already playing broadly speaking a Rugby style game, and the Royal High School, Merchiston Castle and Edinburgh Academy competed with one another from 1858.

Between them they produced enough players in the Edinburgh area to make up old boys' sides, Edinburgh Academicals being one of the earliest clubs ever formed, and the game was also established in the Scottish Universities. Loretto and Fettes soon joined the Edinburgh circuit, while Glasgow Academicals was composed of members connected with Glasgow Academy. Under the leadership of the zealous advocate of sport HH Almond, Loretto pupils achieved astonishing success at the Universities. No less than five Rugby blues at Oxford in 1880 were products of the school. Although there were fewer playing schools in Scotland their social and geographical proximity produced a concentrated playing community. There were many more clubs started in London, but they were fairly widespread, and tended to operate in a series of small groupings. The London clubs, being drawn from a wider base, suffered far more from differences in rules than the Scottish clubs in the early days.

SOURCE 15   *Theories of Football*

FROM THE *NEW RUGBEIAN*, DECEMBER 1861

> *There are more things in this our game, Horatio,*
> *Than are dreamt of in your philosophy.*

We must confess that if there is any single point on which we are more sensitive than another, it is the reverence with which we regard our Rugby Football. Not that we are at all ashamed of such an acknowledgement; on the contrary we should blush if any Rugbeian, whether he play football or not, did not feel as we do. Perhaps our touchiness is increased by the fact that our game is so perpetually attacked by those who have never played it, or are not accustomed to it; and we wish to defend our system against those false charges, since this is the last opportunity that will be offered us for some time of saying anything in favour of our Rugby Football.

We were astonished, and not a little amused to read in *Bell's Life* some short time ago, that a gentleman under the *nom de guerre* of D.D., contemptuously termed our mode of playing 'an indescribable medley of fives, wrestling, racing, and football, not able to lay claim to be termed any game in particular.' He informs us that football (as the name implies) should be a game for the feet and not for the hands. He therefore, of course, disapproves of all touching of the ball with the hands, of all taking up, or running with it.

Now we fancy that the object of Football is to extract the greatest amount of pleasure out of a certain species of game; how this is accomplished does not matter; we should look at the result and not at the means. For this reason we appeal to the proverb, 'The proof of the pudding is in the eating.' Now our argument is perfectly simple; it is this: 'If by making use of your hands in playing you can in any way further the interests of the game, then make use of them by all means.' We have tried the experiment and found it successful; a tolerably sufficient proof, we should imagine, that the system is not wholly without its advantages. Again, these points which are decried by others are the very points which are most admired by us. What universal homage is rendered to the fellow who can effect brilliant run-ins or make splendid drops! And what part of the game is more neat, or more scientific, than the way a half-back player threads a whole crowd of well-meaning but incompetent opponents who are in vain endeavouring to stop him, and touches down the ball between the goal posts?

CHAPTER 15

TO THE UNIVERSITIES

The spread of the Rugby game into the schools was fortuitous. Headmasters were not chosen for their sporting inclinations. Academic distinction, religious and moral principles and personal testimonials were the main criteria for selection, and these were the great strengths of Arnold's men. They therefore achieved a remarkably wide influence at a period when attention was turning to the moral as well as the academic content of education. They could no longer ignore leisure time as irrelevant to their brief, but were wise enough to know that if the boys were to be tamed they must be allowed outlets for their natural energy and aggression. The football they had known at Rugby filled the bill, and Cotton was the first to acknowledge its positive value. Others followed his example, and because so many schoolmasters had come from the same stable, the Rugby game in schools rode on the back of their success.

Where it was transplanted Rugby took root and flourished. Every school sent out ambassadors for the game, and in a remarkably short space of time Rugbeians, who had been blazing a lonely trail for their game, were reinforced by new enthusiasts. In the early days Marlborough in particular made an outstanding contribution to its expansion.

At many schools the same process of incorporating sport into the everyday routine was taking place, though the emphasis may have varied, and the games played differed. From these schools came young men accustomed to athletic sport as part of their daily lives. At the universities in Victoria's day a player would expect to participate in the seasonal activities and, if he had some athletic ability, he could expect to excel in several. Thomas Hughes' brother, George, who was a footballer of repute, played cricket for the Oxford XI. For good measure he stroked the University crew at Henley in 1843 in the extraordinary race against Cambridge which Oxford won, despite having only seven men in their boat. Hughes was not exceptional, and a keen sportsman might have tried his hand at a broad spread of activities ranging from fives to mountain climbing. The link between football and cricket is particularly strong, and many of the nineteenth century footballers had parallel cricketing careers in the summer months.

The natural course for many of the young men emerging from the schools was to progress to Oxford or Cambridge, or to one of the Military Colleges. Here for the first time they encountered the problems of playing team games where large numbers of participants drawn from different backgrounds were simultaneously involved. In sports such as rowing and athletics individuals could be more easily assimilated, and cricket, which had evolved in the community rather than in institutions, had of necessity developed an accepted code. Football, apart from the mass games which took place periodically in the countryside, was a domestic affair, played to different rules in different places.

Albert Pell made the first attempt to organize football outside the school when he went up to Cambridge in 1839. Unfortunately he had rather jumped the gun and, although games took place, he found it virtually impossible to combine players accustomed to a variety of codes in a coherent game. He was the first to discover that there were difficulties in store for the future of football, and that it would not be easy to reach agreement on a single code. There was enthusiasm enough for the *idea* of playing, but too little consensus on the field. The various existing games relied upon customary rules, and the differences presumably only showed up when in the course of play individuals observed the usage to which they had been accustomed. Disputes must have been endless, and players used to school games where procedures were in place for the settlement of differences found themselves at sea, with no recognized authority to turn to.

Pell's initiative appears to have fizzled out, and football continued at Cambridge amid confusion until, in 1846, a new attempt was made to bring some order to the game, this time by a group of Salopians and Etonians who objected in particular to the Rugby habit of running with the ball. It should be remembered that running with the ball was only just coming into regular use at Rugby when Pell left. However by 1846 a generation of Rugbeians had reached Cambridge for whom running in was normal practice, and the clash of cultures became more apparent. What is more, this new Rugby football was supported by printed rules and a much more sophisticated level of organization than had been the case six or seven years earlier. The Rugbeians of this generation were the first to recognize that their game *was* different and to feel strongly enough to defend and promote it.

For the first time the footballers decided to meet together to try and resolve their differences. Eight hours of discussion between representatives of a number of schools resulted in an agreed code which was written up and posted on Parker's Piece where games were played. The Rugby delegates included FJA Hort, a Scholar and Prizeman who was to become Hulsean Professor of Divinity, and must have been one of the very few men in the world qualified by previous experience in the business of putting football rules on paper, having been part of the levee which discussed and sanctioned the first rules at Rugby. He was doubtless supported by the diplomatic efforts of his fellow Scholar of Trinity and football enthusiast, WH Waddington, the future French Minister of Foreign Affairs, Prime Minister, and Ambassador at the Court of St James. The rather simple rules which emerged from this committee were the product of a compromise. They succeeded in discovering a common denominator to resolve the immediate problem of a code for the university, but the results by no means measured up to the expectations of those accustomed to subtler games.

The Cambridge rules were the first to be put together round a table rather than evolved on the field of play. The rules of other games had for their starting point a *status quo*, whereas the Cambridge rules sought to create a workable amalgam of the principal points of a series of codes. The idea of *inventing* a whole set of rules was a novel one, and provided a solution in the long run for the supporters of the 'dribbling game'. These first Cambridge Rules continued to be the subject of extensive debate, but eventually in the early 1860s the whole business came to a head. This time the problems which Cambridge had experienced since the 1840s affected a much wider constituency, as football had greatly increased in popularity and the demand for a uniform code was being urgently pressed by club players in London and elsewhere. The decisions taken at Cambridge in 1863 were to have a fundamental influence on the organization, and discussion belongs more properly in another chapter. At this point it is enough to note that the rules adopted by the Football Association in 1863 were directly derived from the first Cambridge rules of 1846.

Rugby football at Cambridge was challenged continually by supporters of other codes, but optimism that a satisfactory uniform game might eventually be found, and an obvious belief among Cambridge players that such a code was a desirable objective, kept football in the university in a state of flux for twenty years. At Oxford the Rugby game appears to have run an easier course. There were always enough Rugbeians in residence for them to be able to organize games of football played to their own rules for those who wished, and the Old Rugbeian match played annually at Rugby School was chiefly arranged by Oxford men. A charming account of one such match in 1861 lists thirty-eight Rugbeians, mostly Oxford men, on the Close on 1 November, thankful to be free of the 'traditional bad weather which has so often damped this annual match'. The *Bell's Life* report goes on to tell how,

the old ones' nerves were every now and then tried, when Marshall dodged about in his irresistible 'Don't you wish you may get it' sort of style. At last Manwairing found the ball 'going about', and after a twist this way and that dropped a very clever goal. The old ones could not manage a second after Fisher's try falling a few feet short of the bar, and as with other battles 'Darkness put an end to the combat'. To pick out a cause for the old ones' success it might be said that the School's forward play wanted a trifle more skill and purpose.

The high attendance of Old Rugbeians from Oxford may have had something to do with the ease of railway communications between Oxford and Rugby, but the indications are that it was seldom difficult to raise a side from Oxford to play against the school. Since they more often than not won the matches they were certainly getting at least some practice at the university. The Old Marlburians played an annual match against the Old Rugbeians on the Christ Church cricket ground. In one such match, when it was held so late in the term that only twelve Rugbeians faced nineteen Marlburians, the game must certainly have been classed as a 'friendly':

There was the usual amount of good-natured embarrassment about the difference of rules, the usual amount of satisfactory apologies, the usual amount of 'loafing', the usual amount of sudden spurts and equally sudden collapses.

When eventually a club was formed at Oxford in 1869 it was heavily dominated by Rugbeians and Marlburians, and in its early years the captain, secretary and at least one committee man had to be Rugbeians. The club was called the Oxford Football Club, making no acknowledgment at all of the Association game, though it was by then well established. This conceit still prevails today at Rugby School, where 'Football' means only one thing. These days soccer is in fact played at the school, but it is not a major preoccupation. Rugbeians continued to dominate at Oxford until the club changed its rules after seven years to permit all members to be eligible for office. Since then Rugby men who have held the office on merit alone have included such great players as Vincent Cartwright, Adrian Stoop, and Ronnie Poulton-Palmer.

The indifference of the Oxford men to any suggestion of compromise probably did a great deal to help the Rugby game to survive the formation of the Football Association. The formal creation of a club at the University was probably, in spite of the initial Rugby bias, intended to provide a meeting point for the players who were beginning to emerge from the newer schools such as Clifton. Their arrival did much to boost the Rugby game in the face of the new challenge presented by a unification of the dribbling game under Association Rules.

Trinity College, Dublin should not be forgotten in the list of Universities which made a decisive contribution to Rugby. It was the undoubted cradle of Irish Rugby football, and the first club was formed there in 1854. 'In the early days it was probably the only club in the country which played to any defined set of rules', wrote J. W. Whitehead, and he went on to say that he had discovered an old rule book entitled *The Laws of Football, as played at Trinity College, Dublin, and as recommended for adoption by other clubs*, which contained, he said, twenty five rules in all, 'in many ways admirable'. They seem to have been taken directly from the Rugby School rule book, and included the immortal regulation forbidding attempts to 'strangle and throttle' in a maul as being 'totally opposed to all the principles of the game'. This rule was probably needed in Ireland if there was any truth at all in the succinct aphorism coined by JJ McCarthy in his contribution to the original *Marshall's History*, to describe the three versions of football currently in vogue. 'In Rugby you kick the ball, in Association you kick the man if you cannot kick the ball, and in Gaelic you kick the ball if you cannot kick the man.' Hacking was obviously unlikely to prove a major stumbling block in Ireland!

The rulebook founded by Whitehead, quite probably contained the code referred to by GF (a 'Wanderer') in his letter to *The Sporting Gazette* in 1863:

It may be interesting to your readers in general, and a satisfaction to Rugbæans in particular, to hear that at Trinity College, Dublin, and by the 'Wanderers', the Rugby rules, slightly modified have been adopted – the result, I take it, not of any predilection in their favour, but on their own merits, as by far the most scientific mode extant; and, as many of the Irish schools have begun to play by them there is every likelihood of their becoming universal in Ireland.

Trinity educated some Rugbeians in the early 1860s, through whom the game was possibly introduced. As in Wales, Rugby football caught on quickly, and the spread in Ireland owed much to RM Peter, who on his return from Blackheath School, the home of London based Rugby football, started the Wanderers club. Trinity and the Wanderers shared many of their members, and together organized the foundation of the Irish Football Union in 1874. This caused great concern in Belfast, particularly after the North of Ireland FC beat the Wanderers, and claimed the right to represent Ireland. A compromise was reached allowing for ten players each from the North and the South to be nominated to the Irish National XX, an arrangement which prevented a split, but did not do much for the cohesion of the side. What finally brought the two firmly together was a common grievance against the unilateral decision of the RFU in 1877 to reduce international sides to fifteen. This was seen not only as an insult to the Irish Union, but as a severe disadvantage to their chances of success in matches.

Metropolitan Club Football in the 1860s

AG Guillemard

FROM *FOOTBALL: THE RUGBY UNION GAME* BY F MARSHALL

The principal features of the play of the leading clubs both round London and in the North during the years to which my remarks have been directed were the following: Long and sure dropping by the backs, brilliant running by the half-backs, and dogged hard shoving, hacking and following-up by the forwards. It was not until after hacking had been abolished that the scrummages degenerated into shoving matches, for, as soon as the ball had been put down, the solid mass of forwards was loosened by the play of the feet in the centre, and the ball quickly emerged. Indeed, in all matches where the players observed the Rugby School laws and discouraged mauling, the scrummages were never tedious, though, owing partly to the solidity of the formation of a scrummage in those days, and partly to the number of heavy weights, the forwards did not free themselves very quickly. A half-back, therefore, if the ball were kicked fairly to him, and he were a quick starter, had a grand chance, as frequently he had only the two half-backs and three full-backs of the opposite side to account with, and very exciting was the running in consequence. The tackling, however, was surer then than it is now, and there was the chance of a hack over as well. Passing in those days was mainly confined to the forwards, and a half-back who had got well under way kept his eye on his opponents and did his level best to run-in or get within dropping range of goal by his own unaided exertions, for his start as a rule precluded the possibility of anyone but his colleague getting sufficiently near to relieve him of the ball if tackled. As to the backs, of whom the centre player during the latter part of the period alluded to was generally brought forward as three-quarter back, their duties were mainly dropping and tackling. Punting was practically unknown, and, when practised, generally elicited a howl from the crowd in touch.

This review of the game at the time when the Rugby Football Union was founded, may give to players of more recent times some idea of the position.

CHAPTER 16   *YOUNG GENTLEMEN'S CLUBS*

Following the increase in popularity of football of all kinds in the public schools and grammar schools, young men outside the universities began to organize clubs so that they could continue to play after leaving school. The first of the Rugby football clubs is thought to have been formed at Guy's Hospital in 1843, but it was another fifteen years before any further clubs followed. Edinburgh Academicals, with a membership drawn from the old boys of the Edinburgh Schools was the first Scottish club, and the springboard from which Rugby football spread to Glasgow and to the Scottish Universities. The first two clubs in Scotland to be independent of any academic institutions were West of Scotland, formed in Glasgow in 1865 and Edinburgh Wanderers in 1868. However the Scottish game remained closely allied to players from its remarkably strong and geographically concentrated school base throughout the early years of the Scottish Football Union, which was founded in 1873.

Scotland and Ireland both enjoyed the advantage of a close regional organization which allowed for a level of uniformity to be agreed at an early stage in the development of club play. The situation in England was different. Football clubs in the Metropolitan area were beginning to take shape in the late 1850s, but with no clear agreement on codes of play. The Rugby game was favoured by the Old Blackheathen Club (founded 1857), originally consisting of old boys of Blackheath Proprietary School[1] and soon to open its membership,

---

[1] A Proprietary School was one which was initially financed by shareholders, normally parents, who had a proprietary right to nominate pupils. Marlborough, Cheltenham, Rossall and Malvern were among other schools so formed.

changing its name simply to Blackheath Club. Richmond was founded in 1861 and for the first year played by the Harrow School rules, but switched the next year to the Rugby rules under the captaincy of EC Holmes, later to become the first Vice President of the RFU and to assist in drafting its rules. The Secretary of the Richmond Club was Edwin Ash, who worked at the Military College at Richmond and the members were mainly drawn from young men training there. When the Football Association was formed Ash declined to send representatives to the meeting on the grounds that:

As most of our men are only here preparing for the army and do not remain any length of time in Richmond it is useless our trying to form any kind of regular club; we merely club together during the winter for the sake of playing a few matches. I think you will agree with me that under these circumstances it is unnecessary to enrol a club like this as a member of the association, which may not last beyond this season. If the rules of the association are decided upon in time for us to use them this winter we shall no doubt adopt them whatever they may be, as it will be a great convenience to us when we play with other clubs. If we had got a good club at Richmond I should have been only too glad to have done my best to assist in promoting what I think will be a great benefit to us all.

This note from Edwin Ash, who was later to be instrumental in the formation of the RFU and to be the first Secretary, demonstrates clearly the difficulties faced by the early Metropolitan clubs. Membership was fluid, and there was no general agreement on rules of play. Richmond at the time had a heavy preponderance of players from Rugby School and therefore inclined towards the Rugby game, but in another year might expect to draw upon members from other schools with different preferences.

It happened that among the Rugbeians in the early Richmond days were some particularly fine players, including CS Dakyns, Morris Davies and DP Turner, and for two or three years during the 1860s Richmond teams were undefeated. After that there was no further doubt that Richmond would remain firmly with the Rugby code. In other Metropolitan clubs the same pattern was reflected, and the rules adopted varied according to the constituency of the players. Often matches would be played in agreement with the custom of the home team, but this scheme inevitably led to considerable confusion on the field of play. The idea was therefore put forward, as it had been at

An Old Rugbeian at Oxford
(DH Bolton)

Cambridge in 1846, that a single, uniform code should be agreed for football, and a lively discussion followed in the pages of the sporting journals.

All the games played at the various public schools had, like the Rugby game, evolved over a considerable period of time within closed communities. All relied upon an understanding of customary practices easily transmitted from one generation of schoolboys to the next, and none would easily translate into a simple code without severe modification. The differences were neatly summarized in an article in *The Sporting Gazette* written by John D Cartwright.

The following collated summary of the rules will present to the reader at a glance the laws of the principal games, and the differences existing between them. It will also enable him to see at once how far the Cambridge University rules, published last week, accord with those of any particular game, and to ascertain what are the new features introduced. We have not included the dimensions of the grounds or the width of goals. They vary in every case.

Commencement of the game. Rugby, Cambridge, Shrewsbury, Charterhouse, and Harrow, kick off from the middle. Eton begins with a 'bully,' and Winchester with a 'hot,' both in the centre of the ground.

Catching. Harrow, Rugby, Winchester, Shrewsbury, and Charterhouse sanction catching. Eton does not. Cambridge says 'the ball may not be held or hit by the hands.' Catching is not under any circumstances allowed.

Privileges obtained by a catch. At Harrow and Shrewsbury a 'free kick,' with a run of three yards is allowed to the catcher. Charterhouse has no rule on the subject, except that the ball may not be knocked out of a player's hand when caught. Rugby allows the catcher to run with the ball, if he can, into 'touch,' and there 'touch it down.' After which he or one of his side may take a 'punt' toward goal. The catcher may make a mark with his heel on the spot where the ball is caught, beyond which the opposite players may not go until a 'drop kick' or 'place kick,' as may be determined, has been taken. At Winchester a catch from an opponent's kick entitles the player to run with the ball and dodge the players as long as they follow him. When they stop he must do so, and take a free kick at three yards. This he may take at any time after a catch; but he is liable to be pulled down, and have the ball taken from him.

Handling the ball. Harrow and Shrewsbury, except in case of a catch, do not allow the ball to be touched by the hand or arm below the elbow. Eton and Charterhouse sanction the use of the hands to stop the ball. Winchester allows it to be carried under certain conditions. At Rugby, it may be held, carried, and taken up, when bounding, under special circumstances. Cambridge says 'the ball, when in play, may be stopped by any part of the body'.

Running in. This is peculiar to Rugby and Winchester.

Holding. Holding is not allowed at Eton, Harrow, Shrewsbury, or Charterhouse. At Winchester, only when a player has the ball in his hands. At Rugby, in a 'maul' any player may be held; out of a maul, only the one who is carrying the ball. At Cambridge holding is forbidden.

Tripping. Tripping is not allowed at Harrow, Eton, or Charterhouse. Winchester, Rugby, and Eton have no rule on the subject. The two first adopt it in play. The Cambridge rules forbid it.

Hacking and Shinning. Rugby, Shrewsbury, and Eton allow these. Harrow, Winchester, Cambridge, and Charterhouse do not allow either.

Charging. Charging enters into all the games.

Out of bounds. At Harrow, when the ball passes beyond the side-lines, it is kicked straight in again. At Eton, a 'bully' is formed where it is kicked or thrown into the ground again. At Winchester, a 'hot' is formed. At Rugby, it must be thrown in, or any player may take it if he can. At Charterhouse, it is thrown or kicked straight in along the ground. At Shrewsbury, if kicked against the limits of the field in a line with the goal, the opposite side has a fair kick. At Cambridge it is kicked straight in again.

Behind or on the goal lines or bases. At Rugby the ground beyond the goal-sticks is called 'touch in goal.' The player who 'touches the ball down' beyond the line, is entitled to a 'punt,' or it may be taken out and a 'try at goal' made. At Eton a player may not kick the ball behind his own goal; if the opposing player kicking it beyond has been 'bullied,' and it is fact touched by one of his side, he obtains a 'rouge.' If otherwise, the defending side have an uninterrupted kick from the goal line. At Harrow it is always kicked straight in. At Winchester the whole breadth is goal. If it has been unfairly kicked, there it is kicked straight in again along the ground by a player on the side whose goal it passed. At Charterhouse it is always so kicked. At Cambridge, the player who first touches it may bring it 25 yards straight out from the goal line and have a free kick. If it is beyond the goal line, and the side line too, then the kick is made from the 25-yards post.

A goal. At Rugby the ball has to be kicked over a cross-bar ten feet from the ground. Two goals kicked by one side decide a match. At Eton and Harrow, through or above the space marked by the two goal-sticks. At Eton the side obtaining the most rouges wins the game if no goal or an equal number of goals be made. At Winchester the ball has to pass the goal line at any part. At Charterhouse it has to be kicked between the goal-posts and under a cord. If either side kick or hit the ball through their own goal, their adversaries count the game. At Cambridge the ball must be clearly between the goal-sticks, but it may be any height directly over the space marked out. At Shrewsbury it may also be higher than the poles.

Management of the game. At Eton and Winchester two umpires are appointed and stationed at the respective goals. At Rugby heads of sides, or deputies appointed by them, act as arbiters. At Charterhouse a disputed point is left for discussion at the end of the game. After a goal at Rugby, or a base at Harrow, the sides change over. At Eton and Winchester, sides are changed at half time. At Harrow the ball is always kicked from the same end, so that each side kicks it alternately, changing over after every base. The umpires at Harrow follow the game, and can thus give a ready and accurate decision in case of any dispute. When a ball is caught in front of goal, the umpire goes behind the catcher in order to see whether the ball is quite clear of the posts. If exactly over either of them it does not count. The heads of sides settle the details of the Cambridge game. At Shrewsbury the best of three games decides a match. The plan most generally adopted is that of fixing the time when the play shall commence and cease, and victory remains with those who succeed in obtaining most goals.

It might have been possible to take one or another of the school games and to simplify it sufficiently for general use, but each school was strongly attached to its own way of playing. These games were not only finely tuned to suit the circumstances prevailing in the different institutions, but they had a place in the social organization of schools which was central to schoolboy lore and could not easily be abandoned. The schools, who were not involved in inter-school football in the early 1860s, had no pressing need to subscribe to any universal code. The clubs, on the other hand, urgently required uniformity.

Since their players were drawn almost entirely from public school men it was natural that the first attempts to reach a common code were centred upon the idea of some kind of amalgamation of the games with which they were familiar. Lengthy discussions followed, during which it became apparent that it would be virtually impossible to find a solution satisfactory to everyone, and that the Rugby game in particular would be called upon to make such radical changes that its whole character would be altered.

JC Thring, a Salopian who had been involved in the Cambridge Rules of 1846, was the first to suggest that 'it would be quite impossible, even if it were desirable, to induce the different schools to give up their time-honoured vanities, and to adopt a uniform game'. Instead he proposed a form of football 'simple and universal' to be established from the basic premise of the natural game which might emerge if 'two sides were placed in an open field for the purpose of playing it'. The game which he devised reflected his personal dislike of the Rugby game, although his objections were not levelled against carrying the ball, which is nowadays considered to have been one of the fundamental differences between advocates of the dribbling game and Rugbeians. He objected much more strongly to the high goal, the oval ball and above all to hacking. Thring's game was much closer to the principles of Association football, but by no means ruled out handling and running in. One of his more unusual proposals was for a barrel shaped or oval pitch 'as it tends to point the game at the goals'. It is interesting that Australian Rules football, another game which was created from scratch, uses just such a pitch, though the idea never took on in England.

Grounds were a considerable problem for the early London clubs. Most played on common land such as Blackheath, Richmond Green and Clapham Common, but they had no substantive rights and had to stake their claim by going out first thing in the morning to erect goal posts on match days. Richmond Club was eventually prevented from playing on the Green when it was discovered that cricket and bowls were the only games permitted on the Royal enclosures, and the club moved to the Old Deer Park. Football was popular with local spectators whose constant encroachment upon the field plagued the players. At Rugby School this problem was mitigated by praeposters armed with canes 'keeping the line', but such measures could hardly be taken against the general public. Some players made a virtue out of necessity, dodging in and out of the crowd and using spectators to afford defensive cover against their opponents, but the conditions were far from ideal and exasperated players sometimes entered into confrontation with persistent offenders.

Rugby football attracted regular crowds who particularly enjoyed watching the hacking. This they probably witnessed in good measure at Blackheath where there were plenty of Rugbeians and where they were brought up in the belief that 'a tibia covered with an honourably scarred epidermis' was an outward and visible sign of manly virtue. JD Cartwright maintained that above all hacking taught forbearance, and that 'if, as Plato says, "a boy is the most vicious of all wild beasts", the training and taming process begins its work early and does its work well.' Mutilated shins, however, were a good deal less popular with businessmen and lawyers, and it became clear that hacking, however valuable it may have been thought in the education of boys and soldiers, was dangerous and unsuitable for club play. Men are much stronger and heavier than boys, and those who had not learned the 'art' in their youth were often clumsy and could inflict considerable damage. Some clubs dropped the practice of their own accord, but it did not disappear from the Rugby game altogether until hacking and tripping were outlawed, it is said at the insistence of Charles Darwin the younger, when the Rugby Football Union formulated its rules in 1871.

Football's Mental and Physical Advantages as the National Winter Pastime

FROM AN ARTICLE BY A LOVER OF FOOTBALL PUBLISHED IN *THE FIELD*

England is generally admitted to stand first in the list of the countries of the world in national sports. In racing, steeple-chasing, cricket, and gymnastics England has no rival. Though in Africa the pursuit of the lion may be more exciting than partridge or pheasant shooting, – though a combat with a grizzly bear on the Rocky Mountains may have more charms for some than deer-stalking in our Scotish forests, – though Indian officers may declare that wild boar hunting excels a fast run with the foxhounds in Leicestershire or Warwickshire, yet considering all, England is rightly looked on as the mother of national sports. Nor is this all; her energy is displayed to a much larger extent than that of any other land. Her cricketers have visited America, and at the present moment are pursuing their way over 18,000 miles of sea to compete with the Australians, and winter finds many of her aristocracy shooting in the Canadian forests, or cruising in their yachts in the lovely Mediterranean. However, every one does not possess the means whereby to spend his winter thus, and consequently stays at home and seeks to amuse himself as best he may. And since all cannot, or perhaps care not to follow the foxhounds or harriers, these naturally enough look for some game wherein to engage themselves during the few hours of November and December that are suited for remaining out of doors. And games and out-door sports bring not only physical but mental advantages also, and that to a very large extent. To insure vigorous health and a robust frame, they are most strongly to be encouraged, if practised under certain restrictions. Every day, every hour serves to demonstrate how close a relationship mind and body possess, and the great influence they mutually exert on each other; and if the cultivation of the former be a subject deserving especial attention, the proper training of the latter should undoubtedly form a part of every system of youthful education.

And, indeed, it is absolutely needful that pastimes should be diligently and most assiduously looked after. Many very eminent writers have declared that they form a much more necessary portion of the training of youth than is generally supposed to be the case, and that books fall very much into the shade, if school games are exercised with a moderate amount of restriction. They develop themselves very largely in the youthful mind, and the courage with which a mere boy scales the ramparts of the enemy under a withering fire, or leads on his division to death or victory when opposed to fearful odds, may be traced back in a very great measure to his matches at football, cricket, and boxing at our great public schools, and the lessons learned from schoolfellows and college friends. England, of all countries, has great cause to admit the truth of this reasoning, for a very large part of her present greatness is to be attributed to the education of the playground and the lessons taught by the out-door sports at her universities and public schools. How manifestly, too, do games improve the moral qualities, and the good effects on the temper and dispositions of youth. When the ball is in a critical position in front of your own goal, hesitate for a moment and you are lost, prompt decision is an absolute necessity. How well, too, does this game above all others try one's patience and forbearance, and surely these advantages carry great weight.

CHAPTER 17 *THE UNIVERSAL CODE*

The quest for a universal football game was pursued in parallel by the Metropolitan club enthusiasts on the one hand, and Cambridge University on the other. The Cambridge men confined their interest to seeking a suitable game to be enjoyed on Parker's Piece by members of the University, and were following up an idea which had been current since the first set of Cambridge rules were drawn up in 1846. They were well aware of the discussions going on in London and declared no intention of pre-empting the outcome, though in the event the rules agreed at Cambridge were ultimately to find favour with the Association.

Formation of the Cambridge Rules   [1863]

It having been thought desirable to establish a general game for the University of Cambridge, the subjoined rules have been drawn up for that purpose, but without any view of anticipating the labours of the London committee.

The first game was played on Friday, Nov. 20, on Parker's Piece. Any member of the club who wishes to take part in the game can do so on payment of a subscription of one shilling per term.

COMMITTEE

Rev R Burn, Shrewsbury (Chairman) Mr JT Prior, Harrow
Mr RH Blake Humfrey, Eton Mr HL Williams, Harrow
Mr WT Trench, Eton Mr WP Crawley, Marlborough
Mr WR Collyer, Rugby Mr WS Wright, Westminster
Mr MT Martin, Rugby

RULES

1. The length of the ground should not be more than 150 yards, and the breadth not more than 100 yards. The ground shall be marked out by posts, and two posts shall be placed on each side line, at distances of 25 yards from each *goal line*.

2. The goals shall consist of two upright poles at a distance of 15 feet from each other.

3. The choice of goals and *kick off* shall be determined by tossing, and the ball shall be kicked off from the middle of the ground.

4. In a match, when half the time agreed upon has elapsed, the sides shall change goals when the ball is next out of play. After a change, or a goal obtained, the kick off shall be from the middle of the ground in the same direction as before. The time during which the match shall last, and the numbers on each side, are to be settled by the heads of the sides.

5. When a player has kicked the ball, any one of the same side who is nearer to the opponents' goal line is *out of play*, and may not touch the ball himself, nor in any way whatsoever prevent any other player from doing so.

6. When the ball goes out of the ground by crossing the side lines, it is out of play, and shall be kicked straight into the ground again from the point where it is first stopped.

7. When a player has kicked the ball beyond the opponents' goal line, whoever first touches the ball when it is on the ground with his hand, may have a *free kick*, bringing the ball 25 yards straight out from the goal line.

8. No player may touch the ball behind his opponents' goal line who is behind it when the ball is kicked there.

9. If the ball is touched down behind the goal line and beyond the line of the side posts, the free kick shall be from the 25 yards post.

10. When a player has a free kick no one of his own side may be between him and his opponents' goal line, and no one of the opposite side may stand within 10 yards of him.

11. A free kick may be taken in any manner the player may choose.

12. A goal is obtained when the ball goes out of the ground by passing between the poles, or in such a manner that it would have passed between them had they been of sufficient height.

13. The ball when in play may be stopped by any part of the body, but may not be held or hit by the hands, arms, or shoulders.

14. All charging is fair; but holding, pushing with the hands, tripping up, and shinning are forbidden.

At Cambridge where the brief was limited to finding a common game for a limited group of players it had taken more than fifteen years before agreement was reached, and even then the majority of Rugby and Marlborough men, their ranks already being swelled from a rapidly growing number of Rugby football playing schools, continued to play their own game, often in addition to the Cambridge rules game.

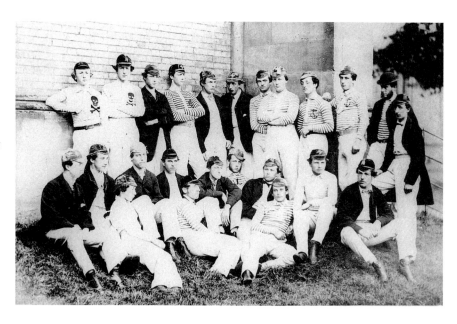

Rugby footballers, including WR Collyer, CS Dakyns, MT Martin and A Rutter, 1859/60

The task before the relatively new London clubs was infinitely greater. Not only were they geographically spread, making communications more difficult, but they included players new to football and with no background in any code of play. Furthermore the idea took hold that they should come up with a game which would be applicable to the country as a whole, not merely a solution to the immediate problems of the Metropolitan clubs. The search was on for a national winter game which would occupy the time when cricket was unseasonable.

Most sportsmen involved in the football discussions made the understandable assumption that football would spread by following cricket into villages and rural communities. Even in the Metropolitan area, places such as Richmond and Blackheath were still villages, and football had proved a popular spectator sport. Discussion was therefore directed towards finding a game which could be easily adopted in the countryside. Arthur Guillemard, later to become one of the founding fathers of the RFU and to serve in turn in all the major offices in the early years, recommended football as being 'quite as exciting as cricket, rather more healthful and much less expensive'. In his letter to *The Field*, though he had made no attempt to press the case for the Rugby game in the text, he enclosed a copy of the Rugby School rules, which was duly published. This gentle suggestion of Guillemard's rather backfired, for it highlighted one of the great problems of the Rugby game – its complexity. 'JH' from Winchester wasted no time in pointing this out:

If the boys waited to begin kicking until this pie, or hash or hodge podge was made intelligible, goodbye to their chance of a game on a winter afternoon . . . forty rules! It's 'jest awful', when the Articles of the Church of England are only thirty-nine!

In reply to JH there came a letter from 'Goalstick', an Etonian whose genuine attempt to consider the broader practical requirements of a game which might be enjoyed in country communities reads some- what condescendingly, but nevertheless makes some pertinent obser- vations about the realities of rural life.

Letter to *The Field*

Sir, – Bowing, as I do, in all humility to the statements of your Wykhamist correspondent J. H. contained in the earlier part of his letter; granting, as I do, that Winchester is the parent of Eton, and still more that Eton is *matre pulchra filia pulchrior*; also that the earlier sons of Mother Winchester may have played with the greater zest from the fact that they were backed by their hopefuls; granting, above all things, the utter hopelessness of the Rugby rules being drummed into the thick heads of our country cousins and dependents (for whose especial benefit the amalgamation idea was started), without the aid of a very superior grammar and glossary to the rules – for the sake of both teacher and pupil, still I do strongly object, and that entirely without prejudice to J. H.'s gentle hint, that the maternal Winchester's game become universal: not that anything can be said against the simplicity of the game itself, but on account of the sundry little additions required. The gentle and unpretending suggestion that thirty or forty players be drawn up to keep the ball in the ground, would be very cheering to Maister Bull and a very entertaining diversion for the poor fellow, doubtless, after a hard day's work. That suspicious boots be examined, and nails and iron tips eschewed, would cause a pull on Pa Bull's purse for light shoes and boots, which might cause the said paterfamilias to regard the game in rather a serious light; for when did such a one as Mr J. Bull appear *sans* nails and tips in his all clophodding soles?

Far from aspiring to interference in any committee which may have been formed for the amalgamation of the public school rules, still, since the main object of the amalgamation is to enable the game, healthy and manly as it is, to become more universally played, and to form a substitute in winter for cricket, as well as to offer an amusement to our country working-classes, I should like to suggest to any correspondent or member of the committee that the game be formed as simple as possible.

We never – or, at all events, very rarely – meet with a sufficient number of educated people in our country villages to enable the game, if a difficult one, to be adopted with zest. Our labourers are not very fond of being pulled up for little trivial errors and omissions which they don't and can't understand in a game, and which must occur if a great many little rules are necessary.

Seldom can we, even in cricket, enforce the more complex rules on our lusty slogging dependents of the plough or spade, whose main delight is to hit a ball as far as they can, and think it the only true way of saving their wicket, and who *will* have noise and laughter without restraint in their pastimes, or else eschew them; and how much more difficult would it be to enforce such in football, where nothing but row and bustle, unknown to cricket, prevail!

To Volunteer correspondents I may suggest the simile of a squad of noisy, uncontrollable recruits for the first time on the drill-ground.

Goalstick is taken to task by later correspondents for his suggestion that village footballers may be too unruly or too stupid to comply with the laws of the game. Citing cricket as an example to refute the charge that country people were 'insubordinate in their pastimes', JH draws upon the example of the men of the border counties of the north:

the northern character is as yet rather rough, hard and disputatious: it likes to have justice and no favour, rather than give a point away. But *they take to cricket*, and take to it kindly: and so far from not adopting the rules of the game I find them rather too keen on this point, and more fond of the letter of the law than the spirit of the game. Bless their hearts! Cricket is the very thing for them; it will make them courteous and indulgent to each other, and to all men, as they are already warm and open-hearted; and when we can get them to play cricket on beer instead of 'whuskey', wrangling and disputes will give way to the amenities of the game.

Football, JH considered, would have similar character building properties to cricket, and rules would present no obstacle, provided that they eliminated any of the elements derived from the public school system of 'fagging'. There should be nothing to encourage 'domineering' on the part of gentlemen, for to achieve its proper purpose all players must be able to mix together on terms of perfect equality. He did, however accept Goalstick's point that the 'genuine, clodhopping hobnailed boots presented a problem, and foretold that if hacking were not abolished 'every football club would require a surgeon, and perhaps a chaplain to be attached to its staff'.

Events were to show that much of the speculation about a suitable game for rural communities had been in vain. One of the most pertinent comments of all came from Arthur Guillemard, who noted that in football 'the need of so many players is often detrimental in village clubs, as a match is very poor if there are less than fifteen on each side'. Numbers have always been a predicament in village sport, and football presented a far greater problem than cricket. Not only did most forms of football assume between thirty and fifty players would be available, but the nature of the game required that those players needed to be drawn from a narrower section of the male population. Whereas in cricket quite young boys or older men often, in an emergency, stepped into the breach, football required a greater uniformity in physical strength and called for much more sustained exertion from players. This difficulty was acknowledged, and was probably the main deterrent to any rapid spread of football of any code into the countryside.

Within a decade of these deliberations the rural communities plunged into a serious decline. There was a series of bad harvests in the 1870s, and the shortfall in grain was made good by imports from the North American prairies. The same faster and cheaper shipping which brought the wheat, also carried wool from Australia and New Zealand, challenging that other great staple of British agriculture, sheep farming. The traditional rural communities collapsed under these new pressures, and village populations were rapidly depleted as labourers sought work in the expanding industrial towns. The younger men were the first to go, and those who were left worked long and exhausting hours for minimal wages, leaving little time or inclination for playing football. The provincial spread of the national winter game did not come, as had been anticipated, into the villages, but into the thriving industrial centres of the midlands and north, where large communities presented few difficulties in assembling teams, and for the first time at least part of the working population, released from the endless demands of agriculture, had some little time to spare for leisure.

The Game Played by the New University Rules, and What the Schools Would Lose and Gain by Adopting Them

(The following article written by John D Cartwright, describes one of the first games played by the 1863 Cambridge Rules from which the Association game was to be taken.)

Rules that read well are not always to be relied on, for it by no means follows as a certainty that they will play well. Our recent studies of the different games now in use have served to show that in practice their interpretation admits of great variations. Before therefore, any definite verdict can be pronounced upon a new set of rules, it is necessary to apply to them the practical test of play, which is to them what the aquafortis is to base metal gilded and pure gold. It is nevertheless possible, on reading a set of rules, and comparing them with others the workings of which are known, to form a tolerable estimate of their qualities. This we have already done with regard to the Cambridge University Football Rules, and have seen that the result is highly satisfactory. For the information of the schools and all football clubs, we now carry our investigation further, and proceed to describe a game we saw played on 'Parker's Piece' by these new rules, on Tuesday last, when sides composed of first and third year men, against students of the second and fourth years, entered into a spirited contest.

The football ground at Cambridge known as 'Parker's Piece' is a large one, upon which the Harrow game is ordinarily played; and many memorable football contests have taken place there in past seasons, as well as in the present, the last being one which we report this week.

The ground is of the dimensions stated in Rule 1 – 150 yards long by 100 yards broad. The corners and sides are marked by play-posts, those at the 25 yards distance being considerably higher than the others. Important features in the game render it necessary to have this point distinctly marked, and flags are placed at each side at the required distance from each goal. It would probably, however, in addition to these, be a convenience to have a mark drawn across the ground from flagstaff to flagstaff, either by white chalk or by the removal of a narrow strip of turf. This would facilitate the play in matches, when it is very desirable that the lines at which such important parts of the game occur should be so distinctly defined that neither delay nor dispute could arise. The goal-posts have no cross-bar, the object being to kick the ball between them, or at any height above that would be between them. They are 15 feet apart.

A vigorous kick off from the middle – the ball, having been placed on the ground – starts the game, and drives the ball half the distance between the goal and the middle of the ground, where the other side are drawn up to receive it. All the players but one goal-keeper played up in the game we saw: this, however, is of course a matter to be decided by the captains of sides. Any player may stop the ball by leaping up, or bending down, with his hands or any part of his body. This stopping is not to include *striking*, which is altogether illegal; and if a player momentarily holds the ball in attempting to stop it, or in recovering it as it descends after a kick, he immediately opens his hands again, and allows it to fall at his feet. The only times when a ball is seen in the hands at Cambridge, in the ground, is when it has been beyond one of the goal-lines and is brought in 25 yards from a free kick. The rapidity with which the game moves about the field is equalled by only one of the present popular modes of play. After the ball has been kicked off – all the players on the side taking the kick off being behind the kicker, and all the opposing players before him – it is returned by a sharp kick, or played up until some of the opponents charge the players, bringing it 'by easy stages.' Quick running, sharp kicking, and clever stopping of the ball, are the main features observable in the play. The game is essentially that of football, as distinguished from others in which as much is done with the hands as with the feet. Collisions do of course occur, and shins do of necessity get kicked, but never wilfully. The players follow the ball, and at times it is completely surrounded by them, when a lively contest ensues, resulting in the ball being cleverly kicked (sideways if it cannot be got out straightforward) through some opening, when the players speed after it.

When the ball is kicked beyond the side limits it is returned into the ground again where it went out, and the play goes on until one side gets the ball near the opponents' goal, and, failing to kick it through, drives it beyond the goal-line on one side or other of the goals, when a race to touch it ensues, the racers being of course allowed to charge – that is, to butt at each other with the shoulder. If first touched by the defending side, it is brought out and kicked toward their opponents' goal. If the opposing side succeed in first touching it, they bring it out to a line with the twenty-five yards posts, directly opposite to the place at which it went out, and a free kick is had. The nearer it is to being in a direct line with the goals, the more chance there is of a game being won, as it is easy to kick the ball over the heads of the opposing players who spread out around the goal to stop it; but in any case, and especially on a windy day, it requires a skilful kick to send the ball through the air between a space of fifteen feet at a distance of twenty-five yards from the place whence it is kicked. The further the ball is from the goal-posts when crossing the line, the more difficult it becomes to kick a goal from the twenty-five yards line, as the distance is increased, and the angle lessens the clear space between the goal-posts. When the ball has been behind both the goal-line and the side-line – that is, at the corner – it is brought to the twenty-five yards post and kicked from thence towards or away from the goal, according to the side entitled to take the kick, but there is little or no hope of obtaining a goal from the single kick under such circumstances. It is therefore obviously advantageous to keep the ball as much as possible in front of the goals. The rule regulating off-side, concerning which we published an explanation last week, is extremely simple. It amounts to this: No player may be in advance of the ball; this is the natural rule for 'off-side,' and no player in such a position ought to take advantage of it when the ball is driven up to him by one of his side until an opposing player has kicked it. As soon as that has been done, or directly he gets behind the ball again, then he ought to be 'on-side' and in play. This seems to be the principle which has guided the gentlemen drawing up these rules, and the result is that they have a very intelligible law on the subject.

It is but a few days since these laws were drawn up, and but few opportunities for playing by them have occurred at Cambridge. The result of the little practice has, however, sufficed to make players used to other forms of football familiar with them, and the game we saw played on Tuesday was as regular as that which is seen at a cricket-match. There is nothing tame about it. That it is not so exciting as those forms of the game which admit 'hacking,' holding, and tripping, no one will be disposed to deny or question any more than they would to question the fact that a faction-fight or a rough 'town and gown' is more exciting than the most boisterous game at football ever known. But, rightly viewed, football does not depend upon the excitement it creates, but rather upon the skill displayed. Victory is not with the strongest in well-constituted games, but rather with those who know how to make the most of the strength they possess. We are far from denying the merits of existing games, or exalting that just introduced at Cambridge to their prejudice. We do not consider it the best game that might be had, but it is a good one. It is more in accordance with the spirit of to-day than those which it is designed to take the place of, now or at some future time.

CHAPTER 18   *THE GREAT FOOTBALL QUESTION*

By the autumn of 1863 the question of a single code for football had spread from the sporting journals to the national press. On 23 September, a 'Football Parliament' was proposed in the correspondence columns of *The Daily Telegraph* and the suggestion was made that the clubs should agree upon a set of rules separate from any of the school codes and to be called the 'London Rules'. In *The Times* under the heading 'The Great Football Question', correspondence raised for the first time the need for the schools also to find a common game so that matches could be played between them. Some schools *were* playing matches, and as early as 1862 Wimbledon School played on Wimbledon Common against a combined team from Mr Fleming's and Mr Murray's Institutions according to the Rugby rules. Wimbledon School was already at that time running a first, second and third fifteen, and must have been one of the earliest schools to be so well organized for external matches. However the majority of schools outside London still confined play to domestic competition, and the headmasters were reluctant to sanction inter-school games. Their reasons are not known, but were presumed to have been based upon the difficulties presented by varying codes of play. In fact they may well have feared that rivalry would be too intense. Certainly the first rugby match to be played between Clifton and Marlborough caused so much bad feeling that the return fixture was postponed for nearly thirty years. On the whole schools were interested in the discussions going on in London and contributed eloquently to the correspondence in the press. Eighteen year-old Arthur Guillemard in particular proved an able and persuasive advocate of the Rugby game, but few schoolboys were able to attend meetings held in London during the term time. At the gathering called in the Freemason's Tavern in November, 1863 at which the Football Association was formed only a handful of schools, all metropolitan, were represented. Charterhouse was the only public school to have a delegate present, and offered to canvass the views of other schools on the Association's behalf. The response was poor, the general attitude being that by far the majority of schools were content with the games they played and were reluctant to abandon them. It was left to their Old Boys to create the universal code. In the first draft of the Association rules drawn up by WC Morley of the Barnes Club, it is interesting to note that clauses nine and ten still allowed the 'distinctive feature of the Rugby game', running with the ball. They read:

IX. A player shall be entitled to run with the ball towards his adversaries' goal if he makes a fair catch, or catches the ball on the first bound; but in the case of a fair catch, if he makes his mark he shall not run.
X. If any player shall run with the ball towards his adversaries' goal, any player on the opposite side shall be at liberty to charge, hold, trip or hack him, or to wrest the ball from him, but no player shall be held and hacked at the same time.

On these two commandments hung the future of Rugby football as a club game. They were all set to be approved at a special meeting of the Football Association held on 24 November, but in the intervening time the Cambridge committee had met and produced their set of rules which disallowed running with the ball and hacking. In a surprise move at the F.A. meeting an amendment was proposed 'That the rules of the Cambridge University Football Club, which have been lately published, appear to be the most desirable code of rules for the association to adopt, and therefore it is proposed that a committee be appointed to enter into communication with the committee of the University, and to endeavour to induce them to modify some of the rules which appear to the association to be too lax and to give rise to disputes'. Various minor amendments were made, followed by the resolution crucial for Rugby men proposed by Messrs

Lawson and Gregory, 'That the committee be empowered not to insist on the clause in the association's proposed rules which allows running with the ball.'

A committee was duly appointed, and immediate protests followed from many of those present who had not understood that agreement to communicate with Cambridge would preclude any further debate on the rules put up by the Association which the meeting had been called to discuss. The President, however, ruled that the motion had been properly carried, and refused the plea that a number of those present would certainly have voted against it had they realised its full implication.

In a last ditch effort to register their views the advocates of the running game proposed that the brief of the committee should include the following words; 'and that the committee do insist upon hacking when running with the ball in their communication with Cambridge'. The amendment was carried by ten votes to nine, and, as it had been intended to do, and as the exasperated President pointed out, 'to all intents and purposes annulled the business of the evening'.

The next meeting was an ill-tempered affair in which the Blackheath representatives openly maintained that the previous meeting had been deliberately designed to outmanoeuvre the strong 'hacking' party and had been improperly conducted. On this occasion they were outnumbered, and the proposed laws numbers nine and ten were finally voted down and eliminated from the Association rules which were passed that night.

The Association Committee's discussions with Cambridge had resulted in the adoption of one of the Cambridge rules and the assimilation of several more, producing closely similar games. The desired Universal Code came very close to achievement in the original draft of the Association rules, and, had Cambridge not arrived at their code just a few days before the date set for final approval, the Association would very probably have adopted the practice of running with the ball. Blackheath had been forced to put up the hacking amendment in an effort to save the carrying game, and it has been generally supposed by modern historians of Rugby football that hacking was the central issue over which the two codes of football finally divided. However if running with the ball had been accepted, then hacking might well have been conceded by the Rugby players, since several clubs had already voluntarily dropped it. There was no rule in the Rugby game which actually *authorised* hacking, and Rugbeians themselves were at pains to point out that the spirit of the

Rugby game, which deplored unnecessary hacking, was in accord with the principle behind the written laws of the Association. The real point at issue was running, without which the whole character of the Rugby game would have been destroyed. It was in the interests of those who preferred the dribbling game to focus attention on hacking as the weak point of Rugby as a club game. After Blackheath's amendment they were immediately dubbed the 'hacking men', and instead of positively debating the merits of running, they allowed themselves to be diverted into a heated defence of hacking.

At the meeting on 8 December, 1863 Mr Campbell of Blackheath declared that, while he approved the objects of the Association, the laws passed would so utterly destroy their game that they could not be adopted in play by the members of his club. Although Blackheath did not immediately withdraw from the Association the real rift between the two codes of football had occurred during those winter meetings in the Freemasons' Tavern. The Association game enjoyed great success both in London and the provinces, where its adoption in Sheffield provided the spearhead for a rapid explosion in popularity in the Midlands and the North. The Rugby game retained support in those metropolitan clubs where it was already played, and their continued growth was ensured by the increasing number of players coming from the many schools which had chosen to follow the Rugby code. The survival of Rugby football following the formation of the Association was largely due to its popularity in those schools which had not developed a game of their own. In such schools and at Oxford University the game flourished, and such was the success of football as a national game that there was room for both codes to grow in their several ways.

SOURCE 19   *Three of the Early Meetings of the Football Association*

THE FIRST MEETING

Pursuant to notice, a meeting of an influential character took place at the Freemasons' Tavern, on Monday, the object of the promoters being to decide upon some plan of action for bringing about a definite code of laws for the regulation and adoption of the various clubs which indulge in this exciting and health promoting winter amusement. There was a large muster of the captains and officers of the metropolitan football clubs present, amongst whom we observed the following: Mr. Morley (Barnes), Messrs. Campbell and Moore (secretary and captain of the Blackheath), Mr. Pomber (N. N.), Mr. McKenzie (Forest), Mr. Bell (Dingley Dell), Mr. Wawn (War-office), Mr. G. Shillingford (Percival House, Blackheath), Mr. W. Macintosh (Kensington School), Mr. S. Day (Crystal Palace), Mr. W. H. Gordon (Blackheath Proprietary School), Mr. J. F. Alcock (Leytonstone), and Mr. B. F. Hartshorne (Charterhouse), &c.

Mr. Pember (N. N.) was voted to the chair, and remarked upon the necessity for the adoption of some settled rules for the regulation of the London clubs. His idea was, that the captains of all clubs should put their names down as members of a society to be called the Football Association.

Mr. E. C. Morley then moved, and Mr. McKenzie seconded, the following resolution: 'That it is desirable that a football association should be formed for the purpose of settling a code of rules for the regulation of the game of football.'

Mr. B. F. Hartshorne quite agreed with the spirit of the foregoing resolution, but regretted that the public schools were not represented there. He supposed it was owing to insufficient publicity being given to the meeting, as only two advertisements had appeared in *Bell's Life*, and none in the other sporting papers or in *The Times*. He should, being the only representative of the public schools present, decline to vote for the resolution, because he might be committing himself thereby, and would therefore prefer to wait until he saw what the other schools intended to do; but, on the part of the Charterhouse, he would be quite willing to coalesce if the other schools would do the same. He would suggest that the chairman should write to the various captains on the subject and obtain their opinions.

The chairman said he did not think the advertisements in *The Times* would aid them much, and his reason for saying this was that, notwithstanding the numerous letters upon the subject that had appeared in those columns, he knew that several had been written by members of the London clubs, but their insertion had been steadily refused. All they wanted that night was a basis of action. He was not aware that Mr. Hartshorne represented a public school, but he should be happy to adopt his suggestion by writing to the various captains and soliciting their co-operation. If the step they were then taking did not answer, it would be very easy to dissolve the association; but everything must have a beginning, and they would be very happy to have the co-operation of the last speaker at a future meeting. The resolution for the formation of the Football Association was then carried *nem con*.

Mr. Pember was then elected permanent president of the association; Mr. E. C. Morley, honorary secretary; and Mr. F. M. Campbell, treasurer. The following rules for the guidance of the Association were agreed to, and, with a vote of thanks to the chairman, the meeting, which was unanimous, terminated:

'That the annual subscription to the association be £1 1s, and all clubs of one year's standing be eligible to membership.

'That a meeting be held in the last week in September in each year for the despatch of business, notice whereof shall be given in sporting newspapers.

'That this meeting be adjourned to such time as shall be appointed by the officers, due notice of such time being given in *Bell's Life*, *The Sporting Life*, and *The Field*.'

A SPECIAL MEETING OF THE FOOTBALL ASSOCIATION TO SETTLE THE LAWS OF THE ASSOCIATION [NOVEMBER 24, 1863]

At this meeting, due to a misunderstanding of procedure, running with the ball was eliminated from the Association game.

Mr Morley, hon secretary, said that he had endeavoured as faithfully as he could to draw up the laws according to the suggestions made, but he wished to call the attention of the meeting to other matters that had taken place. The Cambridge University Football Club, probably stimulated by the Football Association, had formed some laws in which gentlemen of note from six of the public schools had taken part. Those rules, so approved, were entitled to the greatest consideration and respect at the hands of the association, and they ought not to pass them over without giving them all the weight that the feeling of six of the public schools entitled them to. The laws to which he (Mr Morley) referred seemed to embrace every requisite of the game with great simplicity, and before passing the laws that had been proposed it would be well that they should consider every phase of the matter [hear, hear].

Mr Alcock thought that the association could not do better than fall into the views of the gentlemen at Cambridge who had put forward the laws which the hon secretary had referred to; and as there were several members of the public schools who had taken part in the matter, he deemed it well worthy the earnest consideration of the association. Having those views, and feeling that it would be well to have the support of the Universities, he should move 'That the rules of the Cambridge University Football Club, which have been lately published, appear to be the most desirable code of rules for the association to adopt, and therefore it is proposed that a committee be appointed to enter into communication with the committee of the University, and to endeavour to induce them to modify some of the rules which appear to the association to be too lax, and liable to give rise to disputes.'

Mr Turner would willingly second that resolution.

Mr Campbell proposed as an amendment that the words 'The most desirable code of rules for the association to adopt,' be omitted, and to insert instead thereof 'worthy of consideration'.

Mr Lawson seconded.

Mr Morley would suggest the words that they 'embrace the true principles of the game with the greatest simplicity.' He moved the insertion of those words in the resolution as a further amendment, in lieu of the words proposed by Mr Campbell.

Mr Gregory seconded.

On a division there were eight voted for each amendment, and the President gave a casting vote in favour of Mr Morley's amendment.

Mr Lawson moved, and Mr Gregory seconded, the following resolution: 'That the committee be empowered not to insist on the clause in the association's proposed rules which allows running with the ball.' This was carried.

Some further discussion then took place upon the appointment of the committee suggested in the foregoing resolution, and several representative members of school clubs said they had misunderstood the purport of the amendments, and therefore had not voted. They wished to know whether it was not competent for them to ignore the Cambridge rules altogether, which had been referred to as the basis of any proposed rules?

The President said that the question had been decided by the amendment being carried.

A member said that he presumed the non-voters wished to go on with the rules as they had been proposed by the association, and discuss them.

Several members: Yes, yes.

The President said that in the proper course of business the appointment of the committee ought to proceed.

Another member thought that the hon sec should put himself in communication with the Cambridge players, to ascertain whether they would enter into any negociations on the subject.

The proposition received 7 votes, none being held up against it.

Mr Alcock then moved and another gentleman seconded, the appointment of the committee as follows: Messrs Moore, Campbell, Lawson, and Alcock.

On the question being put a member observed that, with many others near him, the resolution had been passed without their fully understanding the matter, but as the President had decided that it had been properly carried, and he (the speaker), with several friends, should certainly have voted against the resolution, he should move as an amendment to the appointment of a committee the addition of the following words, 'And that the committee *do* insist upon 'hacking,' when running with the ball, in their communications with Cambridge.'

On a division the numbers were – for the amendment, 10; against it, 9.

The President pointed out that the vote just passed to all intents and purposes annulled the business of the evening, whereupon Mr Alcock said it was too late to proceed further, and moved that the meeting do adjourn till Tuesday next, Dec 1, and it was so resolved.

THE MEETING AT WHICH, DESPITE PROTESTS, RUNNING WAS FORMALLY DELETED [1 DEC, 1863]

The fourth meeting of the members of this recently-formed association was held on Tuesday evening, Dec 1, at seven o'clock, at the Freemasons' Tavern, Great Queen Street, Lincoln's Innfields, for the further consideration of the laws, and perfecting generally the working arrangements of the association. In our impression of Saturday last we gave a full report of the meeting which was held on the previous Tuesday, and at which meeting considerable discussion arose on a question calculated to lead to a sudden disruption of the association, and the tone taken on Tuesday last evidenced that the Blackheath members were fully bent on preserving their time-honoured institution of 'hacking,' although, as will be seen, the 'non-hackers' carried their point. The meeting was numerous, and comprised the following members, the names of the clubs they represented being also specified: Blackheath Club, Messrs F. M. Campbell and L. A. Campbell; Blackheath Proprietary School, Messrs W. H. Gordon and T. P. Fox; Forest, Leytonstone, Messrs J. F. Alcock and A. W. Mackenzie; Forest School, Walthamstow, Messrs J. Morgan and J. Bouch, jun; Crystal Palace, Messrs F. Urwick and J. L. Siordet; Barnes, Messrs W. C. Morley and T. D. Gregory; N. N.; Kilburn, Messrs A. Pember and G. Lawson; Wimbledon School, Mr A. E. Daltry. The President (Mr A. Pember) took the chair, and called on the hon sec (Mr W. C. Morley) to read the minutes of the last meeting. The hon sec accordingly read the minutes as entered by him, and the President put the question, 'That the minutes as read are correctly entered, and that they be signed accordingly.'

Mr F. M. Campbell (the treasurer) said: I wish to call the attention of the meeting to what took place on the last occasion. It would be remembered that Mr Alcock proposed, 'That the rules of the Cambridge University

Football Club, which have been lately published, appear to be the most desirable code of rules for the association to adopt, and therefore it is proposed that a committee be appointed to enter into communication with the committee of the University, and to endeavour to induce them to modify some of the rules which appear to the association to be too lax, and liable to give rise to disputes.' I then moved an amendment that the words, 'The most desirable code of rules for the association to adopt' be omitted, and to insert instead thereof 'worthy of consideration.' Upon that Mr Morely made another amendment for the insertion of the words in the place of those proposed by me, 'and that they embrace the true principles of the game with the greatest simplicity.' The President, when he put the first amendment, took the number in favour of it, seven, and then put the second amendment, for which eight hands were held up. On neither of those amendments did he take the votes against either of them, and as the number present was 19, if the resolution had been put in the proper form the amendment would have been negatived.

Mr Mackenzie: But everybody might not have voted.

The President: I really think Mr Campbell that you are in error. There certainly was something said, and I replied, 'Why, you did not vote,' on which the gentleman – I think it was Mr Gordon – replied to the effect that the purport of the resolution had not been properly understood, and most certainly put it again, and they did not vote again. I certainly put the question both ways, and I appeal to the recollection of those gentlemen who were present at the last meeting. Besides, I gave a casting vote for Mr Morley's amendment. What is your plan now, then? Do you move that these minutes are not correct?

Mr Campbell: No, I will not say that, but I want the resolutions of Mr Alcock and Mr Morley to be expunged.

Mr Lawson: Then you can move that so much of the minutes as relate to that matter be not confirmed.

Mr Campbell accordingly moved, and Mr Gordon seconded – 'That so much of the minutes as relate to the resolutions moved by Mr Alcock and Mr Morley be not confirmed.'

The President put the question, which was negatived, and the minutes were then confirmed and signed, Mr Campbell entering a formal protest on behalf of the Blackheath players.

Mr Alcock: I think, sir, as the whole of the rules almost depend upon Nos. 9 and 10, as they have been proposed I think we had better proceed with them at once. They are as follows:

IX. A player shall be entitled to run with the ball towards his adversaries' goal if he makes a fair catch, or catches the ball on the first bound; but in the case of a fair catch, if he makes his mark, he shall not then run.

X. If any player shall run with the ball towards his adversaries' goal, any player on the opposite side shall be at liberty to charge, hold, trip, or hack him, or to wrest the ball from him; but no player shall be held and hacked at the same time.

I therefore move, sir, that we proceed with them at once.

Mr Morley (hon sec): I agree with Mr Alcock in thinking that these two rules affect everything so materially that I am strongly of opinion that it would be well if we went into the further consideration of them at once. 'Hacking' and 'running' so much affects every rule, the length of the ground, the tape, the width of the goal posts, and indeed everything connected with the game, that they must be looked upon and dealt with as most vital points. As far as either hacking and running is concerned I do not mind it myself personally, but my object in the matter is that I feel that, if we carry those two rules, it will be seriously detrimental to the great majority of the football clubs. I do not say that they would not play with us, but it is more than probable that they would not; and Mr Campbell himself knows well that the Blackheath clubs cannot get any three clubs in London to play with them whose members are for the most part men in business, and to whom it is of importance to take care of themselves. For my own part, I confess I think that the 'hacking' is more dreadful in name and on paper than in reality; but I object to it because I think that its being disallowed will promote the game of football, and therefore I cordially agree with Mr Alcock. If we have 'hacking,' no one who has arrived at years of discretion will play at football, and it will be entirely relinquished to schoolboys.

Mr Campbell: I have played football ever since I was eight years of age, and certainly approve now of the laws proposed to be expunged. I am much afraid that there are many of the clubs who will not join the association because they fear that our rules will do away with the skill shown in the game at Harrow and Eton, and the pluck so necessary in the game as played at Rugby. 'Hacking' is the true football game, and if you look into the Winchester records you will find that in former years men were so wounded that two of them were actually carried off the field, and they allowed two others to occupy their places and finish the game. Lately, however, the game had become more civilised than that state of things, which certainly was, to a certain extent, brutal. As to not liking 'hacking' as at present carried on, I say they had no business to draw up such a rule at Cambridge, and that it savours far more of the feelings of those who liked their pipes and grog or schnaps more than the manly game of football. I think that the reason they object to 'hacking' is because too many of the members of clubs began late in life, and were too old for that spirit of the game which was so fully entered into at the public schools and by public school men in after life.

The President: Perhaps you will allow me to say that I took down 'Fifteen' the other day to play a match, and I was the only one that had not been at a public school, and we were all dead against 'hacking.'

Mr Campbell: Be that as it may, I think that if you do away with it you will do away with all the courage and pluck of the game, and I will be bound to bring over a lot of Frenchmen, who would beat you with a week's practice [loud laughter]. I think that Mr Alcock ought not to have put such a resolution, and I think it does not denote the opinion of the London clubs. I am sure if you take the votes of all the schools that resolution will be condemned, and why? they all like 'running' and 'hacking,' and will not play any other game. The rule will exclude something, though it is open to running, so that while you can play our game in your way we cannot play it in ours if your resolution is adopted. We have been willing to meet you halfway, but I confess I do not like the spirit in which you propose to deal with this subject, and I hope the meeting will not adopt it. If the rules are to be established they must be gone into from beginning to end, and at the last meeting we ought not to have had the Cambridge rules put before us. We ought to have gone on with the appointement of the committee, who should be unshackled by any recommendations, and made the laws on the basis of the original propositions as printed and now before the meeting. I think that this proposition to expunge rules 9 and 10 would not now be gone on with, but that you see we who are the advocates of running and hacking are in a minority. I will, however, say this, that I represent the true feeling of our club when I say that in the event of this resolution being carried we shall not only feel it our duty to withdraw our names from the list of members of the association, but we shall call a meeting of those who were at the former meeting, and take their opinion on the subject, and shall, besides that, put ourselves into communication with the other clubs and schools to see what they think of it.

The President: I must be allowed to interpose a word. At the outset I must remind Mr Campbell that several of the London clubs were invited to attend to talk the matter over, and when we first started it was agreed that the rules should be arranged upon a certain basis, and put into proper form by Mr Morley, who kindly undertook to do it, but that nothing was to be considered finally settled till they had been confirmed at a subsequent meeting, as appears by the heading of the printed laws, which is in these words, 'to settle the laws, which are proposed to be as follows.' Several gentlemen came, and you, Mr Campbell, amongst the number, and if those who attended and put down the names of their clubs as proposing to join the association, with the intention of adhering to it if all their principles were carried out, or immediately seceding if their notions were not adopted, it certainly is not, in my opinion, a fair and honest way of dealing. You virtually say, 'I will come and join your association, and see if I can get my notions adopted, and if so go on with you, but if not we will secede, and form an association for ourselves.'

Mr Campbell: In reply I will just say that when the Blackheath clubs joined the association they were prepared to carry the laws such as the majority of the meeting agreed to. When the last meeting was held for the express purpose, as the president had said, of settling the proposed laws, they ought to have gone on with the rules as proposed by the association, and not taken the course they did as to the Cambridge rules, but the resolution and amendments had been proposed and passed in the way they had been without being properly put to the meeting, because it was found that the 'hacking' party were too strong.

The President: That is, I think, an accusation of ungentlemanly conduct to which I am not willing to submit, added to which it is not the fact.

Mr Morley: I certainly thought that any member had a perfect right to propose any resolution he though fit.

Mr Alcock: Let me explain that I moved the resolution upon the subject of the Cambridge rules without any previous communication with any one until just prior to the meeting, when they were brought to my notice quite unexpectedly on my part.

Mr Lawson: I saw the rules in one of the sporting papers, and thinking they were just the rules that were wanted, I certainly submitted them to one or two; but I emphatically deny that I had any intention of delaying any fair discussion of the laws. I may observe that the division on the question, 'That the committee *do* insist upon 'hacking' in their communications with Cambridge' was very close, the numbers being 10 to 9, and certainly I had no idea that we should be in a minority.

The President: Well, gentlemen, there is a motion before the meetings, 'That Nos. 9 and 10, of the proposed laws be expunged.'

Mr Campbell: I beg to move as an amendment, 'That this meeting do adjourn until the vacation, so that the representatives of the schools who are members of the association may be enabled to attend.'

Mr Gordon seconded, and on the amendment being put to the vote it was lost by 13 to 4, and the original motion carried.

The President observed that though the rules 9 and 10 were expunged, it was quite competent for Mr Campbell to bring the matter up at the next annual meeting, by which time it would be seen how the laws worked.

Mr Morley said that before the meeting proceeded any further he would suggest that having the Cambridge rules before them the association should, in forming their own laws, see what consideration the others deserved. No communication had taken place with Cambridge since the last meeting, but he (Mr Morley) thought that their hands would be strengthened if the laws of the association were made nearly identical with the Cambridge rules. He thought it a matter worthy of consideration, especially with reference to the influence it might have on some of the public schools.

The President thought it would be better to go on with their own rules.

Mr Alcock would be glad if they could so assimilate the rules as to bring all players within the scope of the association.

The meeting then proceeded to settle the proposed laws, which will have to be confirmed at the next meeting, and we give them now *in extenso* as they will be submitted *verb et lit* for adoption, so that any non-contents may not be able to say they did not know, and there are several very important differences from the code published last week.

LAWS

1. The maximum length of the ground shall be 200 yards, the maximum breadth shall be 100 yards, the length and breadth shall be marked off with flags; and the goal shall be defined by two upright posts, eight yards apart, without any tape or bar across them.

2. A toss for goals shall take place, and the game shall be commenced by a place kick from the centre of the ground by the side losing the toss for goals; the other side shall not approach within 10 yards of the ball until it is kicked off.

3. After a goal is won, the losing side shall be entitled to kick off, and the two sides shall change goals after each goal is won.

4. A goal shall be won when the ball passes between the goal-posts or over the space between the goal-posts (at whatever height), not being thrown, knocked on, or carried.

5. When the ball is in touch, the first player who touches it shall throw it from the point on the boundary line where it left the ground in a direction at right angles with the boundary line, and the ball shall not be in play until it has touched the ground.

6. When a player has kicked the ball, any one of the same side who is nearer to the opponent's goal line is out of play, and may not touch the ball himself, nor in any way whatever prevent any other player from doing so, until he is in play; but no player is out of play when the ball is kicked off from behind the goal line.

7. In case the ball goes behind the goal line, if a player on the side to whom the goal belongs first touches the ball, one of his side shall be entitled to a free kick from the goal line at the point opposite the place where the ball shall be touched. If a player of the opposite side first touches the ball, one of his side shall be entitled to a free kick at the goal only from a point 15 yards outside the goal line, opposite the place where the ball is touched, the opposing side standing within their goal line until he has had his kick.

8. If a player makes a fair catch, he shall be entitled to a free kick, providing he claims it, by making a mark with his heel at once; and in order to take such kick he may go back as far as he pleases, and no player on the opposite side shall advance beyond his mark until he has kicked.

9. No player shall run with the ball.

10. Neither tripping nor hacking shall be allowed, and no player shall use his hands to hold or push his adversary.

11. A player shall not be allowed to throw the ball or pass it to another with his hands.

12. No player shall be allowed to take the ball from the ground with his hands under any pretence whatever while it is in play.

13. No player shall be allowed to wear projecting nails, iron plates, or gutta percha on the soles or heels of his boots.

DEFINITION OF TERMS

A Place Kick – Is a kick at the ball while it is on the ground, in any position which the kicker may choose to place it.

A Free Kick – Is the privilege of kicking the ball, without obstruction, in such manner as the kicker may think fit.

A Fair Catch – Is when the ball is caught, after it has touched the person of an adversary, or has been kicked or knocked on by an adversary, and before it has touched the ground or one of the side catching it; but if the ball is kicked behind goal-line, a fair catch cannot be made.

Hacking – Is kicking an adversary.

Tripping – Is throwing an adversary by the use of the legs.

Knocking On – Is when a player strikes or propels the ball with his hands, arms, or body without kicking or throwing it.

Holding – Includes the obstruction of a player by the hand or any part of the arm below the elbow.

Touch – Is that part of the field, on either side of the ground, which is beyond the line of flags.

The laws and definitions, as amended, having been agreed to, Mr Campbell wished to know whether it was the intention of the association to ignore the public schools as they had done Cambridge.

The President called Mr Campbell's attention to the fact that, so far from ignoring the Cambridge rules, they had adopted their No. 6, and assimilated them where they agreed with the views of the majority of the association. As to the public schools he could confidently state, from information received from a public schoolman, that there was not the least chance of the public schools adopting the rules of any association, or, in fact, departing in any way from their own.

The meeting, after sitting three hours, then adjourned till Tuesday, Dec 8, at seven o'clock.

The President reminded Mr Campbell that if the supporters of 'hacking' (the real bone of contention) had been in the majority the 'non-hackers' must have submitted.

Mr Campbell had only to say, under the circumstances, that he had been instructed by the Blackheath Football Club to say that they perfectly agreed with the object of the association, but at present they wished their names to be withdrawn, otherwise all their members would withdraw in a body.

A long and desultory conversation ensued as to the merits or demerits of 'hacking,' 'running,' 'tripping,' &c, the President facetiously observing that he objected to 'hacking,' not because it was dangerous, but because it was painful, and that deliberate 'hacking' was, to say the least of it, a very brutal practice.

Ultimately it was understood that Mr Campbell would continue to act as treasurer, and it may fairly be presumed that the whole question will be re-opened in September next, when the new laws will have had a fair trial. Subjoined is a complete list of the clubs that have joined the association: Barnes, Blackheath Proprietary School, Blackheath, Percival House; War Office, N. N. Kilburn, Forest Leytonstone, Crystal Palace, Wimbledon School, Forest School, Walthamstow; Kensington School, Royal Naval School, New-cross; Surbiton, Crusaders, Blackheath Lincoln Football Club, Aldershott, Royal Engineers, Chatham; Uppingham, Sheffield Football Club.

CHAPTER 19 *RUGBY*
VERSUS THE WORLD

From the start the metropolitan clubs had been bedevilled by the problem of the variety of codes. In the capital city there were large enough groups of articulate and able men, a remarkable number of them lawyers, who positively enjoyed defending and promoting their views, whether in favour of their own games or of the universal code. It was a different story in the provinces, where football was much more free of the influence of conflicting school and university games.

The Liverpool club was the first in the country to be formed as an open club, entirely independent of any academic institution. It was the brainchild of a group of young men, the sons of prosperous merchant families in Liverpool, who had entered family businesses or were training for the professions in the city. Most had only recently left school and lacked the opportunity to play football which their peers at the universities enjoyed. They had been brought up to play games at school, and once the cricket season was over had little to occupy them in the winter months. 'Surely nothing could be better', observed a correspondent in the sporting press, 'than football in October, an otherwise dull time of year for all except hunting men'. The Merseyside was not hunting country, and these were the sons of a new urban middle class which had no great tradition of field sports. That many of them happened also to be Rugbeians was an accident of geography. The great port of Liverpool was linked by one of the first railways to the capital, and Rugby School chanced to lie along its route. Rugby was a popular choice with the cotton kings and shipping barons of the north west who found the Arnoldian philosophy to their liking, and the result was an unusual concentration of young Rugbeians in the Manchester and Liverpool areas from the 1840s onwards.

These young men came from a background where ideas were put into practice without further ado. Protracted discussions and arguments were not for them. They adopted the characteristic practical approach of Rugby-bred footballers and simply arranged a game to take place on Saturday, 19 December, 1857. The game was played at the Liverpool Cricket Club, where the groundsman, in deference to his turf, marked out the pitch in white chalk rather than cutting the lines as was the practice at Rugby. There was a 'fine and gentlemanly assemblage' present to watch, including members of the impressively tall Gladstone family, two of whom later played for the club. The match was largely arranged by FA Mather, the third son of an athletic Liverpool family, the eldest of whom, JH Mather, was a great runner and featured in *Tom Brown's Schooldays*. He was also a footballer of repute, and later emigrated to Australia. His next brother was another runner who originated the 'Crick Run', an arduous and famous cross country race over fourteen miles which recently celebrated its 150th anniversary at Rugby School. The youngest brother, AS Mather, then a fifteen year-old Rugby schoolboy and later to be Lord Mayor of Liverpool, played in the match and was probably one of the youngest participants.

About fifty players were mustered and, as there was a preponderance of Rugbeians, the game arranged was 'Rugby versus The World', with players for the World coming from as far afield as Yorkshire, Cheshire and other parts of Lancashire. One of Richard Lindon's Big Side balls, still made at that time with a pig's bladder, was brought from Rugby by Richard Sykes, a Manchester boy home for the holidays. Sykes played in the match, and being fully conversant with the rules made a valuable contribution in explaining the game to players used to other versions of football. He must have done his job well, for the game was acclaimed a great success and the Liverpool Club formed there and then with no recorded dispute about the use of the Rugby code.

The early matches played by the Liverpool Club were arranged internally along the same lines as Big Side games at Rugby School. Sides were formed according to any convenient criteria such as Tall v

Short, North v South, Patriarchs v the Rest, and so on. It was not until Richard Sykes left school and returned home to found the Manchester Club in 1860 that Liverpool had any local opposition. Sale followed hard on the heels of Manchester, creating a cluster of clubs within the area from which the Rugby game spread into the North West.

A Big Side game at Rugby School (The Graphic, 1870)

This cluster pattern was repeated in other areas, with Halifax, Bradford and Huddersfield providing a nucleus of clubs in Yorkshire in the mid 1860s from which the game spread rapidly in the following decade. St Peter's School, York, played the game as early as 1850, contributing its share of players to the Ridings. In the west of England groups of clubs formed around Bath, Gloucester, Cheltenham and Bristol, and there was strong early representation in Devon and Cornwall. The west country schools were sending out players in force by the 1870s, and no doubt the popularity of the Rugby code in the south west is attributable to Clifton, Cheltenham, Sherborne, Blundell's and to other educational establishments such as the Agricultural College at Cirencester. The navy also played its part in the westward spread of Rugby football, and ships produced teams trained by officers from the Rugby playing schools. It is perhaps a curiosity that Rugby School itself did not act as a catalyst in the Midlands where very few early clubs were formed. Notable exceptions in the Midland desert of the early days were Coventry, Harbury, Lutterworth and Stratford. Apart from the Old Rugbeians at Oxford the only club directly formed under the school's influence was the Rugby town club, which began in 1867. Most of the early members were masters or old boys of Town House, the dayboy house at Rugby School. Just as the first England XX were to do later, the members adopted the all white uniform they had worn at school, keeping the Lion emblem which Town House still sports today. The Rugby Lions, together with Rugby School, Yorkshire and England are said to be the only English sides traditionally entitled to wear the all-white strip.

In the far north the border counties produced their quota of early clubs. Durham School had been playing since the 1850s, and Darlington dating back to 1863, was followed by Stockton and its Yorkshire neighbour, Middlesbrough. The Cumberland and Westmorland County Union, founded in 1872, was the second to be formed after the Yorkshire Union, and early clubs in the region included Carlisle and Workington, with Sedbergh, under the headmastership of an Old Rugbeian, and St Bees flying the flag for the schools.

The clubs founded before 1863 were all, in the early days, simply football clubs. Some, such as Blackheath or Liverpool favoured the Rugby rules, whilst others elected to play by different codes. At Barnes the dribbling game was preferred, whilst the Sheffield clubs were strongly influenced by the Harrow style of play. Other clubs again switched from one game to another, or adopted new practices to suit the demands of their members. It was all football to the players, with differences of opinion being solved locally.

The formation of the Football Association late in 1863 and the publication of a uniform set of rules, which were adopted by few schools but many clubs, changed the hitherto haphazard organization of the game, and forced those favouring the Rugby rules finally to go their separate ways. The clubs started in the 1860s were consciously choosing one code or the other for the first time, and the Association offered a much better foundation for club competition than rugby. The game might well at this stage have succumbed had it not been by then the most popular choice of football code in the newer independent schools. While the Association rules found favour in many clubs, at precisely the same time the Rugby game was riding on the crest of the wave of the cult of athleticism which was sweeping over the public schools. The older schools retained their traditional games, but reinforcements for rugby were emerging in considerable numbers from those institutions which had no ancient games of their own.

The Association rules had the advantage that they had been tailor made to suit adult club play. The Rugby code, on the other hand, had evolved to suit schoolboys, and really needed *time* to adapt itself to comply with the new demands made by the different circumstances prevailing in the clubs. Change was inevitable, and the flexibility towards innovation which had allowed the game to grow and adapt during the previous thirty or forty years was again called upon to accommodate the new demands of club players. The Rugby approach to innovation had always been empirical. When a new invention was brought in it was generally allowed to run for a while, evaluated on the field of play, and then either accepted or not according to general opinion. Rugby lawmakers were in the business of responding to practice rather than imposing theory, but since the game in the 1860s had no other authoritative body than the boys at Rugby School to govern it, changes emerging from the clubs, such as the abolition of hacking, were likely to take some time to reach the rule book.

There were about twenty clubs playing the Rugby game in London in the 1860s, and more in the country as a whole. All of them broadly accepted the laws published by the school, but in the absence of any parent body it was impossible to standardize on a single code of play while the game was governed by rules explicitly designed to suit the particular circumstances of Rugby School alone. It is perhaps surprising that it was not until a full eight years after the formation of the Football Association that any attempt was made to create a similar organization to bring the Rugby football clubs together. In 1870, when the game came under attack in the correspondence columns of *The Times* for being dangerous, the need for some authoritative control was recognized. At the same time a group of Scots footballers issued a challenge in *The Scotsman* and *Bell's Life* on 8 December, 1870, proposing that a match should be played between England and Scotland under the Rugby rules. This, they claimed, would allow fairer representation of Scottish skills than the matches arranged earlier in the year under the auspices of the Football Association. In response to these two events EH Ash of Richmond and BH Burns of Blackheath appealed in the press for clubs to co-operate. Ash, it will be remembered, had been sympathetic to the idea of a common code in 1863, so it was not surprising that he should be one of those taking the initiative on Christmas Eve, 1870.

An opinion has for some time prevailed among supporters of Rugby football that some code should be adopted by all clubs who profess to play the Rugby game, as at present the majority have altered in some slight manner the game as played at Rugby School by introducing new rules of their own. Each club plays to its own rules on its own ground; so, the strangers in each match finding themselves at once at a disadvantage in not knowing the rules of the ground, confusion and disputes are generally the result. We therefore propose that all the clubs playing the Rugby game will join with us in forming a code to be generally adopted. Secretaries of clubs approving this will greatly oblige by forwarding their names to us.

As a result of this letter twenty-one clubs were represented at a meeting held on 26 January, 1871 at the Pall Mall Restaurant. The Chairman was EC Holmes, the Old Rugbeian under whose captaincy Richmond had adopted the Rugby code. Algernon Rutter, a fellow Rugbeian and Richmond man, was elected the first president, and EH Ash became treasurer. [Ash was not in fact a Rugbeian, though he is often mistakenly so described.] The meeting ran remarkably smoothly, and Rutter, Holmes, and LJ Maton, a third Rugbeian, were designated to draw up a common code of rules. All three men, who represented different clubs, had a thorough knowledge of both club practices and the guiding laws of Rugby School, but it was Maton who did most of the work since he had chanced to break his leg and therefore had time on his hands. He stuck very closely to the Rugby School laws, but made a few significant alterations, notably the prohibition of hacking. Most of the changes were designed to speed up and to simplify play, and were introduced forthwith.

SOURCE 20   *The First International Match*

By AG Guillemard

March 27th, 1871, Edinburgh. Scotland beat England by a goal and a try to a try

The first international match between England and Scotland was played at the Academy Ground in Raeburn Place, Edinburgh, on the 27th March, 1871. The weather was magnificent and the turf in excellent order, and an attendance of some 4,000 spectators showed that Rugby football had already attained considerable popularity north of the Tweed. The ground measured some 120 yards in length by 55 in breadth, and its narrowness compared with English grounds materially handicapped the excellent running of the English half-backs.

It was arranged before kick-off that the match should be played for two periods of fifty minutes each, that no hacking-over or tripping-up should be allowed, and that the ball should not be taken up for a run unless absolutely bounding, as opposed to rolling. There were other points, too, upon which the Scottish fashion of playing the Rugby game had to be followed. The match was very evenly contested until half-time, after which the combination of the Scotsmen, who knew each other's play thoroughly, and their superior training began to tell a tale, and after a maul just outside the English goal-line the umpires ordered the ball to be put down in a scrummage five yards outside the line. It was taken out accordingly, but, instead of putting it down, the Scottish forwards drove the entire scrummage into goal, and then grounded the ball and claimed a try. This, though illegal according to English laws, was allowed by the umpires, and a goal was kicked by Cross. England then penned their opponents for some time, and ultimately R. H. Birkett ran in close to touch, but the captain's place-kick, a long and difficult one across the wind, failed. Scotland gained another try just before 'no side,' Cross touching the ball down after an unintentional knock-on by one of his own side. His place-kick, however, was unsuccessful. The English twenty in this match averaged 12 st. 3 lb. per man, and the Scots probably about the same. J. F. Green and F. Tobin for England and M. Cross for Scotland played splendidly behind the scrummage. The Scottish forwards were distinctly quicker on their feet, and in better training than their opponents.

A few words on the leading English players. F. Stokes, who learnt his football at Rugby, was a most excellent and popular captain of the English twenty for this and the two succeeding years, combining a thorough knowledge of the game with admirable tact and good temper, and being gifted with power of infusing spirit and enthusiasm into his team similar to that possessed by A. N. Hornby on the cricket field. As a player, he was one of the very best examples of a heavy forward, always on the ball, and first-rate either in the thick of a scrummage or in a loose rally, a good dribbler, very successful in getting the ball when thrown out of touch, a very long drop and a particularly safe tackle. For his club he often played half-back with success, as, though not one of the fastest runners, his powers of 'shoving-off' were very great. He was also one of the very longest and best of place-kicks. No fewer than ten of the English twenty – F. Stokes, A. G. Guillemard, A. Lyon, J. F. Green, F. Tobin, J. H. Clayton, A. Davenport, J. N. Dugdale, C. W. Sherrard, and D. P. Turner – were Old Rugbeians.

The First Irish International

By F Marshall

February 19th, 1875, The Oval. England beat Ireland by 2 Goals and a Try

This was the first meeting of the two countries. England penned their adversaries almost throughout the game, and obtained 2 goals, one from a good drop by Nash, the other from a place-kick by Pearson, after a run-in by Cheston. Michell also made a fine run-in, but Fraser's place-kick failed. On the winning side Nash was conspicuous for the way in which he got through the mud. The Irish team showed great want of practice, both in play and dropping, and their backs were badly placed but tackled well. Cronyn was conspicuous on their side. The forwards played a good and plucky game.

Lennard Stokes, a younger brother of F. Stokes, who was captain of the first English twenties, donned an international cap and jersey for the first time in this match. He played in six successive matches *v*. Scotland, five times *v*. Ireland, and also in the first match *v*. Wales. He played full-back in his opening match, but nearly always afterwards three-quarter back, and it is not too much to say that at this post his equal, either in science or play, has never been seen from the date of the foundation of the Union. Six feet in height, and of sinewy frame, he was the very model of an athlete, and his great pace made him the champion sprinter at the sports of the United Hospitals. He was a faultless catch and field, and a very quick starter, and with his speed of foot, wonderful dodging powers, and clever 'shoving-off' was an extremely difficult man to tackle. An excellent place-kick, he was also for several seasons the longest drop in the three kingdoms. Some of his drops at goal from difficult positions when hemmed in by opponents were simply marvellous.

188

The First Welsh International

By F Marshall

*February 19th, 1881, Blackheath. England beat Wales by 8 Goals
and 6 Tries to Nothing*

This was the first international match with Wales, who were thoroughly
overmatched. Stokes kicked 6 goals, Hunt 1, and also dropped 1. The tries
were obtained by Burton (4), Vassall (3), and Budd, Hunt, Fernandes,
Rowley, Taylor, and Twynam, 1 each.

CHAPTER 20 *A NATIONAL WINTER PASTIME*

At the inaugural meeting of the RFU only two schools, Wellington College and St Paul's, were represented. Rugby stood aloof for some time, for in spite of the strong presence of Old Rugbeians involved in setting up the Union and formulating its rules, the Rugby schoolboys remained suspicious of any usurpers. They had fiercely defended their independence in the matter of sport against interference from masters, and they were unwilling to surrender control of their game to any outside body. The school eventually adopted the Fifteen game advocated by the union in 1876 for foreign matches, and in 1888 for internal House matches. Rugby School formally joined the Rugby Union in 1890, after which, as the brief historical resume in the *Football Records of Rugby School* concludes, 'the game itself being standardized, there is little left to say, except that the Sixth Match was given up in 1900, and in 1901 the Old Rugbeian Match was played fifteen aside'. Thus did Rugby School bow out of direct responsibility for the game it had nurtured, though the contribution of the school both to the performance and government of the game continues to the present day. For more than forty-five years Micky Steele-Bodger's commitment to the game has echoed the devotion of the founders of the RFU, and John Simpson, the most recent Rugbeian President, held office in 1988/9.

The RFU at its inauguration was mainly the preserve of the London clubs, but the second season saw a doubling in membership, and the first response from the north and from Scotland. No doubt the first international match between Scotland and England on 27 March, 1871 at Raeburn Place in Edinburgh had something to do with the surge of interest in the game. As captain of the oldest club, Fred Stokes of Blackheath was asked to lead the England side.

Fred Stokes, the first captain of an England XX, as a schoolboy at Rugby

Twenty men, fourteen from London and three nominated by each of the senior northern clubs, Liverpool and Manchester, travelled to Scotland to answer the challenge issued by the leading Scottish clubs. The resulting victory for Scotland fired England to arrange a return fixture on their home territory the following year, and thus began international Rugby football. Ireland entered the arena in 1875, losing to England at the Kennington Oval, and it was for the Irish match two years later that sides were first reduced for international games from twenty players to fifteen. Wales, where the first Rugby clubs had been formed rather later, first played England at Blackheath on February 19, 1881. Their defeat on that occasion was comprehensive, but the following year a victory over Ireland in Dublin made good the Welsh claim to join the international circuit.

Although football had been played in Wales in a variety of ways it was not until after the formation of the Rugby Football Union that rugby clubs were started in the Principality. The pattern of their formation was much the same as had occurred in Liverpool, Manchester and other provincial clubs. Young men from South Wales, the sons of industrialists and clergymen, were anxious to continue playing football when they returned home from school or university and followed the example of their schoolfellows in England by setting up clubs.

AG Guillemard, JF Green and Fred Stokes pictured at the first England v Scotland international (1871)

The Swansea area started the ball rolling in 1870, and, as had happened elsewhere, a cluster of clubs quickly followed. Llanelli, Newport, and two clubs in Cardiff which were amalgamated in 1876 were to form the nucleus. Rugby School played its part in the foundation of Welsh Rugby football through the Nevill family of Llanelli, where William Yalden Nevill, then aged twenty, was one of the prime movers in forming the famous club. At Newport William Phillips, a Rugbeian who had recently moved to the area from Clifton, joined his brother in assisting CH Newman to establish the club there in 1874. The west-country schools supplied much of the early support for the game in South Wales, with local academic 'nurseries' from which home-bred players could be drawn developing at Llandovery and Christ College, Brecon, during the 1870s. The majority of the men who introduced the game to Wales from the English schools seem to have been enthusiasts rather than outstanding players. They did a good job in getting the clubs started, but remarkably few of the early Welsh international players were drawn from the public school men who had initiated the game. Play was inevitably crude until the players they had enlisted gained command of the necessary skills and 'science' through practice and through fixtures against the more experienced English club sides.

St David's College, Lampeter, where football had previously been played to local rules, adopted the Rugby rules and is thought to have assisted in the spread of the game in Wales through the enthusiasm of its graduates. The *skills* of the game were undoubtedly fostered in the clubs, and support was greatly enhanced by the introduction of the South Wales Cup Competition in 1877/8. The South Wales Union was formed in 1875 and dissolved five years later to make way for the Welsh Football Union which was founded at a meeting at Neath in March 1881.

The social background which allowed football to flourish in South Wales was in many ways similar to that which prevailed in the industrial areas of England, where the decline in the rural population was balanced by rapid growth in the mining and manufacturing areas. It was no problem to raise thirty or forty men for football at the pit head or the factory gate, and although times were hard by modern standards for the working population, living standards were improving for labourers who had hitherto survived at more or less subsistence level. The introduction of the six and a half day week allowed a little time for leisure, and improving wages meant that a small proportion of income might now be reserved for pleasure and entertainment.

Both Rugby and Association football experienced an explosion of popularity in the last thirty years of the nineteenth century. Association football had the edge over Rugby, having established a set of rules and a governing body ten years sooner. The FA Cup competition, which was introduced in 1871, provided a focus for local patriotism at a time when the rapidly expanding industrial towns and cities needed to establish a sense of identity among the largely immigrant working populations. The city fathers led the way by putting up magnificent civic buildings, and contributing to the foundation of all manner of public institutions, including football clubs. These were largely run and financed by local businessmen, but the players were drawn from all walks of life.

Association football quickly gained a following in the community at large, and was the first sport to attract large, regular crowds of spectators. Competition helped to sustain and heighten interest throughout the season, and supporters with a modicum of surplus income could afford the occasional train fares to travel in support of their local teams. Spectators in large numbers were a new phenomenon, and inevitably some of the financial rewards from gate money were passed on to the players. Professionalism in Association football became a well established system by the middle of the 1880s.

Rugby football in the industrial north followed much the same pattern as the Association game, spreading rapidly into Lancashire, Yorkshire and the border counties. It was particularly popular in mining areas, possibly reflecting the historical predilection of miners for various local forms of the primitive game. In all these areas Rugby acquired a partisan following of spectators, and great players soon became local heroes. Most of them were working men drawn from the communities they represented, and few had the means to allow them to devote as much time to the game as public expectation demanded. As demands on their time increased, and players could see for themselves that profits were being made from gate receipts, they understandably felt that they deserved at the very least to be financially compensated when they had to take time off work. The managers understood full well that if they were to retain good players and have them available whenever they were required, then some financial reward was needed. What had been purely a leisure activity had now become a business as well and illicit payments to encourage good players to take part became the norm, together with other less obvious incentives such as offers of employment. Financial rewards were sometimes made to induce players to change clubs, and it was an accusation of just such a deal which first brought the question of professionalism in Rugby football out into the open.

In the early 1890s there was a series of cases brought to the Rugby Union Committee, and in 1893 the Yorkshire Committee sought to clarify the situation. They proposed that players 'be allowed compensation for *bona fide* loss of time', a motion strenuously opposed by the southern clubs. It was felt that 'broken time' payments were the thin end of the wedge, and that if they were to be introduced professionalism would inevitably follow. An amendment to the Yorkshire motion was therefore put by William Cail, the President of the RFU, himself a northerner: 'That this Meeting, believing that the above principle is contrary to the true interest of the Game and its spirit, declines to sanction the same'. The President was not a man to be gainsaid. He was a dour and impregnable Northumbrian with a deep and resonant bass voice. Of him it was said that he was 'the one being in the world who had been known to pulverise an opponent with a single blast of two words – SIT DOWN!' Not a man to take on lightly!

To make sure that the equally determined Yorkshire delegation were outvoted, HE Steed put in a great deal of staff work before the meeting. His calculations were aided by one group from Yorkshire getting lost in London on the way to the Westminster Palace Hotel where the meeting was held, but defeat for Yorkshire was already ensured by a full muster of southern clubs answering to Steed's three-line whip. Some clubs were rumoured to have been newly formed specially for the occasion, and representatives of the Oxford and Cambridge Colleges were given one vote each rather than a single vote for each University so that they might swell the ranks in the amateur lobby.

This meeting essentially established the amateur principle in Rugby Union football and two years later, following further measures to eliminate professionalism, the majority of the northern clubs broke away from the RFU. At a meeting in Leeds they formed the Northern Football Union on the principle that payment may be made to players for *bona fide* broken time. The participating clubs from Yorkshire, Lancashire and Cheshire were some of the strongest in the country, and their loss was a grave blow to Rugby Union football. At the time these clubs did not see themselves as opposing amateurism, and even when, at a later date, 'broken time' compensation was replaced by straightforward payment the Northern Union insisted that players should be in other employment. They were, as they saw it, responding to a justifiable need to offer financial support to their players in the interests of better football, and there was no doubt that by drawing on a wider social base these clubs had produced some of the finest players of the day.

The Northern Union ultimately became the Rugby League, organizing competition on a club rather than a county and international basis, and in due course made amendments to the game to suit their own requirements. It is perhaps curious that, although individual Welsh players made their way into the professional game, in Wales itself, where players were drawn from a similar working class community, the amateur principle was retained. This may in part have been due to the fact that the Welsh clubs, with the exception of Cardiff and Swansea, were based upon much smaller towns and villages than their English counterparts, and their supporters, though no less partisan, were far fewer in numbers and generated much less income for the clubs from gate money.

Rugby Football in New Zealand
FROM A COMMEMORATIVE ARTICLE WRITTEN IN THE *RUGBY ADVERTISER*
FOR THE FOOTBALL CENTENARY IN 1923

The following article was compiled by a New Zealand footballer of bygone days, signing himself 'Full Back,' for one of the clients of Mr. J. Gilbert, of St. Matthew's Street, Rugby, by whose permission we publish it. This article is specially interesting in view of the fact that New Zealand is sending over a team to play in England next year, and there is a suggestion that they may be invited to play one of their games in Rugby.

'Drop down a dozen Englishmen anywhere – on an island, in a back-woods clearing, or on the Indian hills – and in a very short time the old schoolboy instinct will out, and the first level sward is turned into a cricket field in summer and a football arena in winter.'

It was some such dozen Englishmen dropped down in this Britain of the South who laid the foundation for what has since become the national game of New Zealand – Rugby football. Every little 'back block' town, whose total inhabitants in many instances do not number more than a couple of hundred, has its Rugby football club. From the North cape to the Bluff there is scarcely a spot worthy of that distinction in which the game is not played. Many of these out-back townships are not connected by railway, and the means of transit from one place to another is often primitive. As showing the zeal which fires the blood of the sons of the Southern Seas, they frequently ride miles on horseback, fording rivers and crossing mountains, to play in an unimportant match.

When such keenness is shown by the footballing enthusiasts of the bush township it can be readily imagined the interest taken in the pastime in principal centres. The tour of the British Rugby team of 1904, captained by D. R. Bedell-Sivright, and again of the British team of 1908, captained by Arthur F. Harding, threw into bold relief the interest in the game and the hold it has on the New Zealand public.

The first evidence of the Rugby football in New Zealand was in the year 1868, when a 'game of ball' was indulged in on Saturday afternoons. About the year 1869 a match was played between a side representing Auckland and a team made up from the crews of two gunboats, the Rosario and Miranda, which were in Auckland Harbour at the time. This match is of importance as marking the beginning of the game in the Auckland province. A number of Irish miners working at the Thames despatched a challenge to Auckland to play a representative team – 100 players aside! The goals were to be goldfields! One goal was to be at one goldfield and the other another goldfield some distance away, and the match was to be played for £200 a side. It is probably unnecessary to say that this unique challenge was not accepted.

In 1875 the first Rugby team sent on tour was despatched from Auckland, which province has always been in the van of Rugby. Some difficulty was experienced in getting the team together, but finally 15 players consented to make the trip. Imagine it, present-day footballers: a team of 15 undertaking a tour of New Zealand, and playing five matches in a fortnight! And the travel! No fast express trains in those days. No big red funnel liners to bridge the waterways. Small boats were the modes of travel and rough it was too. The method of scoring on that tour was somewhat different from what prevails in present rugby. Then six points were counted for a goal, two points for a try, and half a point for a force-down.

In the following year (1876) Canterbury sent on tour as far as Auckland a team captained by an old English Rugby player, W. F. Neilson. At this stage it might not be out of place to mention that wing-forwards were played for the first time in 1876. Thus early the 'winger,' who was to cause a great deal of controversy in later years, was much in evidence. In 1877 Otago despatched a team on a tour of New Zealand as far as Auckland.

The two half-back system, which was afterwards to develop into the now well-known five-eights, prevailed very largely about 1880, and although the wing forward was being developed in the North Island, Otago would have none of it.

In 1881 Otago football was organised seriously, and in that year was formed the Otago Rugby Union. The various other provinces followed the lead of Otago, and established unions, which marked an important epoch in the game of Rugby throughout New Zealand.

In the year 1884 an important step was taken in the despatch of a New Zealand team to Sydney to return the visit of the New South Wales team in 1882. It was a splendid side, captained by W. V. Millton, of Canterbury, and included all the leading Rugby players of the time, H. Braddon, G. Robertson, J. Allan, and J. O'Donnell.

A return visit was paid by a New South Wales team to New Zealand in 1886. J. A. Shaw acted as captain on this occasion, and although the Welshmen were a fairly strong side, the standard of play through the various provinces in New Zealand had improved to such an extent tht the visitors only succeeded in winning two out of the twelve matches played.

From 1886 onwards the progress of the game was not so marked and was more confined to developing methods of attack and defence and in improving the combination. It was some time after this that Rugby broke out in a fresh place, and a new development took place in the scrum formation. The 2–3–2 system, which has stood the test of all these years, and which caused so much discussion during the All Black's tour of England in 1905, was adopted.

The year 1887 saw another Otago team despatched north, and the following year brought out the famous English team captained by the late lamented R. L. Seddon, and afterwards by that prince of three-quarter backs, A. E. Stoddart. Indeed, it is to this day referred to in an appreciative strain as 'Stoddart's team.' The visit of the English team brought about an evolution in Rugby football in New Zealand, for it was 'Stoddart's team' of brilliant exponents who brought to light the possibilities of the spectacular passing game, which has through the years been one of the features of Maoriland Rugby.

The season of the English team's visit to New Zealand in 1888 saw also the departure for England of the famous New Zealand native team of 1888–9.

We were told that the British team of 1904 taught us nothing. New Zealand had arrived at a stage when it thought that it had exhausted the possibilities of Rugby. Yet we found for a season or two afterwards many praiseworthy attempts to bring about the art of the cross punt, so cleverly executed by the Welsh trio. Not that the 'centre' or 'cross' punt was a new thing in Otago. George Stephenson, the representative three-quarter back, saw its possibilities, and attempted to introduce it into Otago. But we at this end were somewhat slow at picking up and attempting a new thing, and the cross punt was laughed at by the unintelligent off the field, and lay buried in the cemetery of dead ideas until revived by Morgan, Cabe, Llewellyn, and Co., of Sivright's British team of 1904.

In 1905 quite the most interesting event in the annals of Rugby Football in New Zealand took place. This was the despatching of a New Zealand team to England, under the auspices of the New Zealand Rugby Union. The team – which was afterwards to be known the world over as the famous All Blacks – was despatched with many misgivings as to its success in Great Britain. For was it not played to a draw on the Caledonian ground by an Otago team, and beaten by a Wellington representative team on the eve of its departure for Great Britain? Yet after the opening matches in England the team never looked back, and the All Blacks became the fashion. The tour is even now fresh in the memories of enthusiasts.

It was in response to the visit to Great Britain of the famous All Black team of 1905 that the British Rugby Team of 1908 set out on a tour of the new Dominion. The team was enthusiastically welcomed through the length and breadth of New Zealand, and the people generally vied with each other in extending true Colonial hospitality. No one really knows to what this hospitality extends until he has undertaken a tour with a British Rugby team through the Wonderland of the World – Maoriland.

CHAPTER 21 *A DOZEN ENGLISHMEN*

'Drop down a dozen Englishmen anywhere – on an island, in a backwoods clearing, or on the Indian hills – and in a very short time the schoolboy instinct will out, and the first level sward is turned into a cricket field in summer and a football arena in winter.'

A glance at the nineteenth century registers of any public school reveals the extraordinary dispersal of their past pupils to all the corners of the earth. Hardly a page is without its record of soldiers and sailors, civil servants and teachers, bishops, farmers, engineers, traders and explorers, seeking their fortunes overseas. Many were young men who had recently left school or graduated from the universities. Their upbringing had been designed to instil a sense of leadership, and they had been responsible at school for the organization of their games, so it was hardly surprising that they should have had no difficulty in arranging clubs or occasional matches as the local conditions allowed. They were natural ambassadors for cricket and football, and if enough experienced players could not be mustered local reinforcements were enlisted and taught to play.

The classic example of such enthusiasm was TW Wills, the son of an Australian farmer who had been sent over to England to be educated at Rugby and Oxford. He played cricket for both the school and the university in the 1850s, and when he returned home he set about teaching the aboriginal labourers on his father's sheep station to play cricket. So successful was his coaching that in 1868 he brought his team to England where they performed 'uncommonly well' and one of their number, Mullagh, was 'equal to playing for his county, if he had had a county to play for'. The tour was enormously popular with the English spectators, as was the first Maori Rugby football side which visited England twenty years later during the 1888/9 season. Wills himself introduced football to his cricketers as a means of keeping them fit during the winter. The game he had played at school he considered to be unsuitable for the hard Australian ground and so he contrived the Australian rules game, which has been described as 'aerial ping pong'. Perhaps the most prominent of the features which he retained from the Rugby game were the oval ball and the 'mark', but he followed the normal practice of his generation in adopting aspects of various codes to suit the needs of his players and the available pitches. In Sydney the first Rugby football club was formed in 1864 with little thought of competitive play. They arranged internal matches, just as Liverpool had done in the first years, and occasionally accepted challenges from visiting ships' crews. The earliest international tour was undertaken by a New South Wales side to New Zealand in 1882. As club play developed the Australians experienced exactly the same difficulties in establishing a common code as their English counterparts, and formed the first Union in New South Wales in 1874.

New Zealand was a favourite destination for young English and Scottish emigrants, and many of them were positively encouraged by schoolmasters like Thomas Arnold to settle there. He believed that it was a duty for England to send her *best* men to help in establishing sound Christian principles and good government in the young nations of the Empire, and the many schoolmasters who were trained or taught by him promulgated his views in their own schools. In the excellent article published in the *Rugby Advertiser* on the occasion of the Rugby Football Centenary match which was played on the Close in 1923 two Rugbeians are mentioned. WF Neilson, who had left Rugby in 1868, captained Canterbury on their first trip to Auckland in 1876, and George Robertson took part in the 1884 match in Sydney between New Zealand and New South Wales. Rugby football was first introduced to New Zealand by CJ Monro, a Sherborne boy,

The captain of football in 1900

who converted the Nelson club to the Rugby code in 1870.

Arnold's conviction that able public school boys should play their part in the foundation of new communities was shared by Thomas Hughes, who lost a great deal of money on a venture in America when he attempted to create a new settlement to be populated in the first instance by just such young men. He founded the small town of Rugby, Tennessee, but his faith was misplaced and the first settlers proved to be, by and large, a bunch of charming idlers. Hughes had far greater influence through *Tom Brown's Schooldays*, which proved a great success in America, and resulted in a stream of American visitors to Rugby. They warmed to Hughes' depiction of Arnold's straightforward morality and the uncomplicated creed of schoolboy life, which encapsulated for many Americans the manly Christian virtues which they sought to promote in their own society. No doubt the spread of football in the USA was helped by the publication of *Tom Brown's Schooldays*, but it was Richard Sykes, the boy who took the ball to that first game in Liverpool, who claimed to have introduced the game to America. Once again he carried the oval ball into new territory, and maintained that he had taken Rugby football to colleges and universities in the west. A man of great energy, he founded the town of Sykeston, Dakota and was involved in extending the railways to the west. At one time he was said to have owned 92,000 acres of land. The game which Sykes knew was the old-style Big Side football he had played at school, and modern American football retains some of the features of the old matches. Although the two games have gone their separate ways, obvious similarities remain in the ball shape, the high goal and the scrummage. The large numbers involved in the American game are a relic of the old days, and the organization of players into teams, or 'rosters' under individual captains each responsible for undertaking particular tasks is reminiscent of Old Brooke's deployment of his side in the match described in *Tom Brown's Schooldays*. Early illustrations of the game being played at Rugby show groups of players sitting and lying on the pitch until they are called into play, rather like players in American football waiting on the sidelines today. The practice of forwards charging in advance to clear a way for the backs following up behind them with the ball derives from the blatant disregard of the off-side rule common in early club play in England when inexperienced players frequently failed to understand the laws of the game. Perhaps Sykes experienced the same problem in America, and simply incorporated the practice by the same token that Rugby schoolboys allowed innovations in their games.

In many places the Armed Services were largely responsible for the spread of the game. The first Canadian match was played by a Montreal side against British officers in 1865, and in South Africa the Military challenged the Civilians in August, 1862 in the first recorded game on the continent. The spread of football in South Africa is attributed to RFC Oddy who introduced 'Gog' football, later switched to the Rugby Union code. HV Ellis, an Old Rugbeian who was in the Cricket XI for three years when at school, and who is thought to be a relative of William Webb Ellis, did much to promote the game in Natal, when he was Headmaster of Hilton College from 1878–1905.

The opportunity to spread the gospel of Rugby football to the remote fastness of Tibet seems to have been missed, but not for want of trying on Rugby's part. In 1914 the Grand Lama elected to send four boys to an English public school, and so it was that Ringrang, Mondo, Kyipup and Gongkar found themselves playing for the Town House 2nd XV one wet, cold, windy day in a game described by Dr Robert Collis in his autobiography *The Silver Fleece* as one of the most remarkable of his distinguished football career.

Ringrang grasped the principles of the game fairly soon and, like William Webb Ellis, took the ball and ran with it whenever the opportunity presented itself to him, though it must be admitted such moments usually occurred after the whistle had blown. Judged by public school standards the behaviour during the match of Mondo and Kyipup was abominable. They would not get into the scrum properly, and their enormous bottoms prevented the rest of us from doing so. As the game progressed they received a number of more or less violent biffs both from before and from behind which, I am sorry to say, they took in quite the wrong spirit and became embittered, showing a tendency to bite and other hasty traits unexpected in good Bhuddists. Gongkar, being of slighter build, had been placed in the three-quarter line where he wandered about miserably, like a lost soul, shivering. I ran up and down the field the whole afternoon tackling people, including occasionally Ringrang, who was apt to run strangely in the wrong direction – till our opponents had piled up 35 points to nil, when, as is the Rugby School tradition, the game ended.'

Ringrang, the youngest and most successful of the four, went on to play football for the School House. He returned to Tibet bearing with him an Old Rugbeian tie and the equipment necessary for him to install, virtually single-handed, an electricity supply in Lhasa. There is, alas, no evidence that he carried a Gilbert ball through the high passes of the Himalayas, but he was enormously proud of his English education and a photograph of him in the School House XV remained in his family's possession until it was destroyed in the Chinese purges of recent times.

Rugby football in continental Europe dates back to the early 1870s when a group of British students founded a club in Le Havre. The game soon became popular in Paris among the sons of the well-to-do, and flourished as it had done in England in the wake of a new enthusiasm for athletic sports. Baron Pierre de Coubertin, the founder of the modern Olympic movement, believed that sport should be an integral part of French education, and promoted his conviction vigorously. He was another disciple of the Arnoldian tradition, and may have had his first introduction to Rugby through the popular French edition of *Tom Brown's Schooldays*. At any rate he maintained that it was in the Rugby School Chapel, whilst on a visit to observe the school at first hand, that he was first inspired by the idea of the Olympic movement, although Rugby football was not to be an Olympic sport. France made her contribution to the international scene by taking the game eastwards to Romania and Yugoslavia, where French students introduced the game. As the notion of athletic sports grew in France, British Naval vessels began to play matches when they put in to southern ports, and encouraged Rugby football in the areas which have since become the heartland of French rugby. Appropriately it is there, in Menton on the French Mediterranean coast that William Webb Ellis lies buried.

SOURCE 22 | *The First Matches Against Australia and New Zealand*

FROM F MARSHALL'S *FOOTBALL: THE RUGBY UNION GAME*

The first tour by a British team in the Dominions was that of what was known as 'Shaw and Shrewsbury's Team,' which visited Australia and New Zealand in 1888, sailing on March 8th and returning on November 11th. Messrs. Shaw and Shrewsbury had been managers of a cricket team which visited Australia in the preceding winter and, while there, saw the possibilities of a successful tour of Rugby players. They applied to the Rugby Union for permission to arrange this, but without success, for the Rugby Union formed the opinion that the tour was being proposed more with a view to the benefit of the promoters than as a means of spreading a knowledge of the game and improving it in the Dominions. At the same time, they did not feel justified in prohibiting the tour altogether, and so it came about. This unofficial character of the venture had influence on the composition of the team, which eventually sailed with only three international players, four North or South 'caps,' and eight county players. T. Kent, another member of the team, gained his international cap for England later (in 1891), and A. E. Stoddart, another International, joined the team in Australia. Some doubt has been expressed about H. Eagles' right to be styled an International. He was one of the XV selected to represent England and awarded caps in 1887–8, though no matches were played against other countries owing to an international dispute. Trouble arose through the terms arranged with the players by Messrs. Shaw and Shrewsbury's agent in England, and, as a sequel J. P. Clowes (Halifax) was declared a professional and, although he accompanied the team during its tour, did not take part in any of the matches. The results of the tour were fairly satisfactory while the team played under Rugby Union rules. Out of 35 matches played, 27 were won, 2 lost, and 6 drawn. Unfortunately, a series of 18 matches was also arranged under Victorian rules, and of these 6 were won, 11 lost, and 1 drawn. The features of the tour were the fine play of A. E. Stoddart, the death by drowning of R. L. Seddon, the captain, which cast a gloom over the whole tour, and the kindness and hospitality received by the visitors everywhere. H. Eagles played in every match.

The First Tour by New Zealand Players

FROM F MARSHALL'S *FOOTBALL: THE RUGBY UNION GAME*

During the winter 1889–9 the first 'Maoris' team visited this country. This was composed mainly of native players with a few half-castes and New Zealanders. The tour was officially recognised, and the matches were arranged by Mr. Rowland Hill. The 'Maoris' were a fine body of men, and in their earlier matches appeared in their native mats and head-dresses. Even then, as in 1924, the native war-cry was given by the team before each match. Games were played against clubs, counties and countries. The list of fixtures was far too long, but this was inevitable in order to cover the heavy cost of the tour. In twenty-five weeks 74 matches were played, of which the Maoris won 49, lost 20, and drew 5. The strength of the team was in the fine physique and strong play of their forwards, though P. Keogh, who was declared a professional in 1891, was a very fine half-back, and E. M'Causland was an excellent place-kick. Among the matches won were those against Ireland, Swansea, Newport, Blackheath, Halifax, Manchester, Gloucestershire and Somerset. The tour was marred by a tendency to roughness and a habit of cavilling at the decisions of the referee, which reached a climax in the match against England, when five of the team left the field as a protest against one of Mr. Rowland Hill's decisions. The men were persuaded to return by their manager, and an apology was demanded subsequently by the Rugby Union. Apart from this incident, the Maoris put up a gallant fight against England, and the score – 4 goals 1 try, to 1 goal 1 try – did not represent the closeness of the game.

The First South African Tour

FROM F MARSHALL'S *FOOTBALL: THE RUGBY UNION GAME*

In 1891 the Rugby Union decided to send a team to South Africa with the idea of giving a healthy stimulus to the game there. It was at that time a critical period for the game in South Africa, for both Association and Rugby football were being played and there was some danger of a hybrid form of game being adopted. With a vivid recollection of the 'Victorian' business in the Australian tour, the Rugby Union made cautious arrangements. The length of the tour was limited to fifty days, and it was stipulated that games should only be played under Rugby Union rules. Mr. Cecil Rhodes, the Prime Minister of the Cape, made himself personally responsible for the expenses. The team was selected by a sub-committee consisting of Rowland

Hill, R. S. Whalley, Harry Vassall, Arthur Budd, and J. H. S. McArthur. W. E. Maclagan, the famous Scottish International, was elected captain, and Edwin Ash, a former secretary of the Union, was appointed manager. The tour was a great success from every point of view. The team won all its matches, they were received royally wherever they went, and an immense impetus was given to the game in South Africa. Only one try was scored against the visitors – in the first match at Cape Town – and R. L. Aston's play was a revelation to all who saw him; he scored 30 tries himself. The South African teams played a hard game and shone in kicking, tackling and saving, but they had little knowledge of the finer points of the game, such as passing, wheeling the scrum, etc., and lacked the combination of the visitors. They steadily improved during the tour, and gave the English team a very hard fight in the second international match at Kimberley, which was only won by a goal from a mark to nil.

The visitors found the hard grounds very trying – as other teams who have gone to South Africa in later years have done – but there do not appear to have been many casualties, in spite of this. The best of the South Africans were H. H. Castens, an old Oxford and South of England forward; A. Richards, an Old Leysian and a first-class half-back; B. Duff, a cool and reliable full-back; and C. Versfeld, a wing three-quarter who had the honour of scoring the only try of the tour against the Englishmen. Of the 89 tries scored by Maclagan's team, 30 were scored by R. L. Aston, 9 by Bromet, and 8 each by the captain and Marshall. Rotherham only scored 2 tries, but he placed 39 goals.

The results of the international matches were: played, 3; won, 3 (4–0, 2–0, 4–0 points).

CHAPTER 22   *A FINE DISREGARD . . .*

Rugbeians reverence their game, they adore it, not with love, for that does not express the depth of their affection, but with passion – with a deep, lasting, fervid passion equal to any imagined in a German poet's dream.

This indomitable enthusiasm is revealed again and again in the words of players, and is probably the single most important agent in the survival of Rugby football as a major sport. When the game spread beyond the confines of the school Rugbeians promoted it by example. Their experience of other codes at the universities and in the clubs served to confirm their unshakable belief in their own game, and they therefore remained constant to it despite considerable pressure to compromise.

Football was taken seriously at Rugby. Throughout the formative years it was the sole province of the boys themselves, and this independence was jealously guarded. The government was in the hands of the Sixth Form who were *ipso facto* praeposters. They had achieved their position by their academic performance rather than their athletic ability, and the organization of the game was therefore in the hands of the most able boys. Many of them were later to achieve distinction in their future careers, and these early administrators included boys who were to become ambassadors, cabinet ministers, professors, bishops, judges, poets, philosophers and Governors in all the corners of the British Empire. Their youthful talents were brought to bear upon the administration of football, and they developed a sophisticated system of democratic government which allowed even the youngest boys to take part in some decision making. All could vote, for instance, on the great question each year of the date on which football should be introduced. Innovations in the laws were decided by discussion and, when it was considered appropriate, good players who were not praeposters were invited to contribute. The first written rules were in fact drawn up at the request of the Sixth Form by boys who were not of their number. The Head of the School retained his right to be Captain of Football until 1870, and even then a separate Football Captain could only be appointed if the Head of School chose to resign in his favour.

The minute books were kept meticulously, and provide a record of the formal and orderly conduct of all aspects of the organization. Subscriptions were collected for the provision of equipment and the maintenance of the grounds, the dates of matches were fixed, and the laws of the game developed on a system of 'case law'. Disputed points of play were discussed, and the conclusions recorded to provide precedents for the future. The earliest surviving minute book dates from 1844, but records had been kept before that date, and the first written rules, which were drawn up in only three days and immediately confirmed with only slight amendment, were no doubt based upon written precedent as well as custom.

Scrupulous attention to the details of play and regular revision of the laws enabled Rugby football to be refined to the extent that the various points of play were so closely integrated into the whole that few, if any, could be removed without significantly altering the character of the game. That so many of the great players in the formative years of the game were also able and intelligent contributed positively to the considerable level of sophistication in the development of 'scientific' play.

During the debates which came later on a universal code for football it became increasingly apparent that the Rugby game was not only different in many significant respects from those played elsewhere, but that it was so well integrated that if elements were to be extracted in the interests of simplification its nature would be destroyed. The men who were to be advocates of Rugby's football in the wider constituency of the universities and clubs had all been personally involved during their schooldays in the formation of the game, and were well versed not only in its laws but in the reasoning which had led to their enactment. Furthermore they had the skill to present their case with eloquence, and it is unsurprising that the majority of the men who were later to set up the Rugby Football Union were lawyers by profession.

As time went on at Rugby the Sixth delegated much of the responsibility for football to the 'Big Side Levee', which was a committee consisting of the best players. The organization of games was thus shared with others who had a proven interest. In practice this committee was still dominated by members of the Sixth, but it allowed enthusiasts as well to make their contribution. These boys all left the school well versed in the business of administering their game, and they were to use this experience later in setting up clubs with considerable efficiency. They were well used to taking charge, and not inclined to relinquish their accustomed authority in football matters to outside interference.

The fact that Rugby was predominantly a boarding school undoubtedly influenced the spread of the game. Day schools also had their own versions of football, but their pupils more often settled within the area and were less likely to gather in sufficient numbers to play their own games elsewhere. Sheffield is an example of just such a school, which generated a strong local game but made little headway nationally until its early alignment with the Football Association provided a channel for expansion. Rugbeians, on the other hand, were dispersed worldwide. Even the dayboys were frequently the sons of families who settled briefly in the town in order to take advantage of the free education provided for residents by the Founder's bequest. In particular many of the wives of Indian army officers and civil servants would rent houses in Rugby for the duration of their children's education. These boys often followed the family tradition in overseas careers, and very few remained in the locality.

Rugbeians of the Arnold generation and after were perhaps unusual among public school men of their day in their strong conviction that they had a duty to propagate the ideals which had been impressed upon them at school. Arnold's declared purpose to educate 'Christian gentlemen' had little to do with modern conceptions of class. By 'gentlemen' he meant men who embodied a code of behaviour which combined manliness with Christian values. Many Rugbeians emerged with a highly developed sense of social responsibility and inherited Arnold's concern to improve the lot of their fellow men. Thomas Hughes was a classic example of an Arnoldian who shared with many other Rugbeians a lifelong conviction of the Christian socialist ethic.

This philosophy was reflected in the genuine desire which emerged during the discussions about the universal football code to promote the expansion of the game into British society. The debate, begun as an attempt to make it possible for matches to be played between the Metropolitan clubs, quickly developed into the quest for a national winter game which might act as a unifying agent in society. 'The very essence of our English games and pastimes must be, that rich and poor, high and low, mix together on terms of perfect equality in them'. Through such games it was hoped that the qualities of courage, forbearance and good fellowship which school football was thought to inspire would be propagated by example through society at large.

Because football at Rugby had grown hand-in-hand with the strong Arnoldian ethic it was firmly believed by Rugbeians to be a finer vehicle for the development of character than other forms of the game. Time and again advocates in favour of the Rugby game stress this character-building quality, and there is an almost missionary fervour in their determination that the challenges it made upon the individual courage, self-discipline and initiative of players should not be diluted merely in the interests of simplicity.

Rugbeians believed, and were to be proved right in their belief, that although it was superficially complex their code was well within the grasp of the working man. It was a game which had been evolved through play rather than created from theory, and was therefore, as they saw it, a 'natural' game with a universal application. The Rugby men were accustomed to incorporating innovation, and were not concerned to preserve the game immutably. However they preferred that it should continue in its traditional pattern of empirical development, rather than that it should be allowed to be diminished in the interests of theoretical simplification.

The Rugby football players therefore chose to follow an independent course in the steadfast belief that their game was too good to submit to compromise. It is to these Victorian men who maintained 'the fine disregard' for the powerful opposition they faced from the advocates of the dribbling game, that modern Rugby football owes its place in twentieth century sport.

BIBLIOGRAPHY

Books

Apperly, CJ, *My Life and Times*

Arbuthnot, Sir A, *Memories of Rugby and India* [Fisher Unwin, 1910]

Bettinson, GH, *Rugby School* [Privately printed, 1929]

Bloxam, MH, *Rugby: the School & the Neighbourhood* [AJ Lawrence, 1889]

Burnell, RD, *The Oxford & Cambridge Boat Race* [Oxford, 1954]

Butler, AG, *The Three Friends* [1900]

Daglish, JRA, *Red, Black and Blue* [Neil Richardson, 1983]

Dunning, E & Sheard, K, *Barbarians, Gentlemen and Players* [Oxford, 1979]

Holt, R, *Sport and Society in Modern France* [Macmillan, 1981]

Hope Simpson, JB, *Rugby Since Arnold* [Macmillan, 1967]

John, Brian, *The Ancient Game of Cnapan* [Greencroft Books]

Mangan, JA, *Athleticism in the Victorian and Edwardian Public School* [Cambridge, 1981]

Marshall, F & Tosswill, LR, *Football: The Rugby Union Game* [Cassell, 1925]

Mason, Tony, *Sport in Britain* [Cambridge, 1989]

Mutimer, TP, *Arnold & Organized Games* [University of Alberta, 1971]

Old Rugbeian Soc, *The Origin of Rugby Football* [AJ Lawrence, 1897]

Old Rugbeian Soc, *Football Records of Rugby School* [George Over, 1930]

Rouse, WHD, *A History of Rugby School* [Duckworth, 1898]

Salt, FJ, *Rugby School Register 1858–1891* [George Over, 1952]

Selfe, Sydney, *Chapters from the History of Rugby School* [Privately published, 1910]

Shearman, M, *Badminton Library: Athletics and Football* [Longmans, 1887]

Solly, GA, *Rugby School Register 1675–1857* [George Over, 1933]

Stanley, AP, *Life of Dr. Arnold* [Murray, 1904]

Titley, UA & McWhirter, R, *Centenary History of the RFU* [RFU, 1970]

Newspapers and Periodicals

Bell's Life
The Daily Telegraph
The Field
Meteor, 1867–1900
New Rugbeian
Northampton Past & Present, Vol IV No 3
Rugbeian
Rugby Advertiser
Rugby Football
Rugby Miscellany
The Scotsman
The Sporting Gazette

Index